Merriam-Webster's Student Atlas

®

Merriam-Webster

Merriam-Webster, Incorporated
Springfield, Massachusetts

GLOBE TURNER

ISBN: 978-0-87779-638-1
10th printing Frederic Printing Aurora, CO September 2018

Material on the inside covers and on pages 113–132
© Merriam-Webster, Incorporated.

Merriam-Webster's Geographical Dictionary, 2007 was used as a source of information throughout.

The Merriam-Webster logo and *Merriam-Webster's Collegiate* are registered trademarks of Merriam-Webster, Incorporated.

Acknowledgments:
"How to use this Atlas" written by Elspeth Leacock.

Photograph on page 1 © 2016 JupiterImages Corporation.

Photographs on pages 24–25 Copyright © 2016 Corel Corp. Except "Arid" World Landmarks and Travel/Getty Images and "Tropical Wet" World Commerce and Travel/Getty Images.

Photographs on pages 26–27 Copyright © 2016 Corel Corp. Except "Midlatitude grassland" US Landmarks and Travel/Getty Images; "Coniferous forest," "Subtropical broadleaf evergreen forest" US Landmarks and Travel 2/Getty Images and "Mixed forest," "Tropical rain forest" Nature, Wildlife and the Environment/Getty Images.

Photograph on page 40 by Nancy Yatabe.

Photograph on page 42 Library of Congress, LC-W861-35.

Photographs on pages 58–59 "Earthquakes" © Royalty-Free/Corbis, "Fall line" Copyright © 2016 Corel Corp. and "Fault" US Landmarks and Travel/Getty Images.

Photographs on pages 60–61 US Landmarks and Travel/Getty Images. Except "Tropical Wet" US Landmarks and Travel 2/Getty Images and "Mediterranean," "Tundra" Copyright © 2016 Corel Corp.

Photographs on pages 62–63 Copyright © Corel Corp. Except "Coniferous forest" Copyright © 2016 FreeStockPhotos; "Midlatitude scrubland" US Landmarks and Travel/Getty Images and "Mixed forest" Nature, Wildlife and the Environment/Getty Images.

Photograph on pages 68–69 © Royalty-Free/Corbis.

Sources for statistical information in International Data section: CIA World Factbook, (www.cia.gov/library), updated May 31, 2007, and Flags of the World (www.fotw.net)

WORLD FACTS AND FIGURES . Inside front and back covers

AN ATLAS is a collection of

maps that can be used to find information about your world. The very latest data has been collected to make these maps. Hundreds of satellite images were used to map the dramatic shrinking of Earth's forests. The latest census data from each and every country was used to build a picture of Earth's current population. The most recent scientific research was used to create thematic maps of continental drift, the ocean floor, the environment and our natural resources. Look closely and you will see that the information for the maps comes from many different sources such as NASA, the U.S. Department of the Interior or the World Bank. You can use these maps to explore your world, discover connections between places, and see relationships between places and peoples.

But this atlas is more than just a wealth of information. It is fun to look at too. You will find that these maps and photographs can evoke images of far away places. They invite you to pause and to dream. With a map you can journey the world without ever getting wet, cold, tired or hungry. You can imagine great adventures and not leave the comfort of your favorite chair!

To get the most out of this atlas you need to know how to read maps. Just as you learned to read words like the ones on this page, you can learn how to read the language of maps. The map skills you need to know are:
1. locating places
2. measuring distance
3. finding direction
4. reading map symbols

Locating Places

To find places in this atlas, you can begin with the index. To find Dallas follow these steps.

1. Look up Dallas in the index at the end of this book.
2. The index tells you that Dallas is a city in Texas and that it can be found on page 50. You will also learn that Dallas is located at 32°47'N (32 degrees 47 minutes north) and 96°48'W (96 degrees 48 minutes west.)
3. Go to page 50 and find the line of latitude nearest to the number 32°N and the line of longitude nearest to the number 96°W. You will find Dallas close to where those two lines meet. You can learn more about latitude and longitude on pages 8–9.

Measuring Distance

To measure distance most maps have a distance scale. You can learn more about measuring distance on page 7.

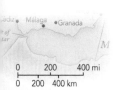

Finding Direction

To find directions use the map's compass rose. You can also use lines of latitude and longitude to find direction. Every line of longitude points north and south. Every line of latitude points east and west. You can learn more about latitude and longitude on pages 8–9.

Reading Map Symbols

Every map symbol shows the location of something. It could be something as large as a continent or as small as a bird-house. A dot shows the location of a city. A blue line shows the course of a river. But map symbols are not the same on all maps. One map might show a city with a square. Map legends or keys help explain the symbols used on a map. You can find out more about legends and the map symbols used in this atlas on page 6.

Special Features of this Atlas

This atlas has been designed and organized to be easy for you to use. Here is a "road map" to your atlas.

The Blue Tab Bar

Somewhere along the top blue tab bar of each spread you will see a darker blue tab. It tells you

| Geographic Features | **Climate** | Land Cover |

the subject of the map or maps you are looking at. The light blue tabs tell you the subjects of the surrounding map spreads. If, for example, you are looking at the World Climate map and would like to compare it to the World Vegetation map, you can use the tabs to find that map quickly and easily.

Map Skills

Look at the blue tab bar above and you will see that you are in the map skills section. This section should be called "Read Me First" because it is here that you will find all sorts of helpful information about maps and how to read them. Even if you are a practiced map reader, read this section!

The World

In this section you will find a world political map, a world physical map, and 35 world thematic maps. The world political map shows the most up to date national boundaries. On the world physical map you can see huge deserts, great mountain ranges, and even the sea ice that covers much of the Arctic. The thematic maps include the most up to date information on everything from the world distribution of computers and televisions to life expectancy, religion and literacy. If you want to see the ocean floor, or to find where in the world volcanoes form, this is the section to look in.

Continents

The continent units are designed to all have the same kinds of maps. This will enable you to compare and contrast one continent with another with ease and accuracy. There is a political map, a physical map, and a total of seven thematic maps per continent.

Used individually each map can provide answers to many questions. But all together, each set of maps can be used to tell a story.

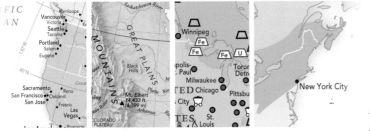

Imagine a journey crossing a continent. You can see the regions visited, the mountains climbed, or the deserts crossed. You can tell if many people are passed along the way or few. You can describe the activities of the people. Will you see miners or ranchers or farmers? And you can tell about the different climates experienced along the way. All of this information and more is on the maps for every continent but Antarctica.

Environmental Issues

There is a special "Environmental Issues" feature for each continent and one for the world. To create these features the latest scientific information was gathered and organized for you. The topics cover the three major environmental issues faced by citizens today, desertification, deforestation, and acid rain.

The United States

In the section on the United States you will find a political map with two pages of political facts, a physical map with two pages of physical facts, and seven thematic map spreads.

Canada and Mexico

Canada and Mexico both have their own spreads that include a political and physical map.

Geographic Features

There are two special "Geographic Features" included in this atlas. To find out how the continents, Earth's greatest land features, have been drifting around the globe, turn to pages 22–23. To take an in depth look at fall lines, divides, and faults turn to the United States Geographic Features spread on pages 58–59.

Charts and Graphs

This atlas is filled with charts, graphs and diagrams. They are used to give more information about subjects shown on the maps. To make these charts and graphs, long lists of the most up to date data was gathered. Then all those numbers were organized into graphic displays that can be read simply and accurately.

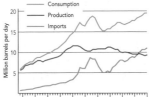

Line graphs are used to show change in amounts over time.

Bar graphs are used to compare amounts.

Pie charts show percentages of a total.

Glossary

There are many geographic terms found on maps such as *fjord*, *isthmus*, or *plateau*. You can find the meaning of these and other terms in the geographic glossary located on pages 129–132.

Legend

The following symbols are used here for general reference maps. Maps with special subjects (thematic maps) have their own unique legends.

General Reference Maps

- ⊛ National capital
- ★ Other capital
- • Other city
- International boundary (political map)
- International boundary in dispute/undefined (political map)
- State or provincial boundary
- International boundary (physical map)
- International boundary in dispute (physical map)

- Nonsubject area
- ▲ Mountain peak
- ▽ Lowest point
- Perennial lake
- Intermittent lake
- Perennial river
- ≈ Falls

Physical Maps Legend

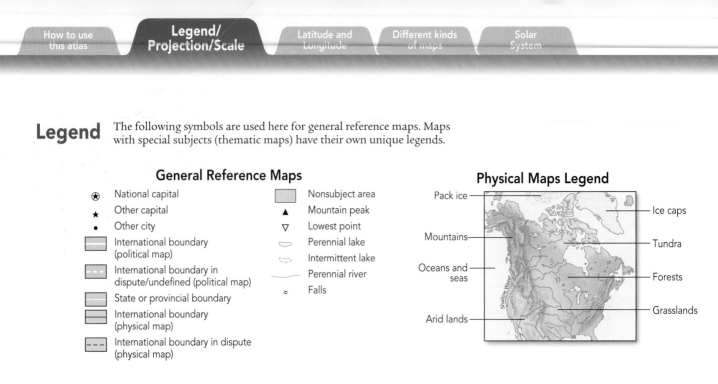

Pack ice · Ice caps · Mountains · Tundra · Oceans and seas · Forests · Arid lands · Grasslands · Shallow Water

Projections

A globe is the most accurate picture of the Earth. Only a globe can show distance, direction, and the true shape and area of land and sea. Mapmakers struggle with how to show the round world on a flat map.

Imagine the Earth as a large balloon.

Cut it apart, and flatten it to make a map.

To show the round Earth on flat paper, mapmakers used different **projections**, or ways of showing a round shape on a flat surface.

With every projection the shapes of places are changed somewhat. This is called distortion. To find distortion, you can compare the latitude and longitude lines of a map to those same lines on a globe.

Mercator Projection

Gerardus Mercator, a Dutch mapmaker, wanted a map projection that showed direction and shape accurately. The problems with distortions are more obvious on this projection. You can see that the land areas are very distorted the closer to the poles that you get. So, this projection ended up greatly distorting distance and size.

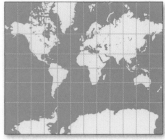

This diagram shows how a Mercator projection distorts the sizes of places. Compare Greenland on the map and the globe.

Projections – Making the Round World Flat

Robinson Projection

Arthur Robinson, an American mapmaker, wanted to develop a map projection that "looked" right. This projection uses many distortions but none are significant. You can see this by comparing one of the large scale World maps in this atlas to a globe.

Azimuthal Projection

This is a projection used to show Antarctica and the Arctic. Azimuthal maps show direction and distance accurately, if measured from the center of the map. But, other distances, shape and size are distorted.

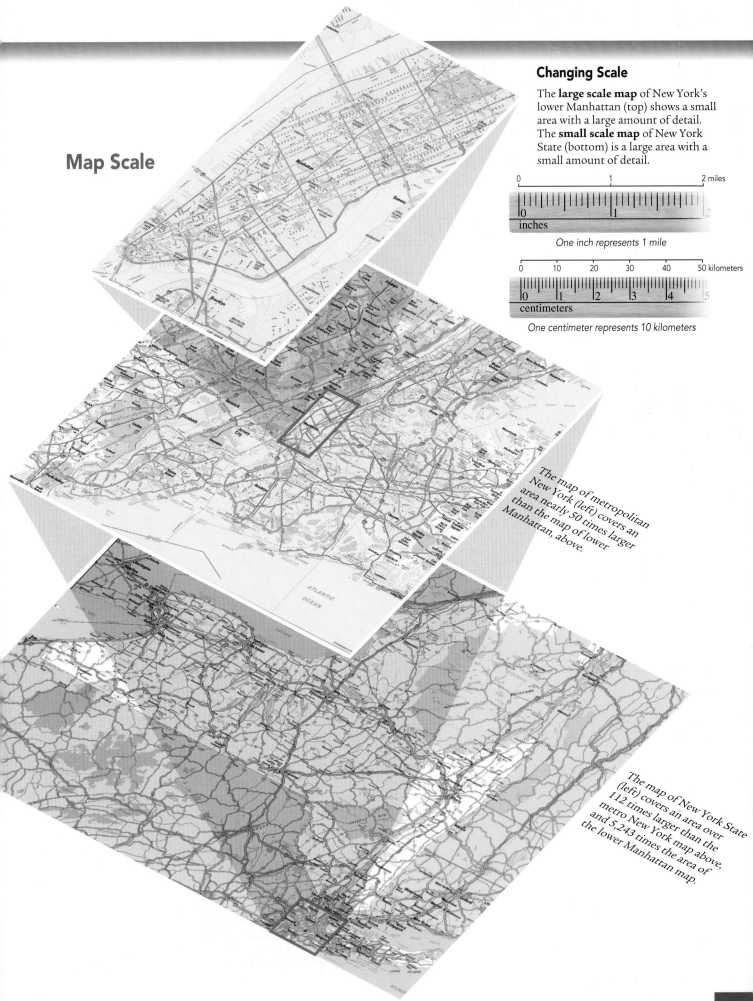

Map Scale

Changing Scale

The **large scale map** of New York's lower Manhattan (top) shows a small area with a large amount of detail. The **small scale map** of New York State (bottom) is a large area with a small amount of detail.

0   1   2 miles

inches

One inch represents 1 mile

0   10   20   30   40   50 kilometers

centimeters

One centimeter represents 10 kilometers

The map of metropolitan New York (left) covers an area nearly 50 times larger than the map of lower Manhattan, above.

The map of New York State (left) covers an area over 112 times larger than the metro New York map above, and 5,243 times the area of the lower Manhattan map.

Latitude and Longitude

Since ancient times, mapmakers, geographers, and navigators have worked to develop a system for accurately locating places on the Earth. On a sphere, such as the Earth, there are no corners or sides, no beginning or end. But since the Earth rotates on an axis, there are two fixed points: the North Pole and the South Pole. These points make a good starting place for a system of imaginary lines.

These imaginary lines form a grid over the Earth, allowing us to pinpoint the exact location of any spot on the Earth. This spherical grid is called the **graticule**. It is formed by lines called **latitude** and **longitude**.

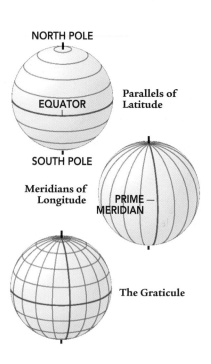

NORTH POLE

EQUATOR

Parallels of Latitude

SOUTH POLE

Meridians of Longitude

PRIME MERIDIAN

The Graticule

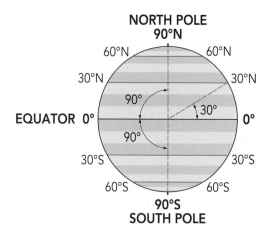

NORTH POLE
90°N

60°N — 60°N
30°N — 30°N
90°
30°
EQUATOR 0° — 0°
90°
30°S — 30°S
60°S — 60°S
90°S
SOUTH POLE

Latitude

Halfway between the poles the Equator circles the globe in an east-west direction. Latitude is measured in degrees north or south of the Equator, which is 0 degrees (°). Lines of latitude are called **parallels** because they circle the globe parallel to the Equator. Parallels are numbered from 0° at the Equator to 90°N at the North Pole and 90°S at the South Pole.

Longitude

Running from pole to pole, lines of longitude—called **meridians**—circle the globe in a north-south direction. As in any circle or sphere, there are 360 degrees (°) of longitude. The meridians are numbered from the Prime Meridian which is labeled 0°. Meridians east or west of the Prime Meridian are labeled E or W up to 180°. The International Date Line generally follows the 180° meridian, making a few jogs to avoid cutting through land areas.

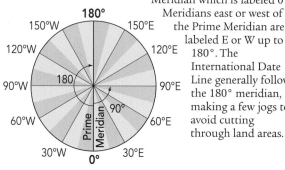

180°
150°W — 150°E
120°W — 120°E
180
90°W — 90°E
90°
60°W — 60°E
Prime Meridian
30°W — 30°E
0°

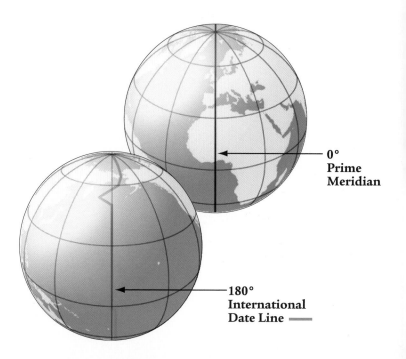

0° **Prime Meridian**

180° **International Date Line**

Parallels and Meridians—The Facts

Parallels
- are lines of latitude used to measure location north or south of the Equator
- are always the same distance apart (about 70 miles)
- differ in length
- The Equator, the longest parallel, is almost 25,000 miles long

Meridians
- are lines of longitude used to measure location east or west of the Prime Meridian
- meet at the poles
- are all the same length

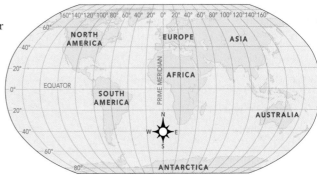

Which way north...

The geographic North and South Poles are fixed points located at each end of the Earth's axis. The Earth's magnetic fields cause the needle of a compass to point toward magnetic north, not geographic north. The north magnetic pole is located in the northern territories of Canada. The south magnetic pole is located near the coast of Antarctica. The magnetic poles are constantly moving.

Degrees, Minutes, Seconds

A degree (°) of latitude or longitude can be divided into 60 parts called minutes ('). Each minute can be divided into 60 seconds ("). The diagram at right is an example of a place located to the nearest second.

It is written as:
42° 21′ 30″ N   71° 03′ 37″ W

● This place is city center, Boston, Massachusetts.

The index at the back of this Atlas uses degrees and minutes of latitude and longitude to help you find places.

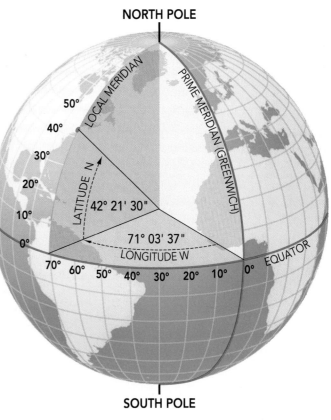

Different Kinds of Maps

Maps are special pictures of places on Earth.

[...] maps are alike in these important ways:
- [...] maps are a view from above
- [...] maps show selected information using symbols
- All maps are smaller than the real place on Earth that they show.

Because people want to show many different things on Earth, they create many different kinds of maps.

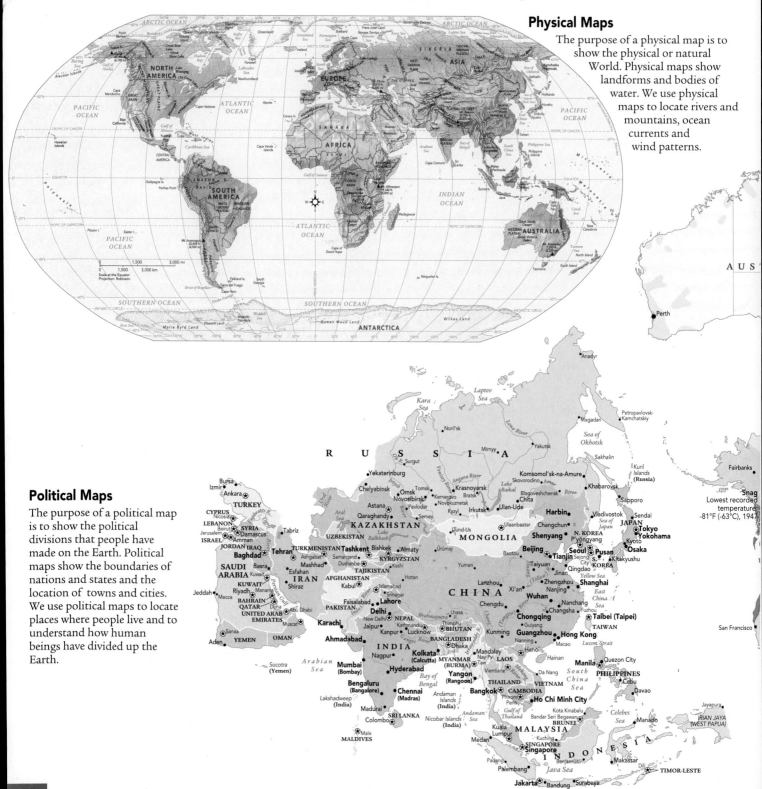

Physical Maps

The purpose of a physical map is to show the physical or natural World. Physical maps show landforms and bodies of water. We use physical maps to locate rivers and mountains, ocean currents and wind patterns.

Political Maps

The purpose of a political map is to show the political divisions that people have made on the Earth. Political maps show the boundaries of nations and states and the location of towns and cities. We use political maps to locate places where people live and to understand how human beings have divided up the Earth.

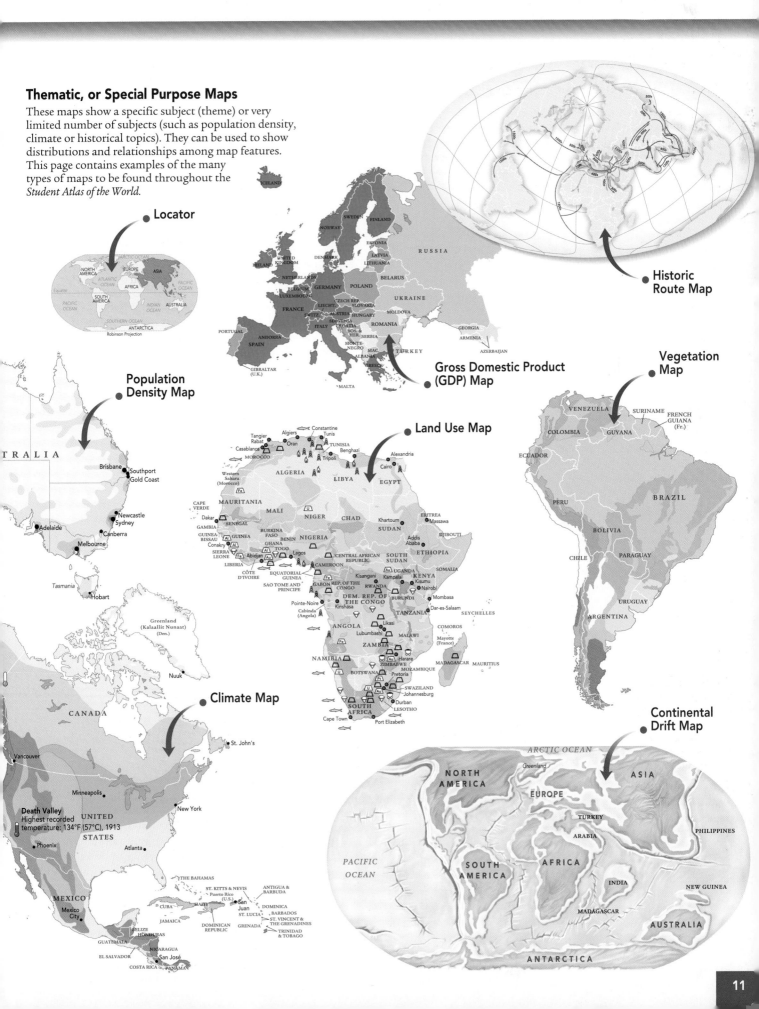

Thematic, or Special Purpose Maps

These maps show a specific subject (theme) or very limited number of subjects (such as population density, climate or historical topics). They can be used to show distributions and relationships among map features. This page contains examples of the many types of maps to be found throughout the *Student Atlas of the World*.

Locator

Historic Route Map

Gross Domestic Product (GDP) Map

Vegetation Map

Population Density Map

Land Use Map

Climate Map

Continental Drift Map

11

Our Solar System

SUN
Jupiter
Mercury
Venus
Earth
Mars
Asteroid belt
Saturn
Uranus

Titan
Rhea
Tethys
Mimas
Dione
Saturn
Jupiter
Miranda
Triton
Nereid
Pluto
Neptune
Uranus
Ganymede

	Pluto	Neptune	Uranus	Saturn	Jupiter
Diameter	1,485 mi (2,390 km)	30,602 mi (49,249 km)	31,518 mi (50,723 km)	72,368 mi (116,465 km)	86,882 mi (139,823 km)
Mean distance from Sun (millions of miles/millions of km)	3,670 mi (5,906 km)	2,793 mi (4,495 km)	1,785 mi (2,873 km)	891 mi (1,434 km)	484 mi (779 km)

Pluto

Neptune

	Approximate time to orbit the Sun	Average surface temperature
Sun	---	9,941°F (5,505°C)
Mercury	0.2 Earth year (88 days)	333°F (167°C)
Venus	0.6 Earth year (225 days)	867°F (464°C)
Earth	1 Earth year	59°F (15°C)
Mars	1.9 Earth years	-81°F (-63°C)
Jupiter	12 Earth years	-162°F (-108°C)
Saturn	29.5 Earth years	-218°F (-139°C)
Uranus	84 Earth years	-323°F (-197°C)
Neptune	165 Earth years	-330°F (-201°C)
Pluto	248 Earth years	-369°F (-223°C)

Pluto: a dwarf planet
In 2006, the International Astronomical Union revised the system of classifying bodies that orbit the Sun. These objects are now classified either as planets, dwarf planets, or small solar system bodies. Under the new method's definitions our solar system contains just 8 planets; Pluto has been designated a dwarf planet. Joining Pluto in the dwarf planet category are Ceres (orbiting within the asteroid belt) and Eris (orbiting beyond Pluto). A dozen more objects are potential dwarf planets, and that list is expected to grow.

Callisto

SUN

Io   Europa

Asteroid
Belt   Mars   Earth   Venus   Mercury

Moon

Phobos

Deimos

Note: Distances on the lower diagram are not shown to scale, and only major satellites are shown.

Mars	Earth	Venus	Mercury	Sun
4,212 mi (6,779 km)	7,926 mi (12,756 km)	7,521 mi (12,104 km)	3,032 mi (4,879 km)	865,000 mi (1,392,000 km)
142 mi (228 km)	93 mi (150 km)	67 mi (108 km)	36 mi (58 km)	-----

Sources: JPL/NASA; World Almanac, 2006

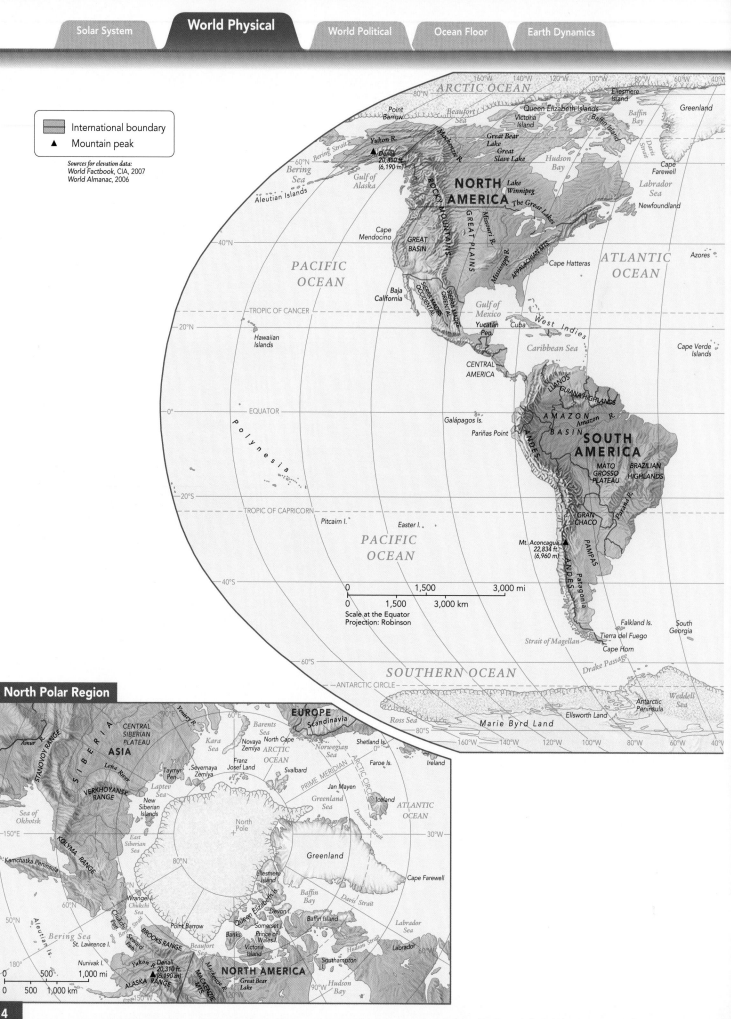

International boundary
▲ Mountain peak

Sources for elevation data:
World Factbook, CIA, 2007
World Almanac, 2006

ARCTIC OCEAN

Point Barrow
Beaufort Sea
Queen Elizabeth Islands
Victoria Island
Great Bear Lake
Great Slave Lake
Ellesmere Island
Baffin Island
Baffin Bay
Greenland
Davis Strait
Cape Farewell

Yukon R.
Mackenzie R.
Denali 20,310 ft (6,190 m)
Bering Strait
Bering Sea
Gulf of Alaska
Aleutian Islands

NORTH AMERICA
Lake Winnipeg
The Great Lakes
Hudson Bay
Labrador Sea
Newfoundland

ROCKY MOUNTAINS
GREAT PLAINS
Missouri R.
Mississippi R.
APPALACHIAN MTS.

Cape Mendocino
GREAT BASIN
ATLANTIC OCEAN
Azores
Cape Hatteras

PACIFIC OCEAN

TROPIC OF CANCER
Baja California
SIERRA MADRE OCCIDENTAL
SIERRA MADRE ORIENTAL
Gulf of Mexico
Yucatán Pen.
Cuba
West Indies
Caribbean Sea
Cape Verde Islands

Hawaiian Islands
CENTRAL AMERICA

EQUATOR
Galápagos Is.
Pariñas Point
LLANOS
GUIANA HIGHLANDS
AMAZON BASIN
Amazon R.
SOUTH AMERICA
MATO GROSSO PLATEAU
BRAZILIAN HIGHLANDS
ANDES

Polynesia

TROPIC OF CAPRICORN
Pitcairn I.
Easter I.
GRAN CHACO
Paraná R.
PAMPAS

Mt. Aconcagua 22,834 ft (6,960 m)
PACIFIC OCEAN
ANDES
Patagonia

0   1,500   3,000 mi
0   1,500   3,000 km
Scale at the Equator
Projection: Robinson

Falkland Is.
South Georgia
Tierra del Fuego
Strait of Magellan
Cape Horn
Drake Passage

SOUTHERN OCEAN
ANTARCTIC CIRCLE

EUROPE
Scandinavia
Ross Sea
Marie Byrd Land
Ellsworth Land
Antarctic Peninsula
Weddell Sea

North Polar Region

SIBERIA
ASIA
CENTRAL SIBERIAN PLATEAU
STANOVOY RANGE
Amur
Yenisey R.
Lena River
VERKHOYANSK RANGE
Taymyr Pen.
Severnaya Zemlya
Barents Sea
North Cape
Novaya Zemlya
Kara Sea
Franz Josef Land
Svalbard
Norwegian Sea
Shetland Is.
Faroe Is.
Ireland
ARCTIC OCEAN
PRIME MERIDIAN
ARCTIC CIRCLE
Jan Mayen
Iceland
ATLANTIC OCEAN
Greenland Sea
Denmark Strait

Sea of Okhotsk
KOLYMA RANGE
Kamchatka Peninsula
Laptev Sea
New Siberian Islands
East Siberian Sea
North Pole
80°N
Greenland
Cape Farewell

Aleutian Is.
Bering Sea
St. Lawrence I.
Nunivak I.
Chukchi Sea
Wrangel I.
Chukchi Pen.
Seward Pen.
Bering Strait
Ellesmere Island
Baffin Bay
Devon I.
Baffin Island
Davis Strait
Labrador Sea

BROOKS RANGE
Beaufort Sea
Banks I.
Somerset I.
Prince of Wales I.
Victoria Island
Hudson Strait
Southampton

Yukon R.
Denali 20,310 ft (6,190 m)
ALASKA RANGE
MACKENZIE MTS.
Mackenzie R.
NORTH AMERICA
Great Bear Lake
Labrador
Hudson Bay

0   500   1,000 mi
0   500   1,000 km

14

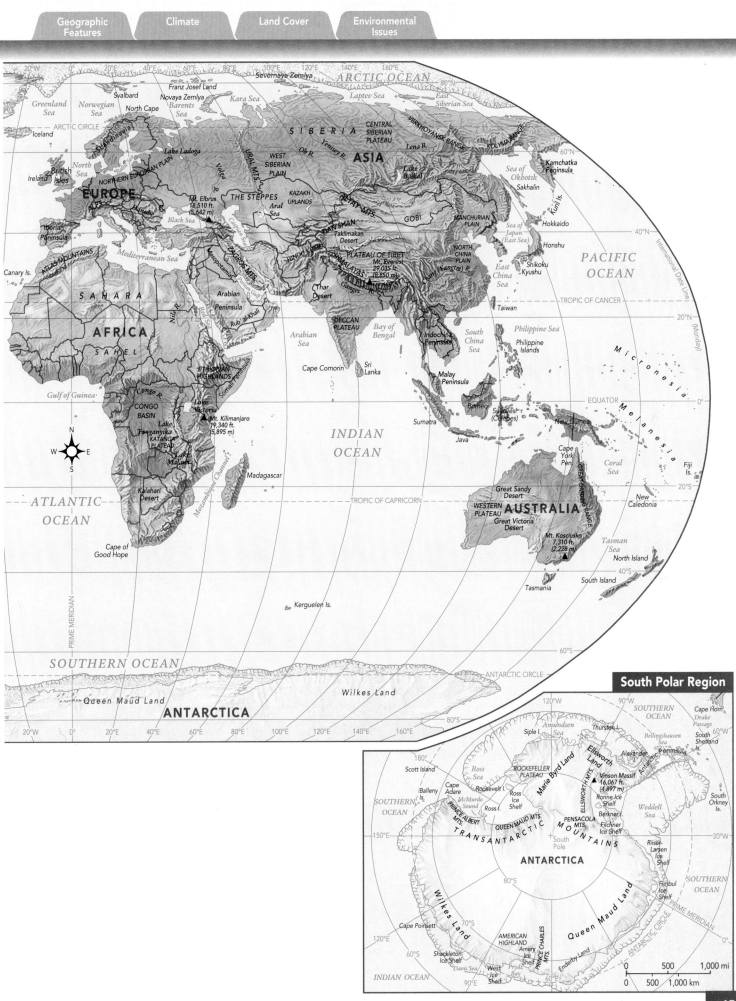

South Polar Region

15

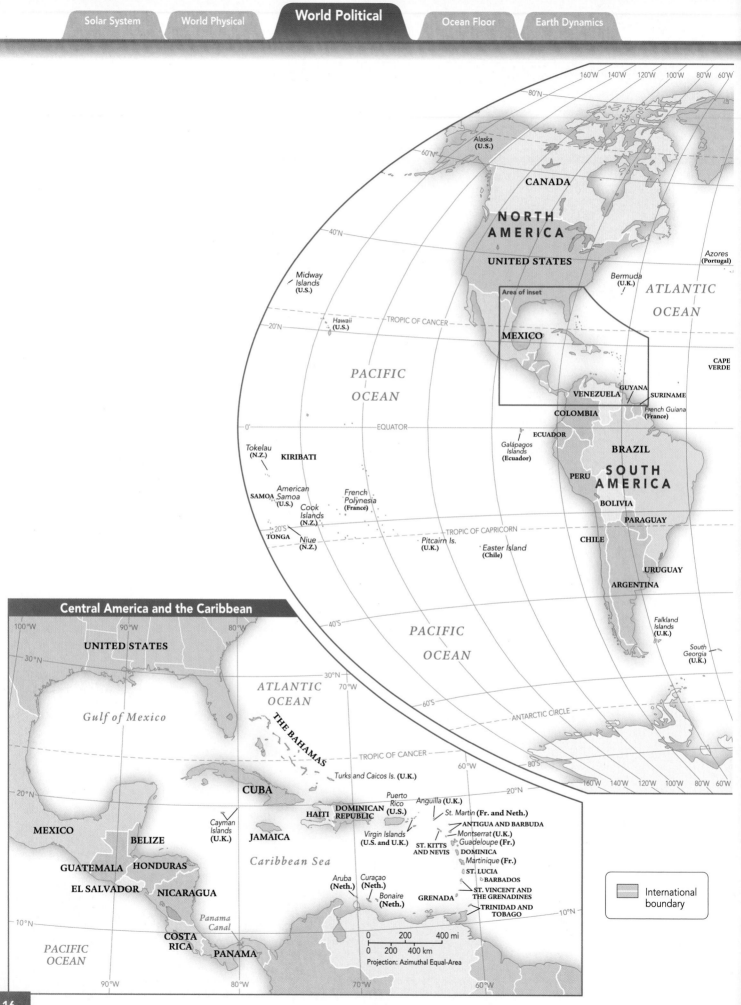

160°W 140°W 120°W 100°W 80°W 60°W

80°N

Alaska (U.S.)

60°N

CANADA

NORTH AMERICA

40°N

UNITED STATES

Azores (Portugal)

ATLANTIC OCEAN

Bermuda (U.K.)

Area of inset

Midway Islands (U.S.)

TROPIC OF CANCER

20°N

Hawaii (U.S.)

MEXICO

CAPE VERDE

PACIFIC OCEAN

VENEZUELA GUYANA SURIName

COLOMBIA *French Guiana (France)*

0° EQUATOR

ECUADOR

Galápagos Islands (Ecuador)

BRAZIL

Tokelau (N.Z.) KIRIBATI

SOUTH AMERICA

PERU

American Samoa (U.S.) *French Polynesia (France)*

SAMOA

BOLIVIA

Cook Islands (N.Z.)

PARAGUAY

20°S

TONGA *Niue (N.Z.)* *Pitcairn Is. (U.K.)* *Easter Island (Chile)* CHILE

TROPIC OF CAPRICORN

URUGUAY

ARGENTINA

Falkland Islands (U.K.)

40°S

PACIFIC OCEAN

South Georgia (U.K.)

60°S

ANTARCTIC CIRCLE

80°S

160°W 140°W 120°W 100°W 80°W 60°W

Central America and the Caribbean

100°W 90°W 80°W

UNITED STATES

30°N

ATLANTIC OCEAN

70°W

Gulf of Mexico

30°N

THE BAHAMAS

TROPIC OF CANCER

Turks and Caicos Is. (U.K.)

60°W

20°N 20°N

CUBA

Puerto Rico (U.S.) Anguilla (U.K.)

DOMINICAN REPUBLIC St. Martin (Fr. and Neth.)

Cayman Islands (U.K.) HAITI **ANTIGUA AND BARBUDA**

MEXICO JAMAICA *Virgin Islands (U.S. and U.K.)* *Montserrat (U.K.)* *Guadeloupe (Fr.)*

BELIZE *Caribbean Sea* **ST. KITTS AND NEVIS** **DOMINICA**

GUATEMALA **HONDURAS** *Martinique (Fr.)* **ST. LUCIA**

EL SALVADOR **NICARAGUA** *Aruba (Neth.)* *Curaçao (Neth.)* **BARBADOS**

Bonaire (Neth.) **GRENADA** **ST. VINCENT AND THE GRENADINES**

10°N 10°N

Panama Canal **TRINIDAD AND TOBAGO**

PACIFIC OCEAN **COSTA RICA** **PANAMA**

0   200   400 mi
0   200   400 km
Projection: Azimuthal Equal-Area

90°W 80°W 70°W 60°W

International boundary

16

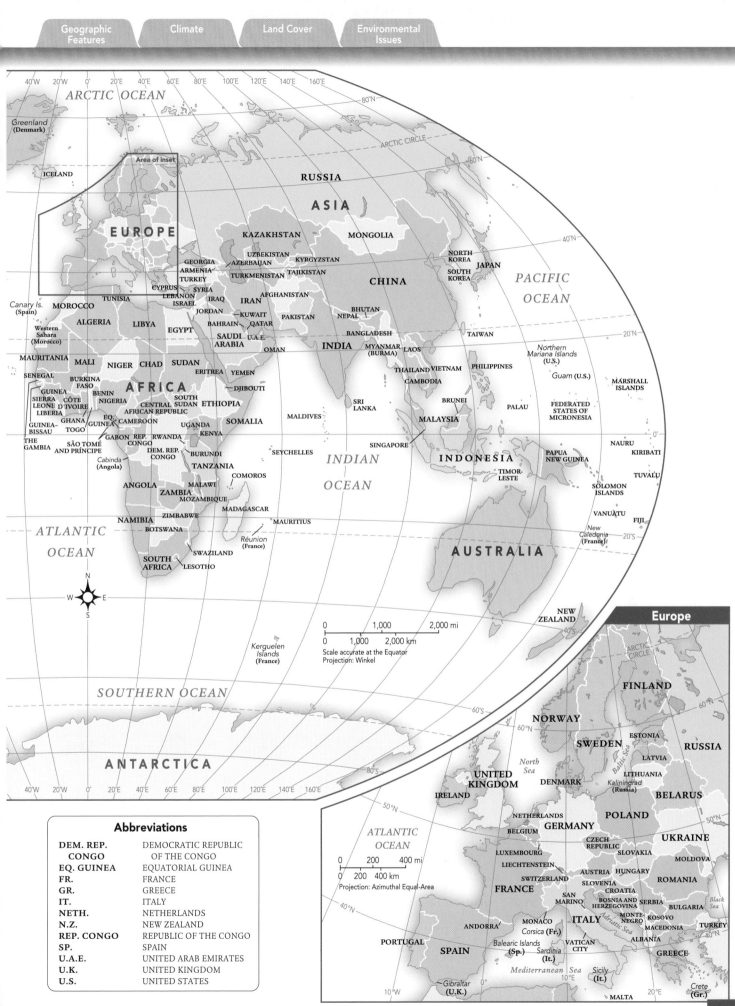

ARCTIC OCEAN

Greenland (Denmark)

ICELAND

Area of inset

EUROPE

RUSSIA

ASIA

ARCTIC CIRCLE

KAZAKHSTAN

MONGOLIA

GEORGIA
ARMENIA
TURKEY
CYPRUS
LEBANON
ISRAEL
SYRIA
IRAQ
JORDAN

AZERBAIJAN
TURKMENISTAN
UZBEKISTAN
TAJIKISTAN
KYRGYZSTAN

AFGHANISTAN

CHINA

NORTH KOREA
SOUTH KOREA

JAPAN

PACIFIC OCEAN

Canary Is. (Spain)

MOROCCO

TUNISIA

ALGERIA
LIBYA
EGYPT

Western Sahara (Morocco)

IRAN
KUWAIT
BAHRAIN
QATAR
SAUDI ARABIA
U.A.E.
OMAN

PAKISTAN
NEPAL
BHUTAN
BANGLADESH
INDIA

TAIWAN

MAURITANIA
MALI
NIGER
CHAD
SUDAN

SENEGAL
BURKINA FASO
GUINEA
SIERRA LEONE
LIBERIA
CÔTE D'IVOIRE
BENIN
NIGERIA
GHANA
TOGO
EQ. GUINEA
CAMEROON
GUINEA-BISSAU
THE GAMBIA
SÃO TOMÉ AND PRÍNCIPE
GABON
REP. CONGO
DEM. REP. CONGO
Cabinda (Angola)

AFRICA

ERITREA
YEMEN
DJIBOUTI
SOUTH SUDAN
CENTRAL AFRICAN REPUBLIC
ETHIOPIA
SOMALIA
UGANDA
KENYA
RWANDA
BURUNDI
TANZANIA

MYANMAR (BURMA)
LAOS
THAILAND
VIETNAM
CAMBODIA

Northern Mariana Islands (U.S.)

Guam (U.S.)

MARSHALL ISLANDS

SRI LANKA

MALDIVES

SEYCHELLES

INDIAN OCEAN

PHILIPPINES

BRUNEI

MALAYSIA

SINGAPORE

PALAU

FEDERATED STATES OF MICRONESIA

NAURU
KIRIBATI

INDONESIA

PAPUA NEW GUINEA

TIMOR-LESTE

COMOROS

ANGOLA
ZAMBIA
MALAWI
MOZAMBIQUE
ZIMBABWE
MADAGASCAR
NAMIBIA
BOTSWANA
SOUTH AFRICA
SWAZILAND
LESOTHO

MAURITIUS

Réunion (France)

SOLOMON ISLANDS

VANUATU

FIJI

New Caledonia (France)

AUSTRALIA

ATLANTIC OCEAN

Kerguelen Islands (France)

NEW ZEALAND

SOUTHERN OCEAN

ANTARCTICA

| 0 | 1,000 | 2,000 mi |
| 0 | 1,000 | 2,000 km |

Scale accurate at the Equator
Projection: Winkel

Europe

ARCTIC CIRCLE

FINLAND

NORWAY
SWEDEN

ESTONIA

RUSSIA

LATVIA

LITHUANIA

Kaliningrad (Russia)

BELARUS

North Sea

UNITED KINGDOM
DENMARK

IRELAND

ATLANTIC OCEAN

NETHERLANDS
BELGIUM
GERMANY
POLAND
UKRAINE

LUXEMBOURG
CZECH REPUBLIC
SLOVAKIA
MOLDOVA

LIECHTENSTEIN
AUSTRIA
HUNGARY
ROMANIA

SWITZERLAND
SLOVENIA
CROATIA

FRANCE
SAN MARINO
BOSNIA AND HERZEGOVINA
SERBIA
BULGARIA

MONTE-NEGRO
KOSOVO
MACEDONIA

ANDORRA

MONACO
Corsica (Fr.)
ITALY
ALBANIA
TURKEY

Black Sea

PORTUGAL
SPAIN

Balearic Islands (Sp.)
Sardinia (It.)
VATICAN CITY

GREECE

Gibraltar (U.K.)

Mediterranean Sea

Sicily (It.)

MALTA

Crete (Gr.)

| 0 | 200 | 400 mi |
| 0 | 200 | 400 km |

Projection: Azimuthal Equal-Area

Abbreviations

DEM. REP. CONGO	DEMOCRATIC REPUBLIC OF THE CONGO
EQ. GUINEA	EQUATORIAL GUINEA
FR.	FRANCE
GR.	GREECE
IT.	ITALY
NETH.	NETHERLANDS
N.Z.	NEW ZEALAND
REP. CONGO	REPUBLIC OF THE CONGO
SP.	SPAIN
U.A.E.	UNITED ARAB EMIRATES
U.K.	UNITED KINGDOM
U.S.	UNITED STATES

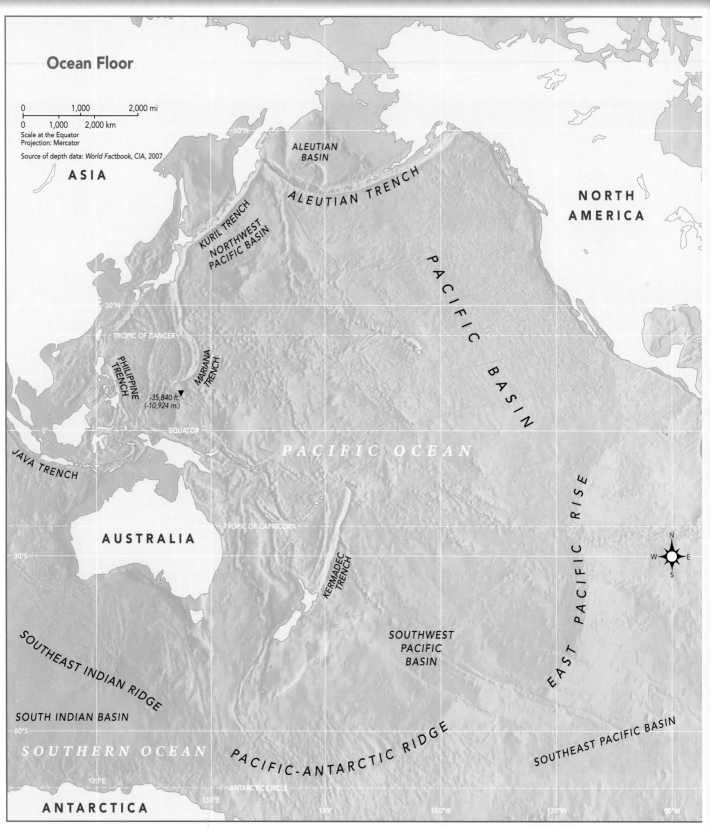

Ocean Floor

0   1,000   2,000 mi

0   1,000   2,000 km

Scale at the Equator
Projection: Mercator

Source of depth data: *World Factbook*, CIA, 2007

ASIA

ALEUTIAN BASIN

ALEUTIAN TRENCH

NORTH AMERICA

KURIL TRENCH

NORTHWEST PACIFIC BASIN

PACIFIC BASIN

60°N

30°N

TROPIC OF CANCER

PHILIPPINE TRENCH

MARIANA TRENCH

-35,840 ft. (-10,924 m.)

0°

EQUATOR

PACIFIC OCEAN

JAVA TRENCH

AUSTRALIA

TROPIC OF CAPRICORN

30°S

KERMADEC TRENCH

SOUTHWEST PACIFIC BASIN

EAST PACIFIC RISE

SOUTHEAST INDIAN RIDGE

SOUTH INDIAN BASIN

60°S

SOUTHERN OCEAN

PACIFIC-ANTARCTIC RIDGE

SOUTHEAST PACIFIC BASIN

120°E

150°E

ANTARCTIC CIRCLE

180°

150°W

120°W

90°W

ANTARCTICA

Surrounding most of the continents are gently sloping areas called continental shelves, which reach depths of about 650 ft. (200 m). At the edges of the continental shelves lie steeper continental slopes leading down to the deep ocean basin, or abyss. The abyss contains many of the same features we see on land, including plains, mountains ranges (ridges), isolated mountains (known as sea mounts or guyots), and trenches. The Mid-Ocean Ridge system marks the areas where crustal plates are moving apart, and is very active geologically, as molten rock rises and erupts to create new crust. Earthquakes and volcanoes are common along many undersea trenches and ridges.

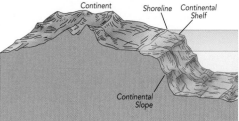

Continent   Shoreline   Continental Shelf

Continental Slope

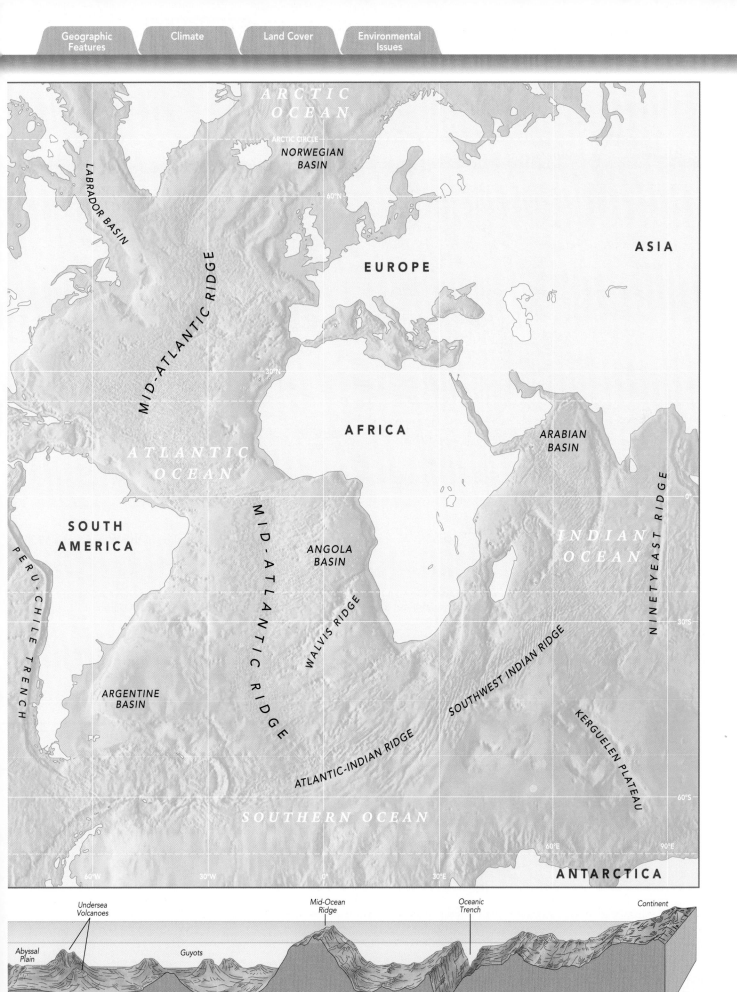

ARCTIC OCEAN

NORWEGIAN BASIN

ARCTIC CIRCLE

60°N

LABRADOR BASIN

EUROPE

ASIA

MID-ATLANTIC RIDGE

30°N

AFRICA

ATLANTIC OCEAN

ARABIAN BASIN

0°

SOUTH AMERICA

MID-ATLANTIC RIDGE

ANGOLA BASIN

INDIAN OCEAN

NINETYEAST RIDGE

WALVIS RIDGE

30°S

PERU-CHILE TRENCH

ARGENTINE BASIN

SOUTHWEST INDIAN RIDGE

ATLANTIC-INDIAN RIDGE

KERGUELEN PLATEAU

60°S

SOUTHERN OCEAN

60°W | 30°W | 0° | 30°E | 60°E | 90°E

ANTARCTICA

Undersea Volcanoes

Mid-Ocean Ridge

Oceanic Trench

Continent

Abyssal Plain

Guyots

19

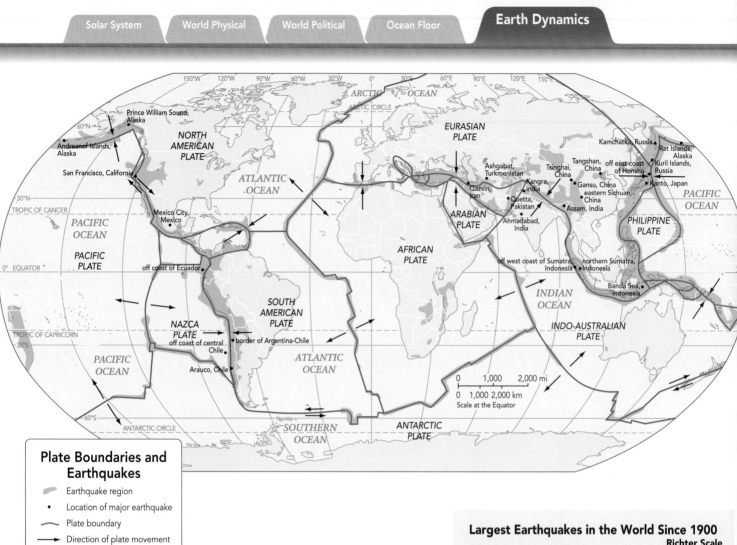

Plate Boundaries and Earthquakes

- Earthquake region
- Location of major earthquake
- Plate boundary
- Direction of plate movement

The movement of Earth's crustal plates causes the phenomena known as earthquakes. The surface of the Earth actually moves or quakes. An **earthquake** can have the destructive energy of an atomic bomb. However, thousands of earthquakes occur each day all over the world without most people realizing it.

The majority of earthquakes occur along a **fault.** A fault is usually a weak or broken area in the rocks beneath the surface of the Earth, but some, like the *San Andreas Fault* in California, can be seen on the surface. See pages 58–59 to learn more about faults.

The Richter Scale measures the energy of an earthquake. This measurement is obtained from the focus, or hypocenter, the spot where the first break in the rock layers occurs. The spot on the surface of the Earth, directly above the focus and nearest to the source of energy is called the epicenter.

Earthquake damage is caused by this energy, called seismic energy, moving through the rocks or along the surface. Many geographic factors, both physical and human, determine how much damage is done by these seismic waves of energy.

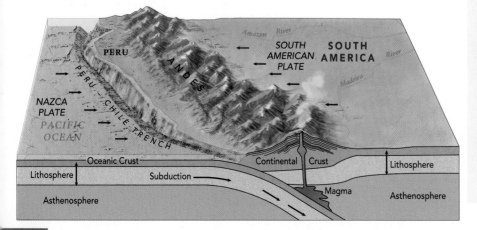

Largest Earthquakes in the World Since 1900

Date	Location	Richter Scale Magnitude
May 22, 1960	Arauco, Chile	9.5
March 27, 1964	Prince William Sound, Alaska	9.2
Dec. 26, 2004	off west coast of Sumatra, Indonesia	9.1
March 11, 2011	near east coast of Honshu, Japan	9.0
Nov. 4, 1952	Kamchatka, Russia	9.0
Feb. 27, 2010	off central coast of Chile	8.8
Jan. 31, 1906	near coast of Ecuador	8.8
March 28, 2005	northern Sumatra, Indonesia	8.7
March 9, 1957	Andreanof Islands, Alaska	8.6
Aug. 15, 1950	Assam, India	8.6
Sept. 12, 2007	Southern Sumatra, Indonesia	8.5
Oct. 13, 1963	Kuril Islands, Russia	8.5
Feb. 1, 1938	Banda Sea, Indonesia	8.5
Nov. 11, 1922	border of Argentina-Chile	8.5

Other Significant Earthquakes Since 1900

Date	Location	Richter Scale Magnitude
Sept. 19, 1985	Mexico City, Mexico	8.0
May 12, 2008	eastern Sichuan, China	7.9
May 22, 1927	Tsinghai, China	7.9
Sept. 1, 1923	Kanto, Japan	7.9
Dec. 16, 1920	Gansu, China	7.8
April 18, 1906	San Francisco, California	7.8
Jan. 26, 2001	Ahmadabad, India	7.7
June 20, 1990	western Iran, near Qazvin	7.7
July 27, 1976	Tangshan, China	7.5
May 30, 1935	Quetta, Pakistan	7.5
Oct. 5, 1948	Ashgabat, Turkmenistan	7.3

Source: National Earthquake Information Center, U.S.G.S

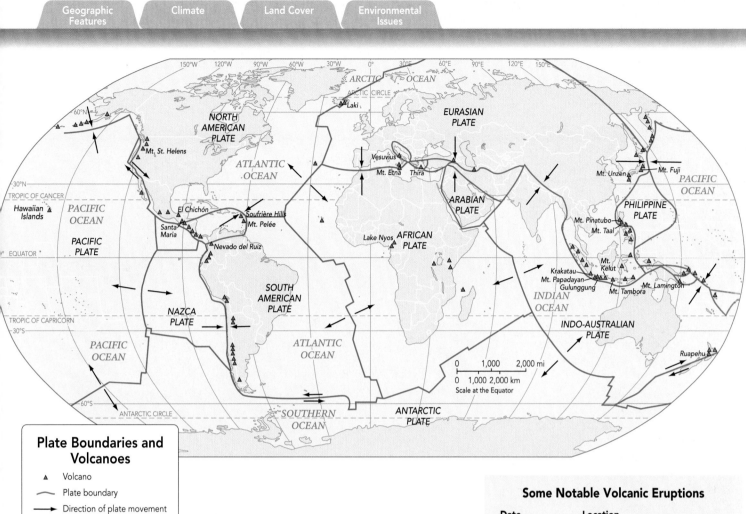

Plate Boundaries and Volcanoes

▲ Volcano

⌒ Plate boundary

→ Direction of plate movement

A **volcano** is an opening in the Earth's crust often capped by a cone-shaped hill or mountain formed from erupted lava and ash.

Volcanoes are associated with plate boundaries. Powerful forces occurring far beneath the surface at the edges of plates cause rock to melt and, at the same time, open cracks in the crust. An eruption occurs when magma (melted rock) flows, and many times explodes, through a weakness, such as a crack in the Earth's crust. Once magma is flowing on the Earth's surface it is called lava. Flowing lava can be several thousand degrees Fahrenheit.

In a few cases, volcanoes exist without being near the edge of a plate. In these cases, such as the Hawaiian Islands, a powerful and persistent flow of magma has broken through the crust.

Some Notable Volcanic Eruptions

Date	Location
1500 B.C.	Thira (Santorini), Greece
Aug. 24, A.D. 79	Vesuvius, Italy
1169	Mt. Etna, Italy
1586	Mt. Kelut, Java, Indonesia
Dec. 15, 1631	Vesuvius, Italy
March–July, 1669	Mt. Etna, Italy
Aug. 12, 1772	Mt. Papandayan, Java, Indonesia
June 8, 1783	Laki, Iceland
May 21, 1792	Mt. Unzen, Japan
Apr. 10–12, 1815	Mt. Tambora, Sumbawa, Indonesia
Oct. 8, 1822	Galunggung, Java, Indonesia
Aug. 26–28, 1883	Krakatau, Indonesia
Apr. 24, 1902	Santa Maria, Guatemala
May 8, 1902	Mt. Pelée, Martinique
Jan. 30, 1911	Mt. Taal, Philippines
May 19, 1919	Mt. Kelut, Java, Indonesia
Jan. 17–21, 1951	Mt. Lamington, New Guinea
May 18, 1980	Mt. St. Helens, United States
Mar. 28, 1982	El Chichon, Mexico
Nov. 13, 1985	Nevado del Ruiz, Colombia
Aug. 21, 1986	Lake Nyos, Cameroon
June 15, 1991	Mt. Pinatubo, Philippines
June–Sept., 1997	Soufrière Hills, Montserrat

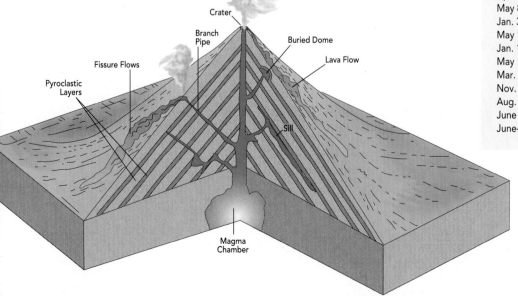

237 Million Years Ago

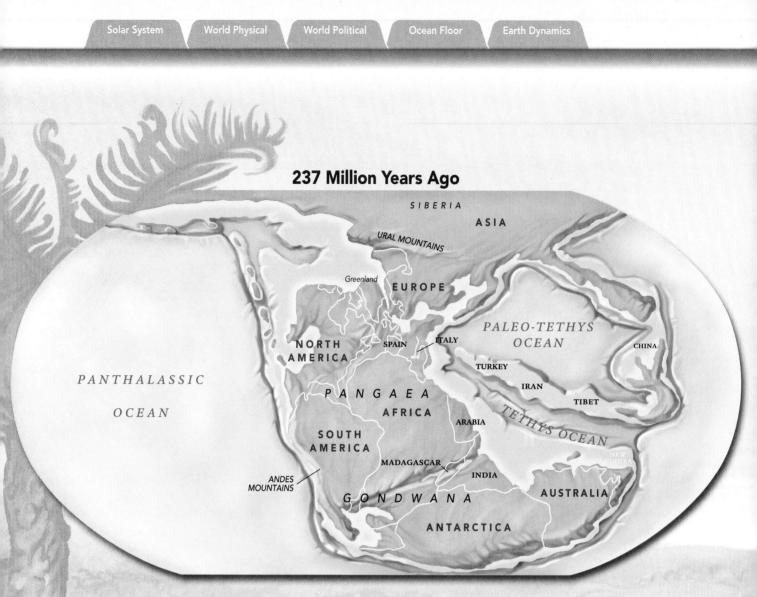

This peculiar—to our eyes—arrangement of continents with its unfamiliar oceans and seas, mountains and plains, and peninsulas and islands reminds us that the dinosaurs lived in a far different landscape than our own. As the last dinosaurs receded into memory, the future Atlantic Ocean and Mediterranean Sea were becoming more substantial and recognizable, and the continents, except for Australia and Antarctica, were nearing their present latitudes. Within the last 65 million years, most continents nestled unhurriedly into their current positions. However, the Indian sub-continent "sprinted" north, crashing into Asia and bulldozing up the Himalayas, earth's loftiest mountain range.

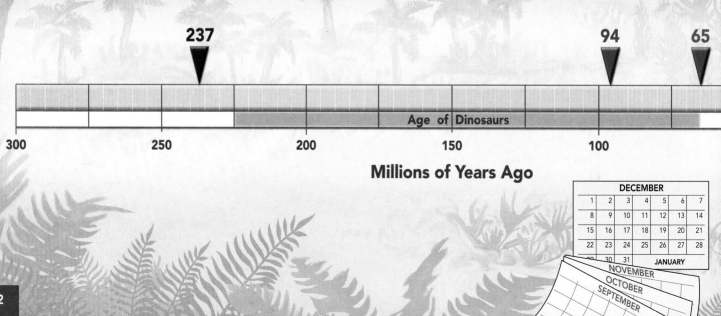

Millions of Years Ago

94 Million Years Ago

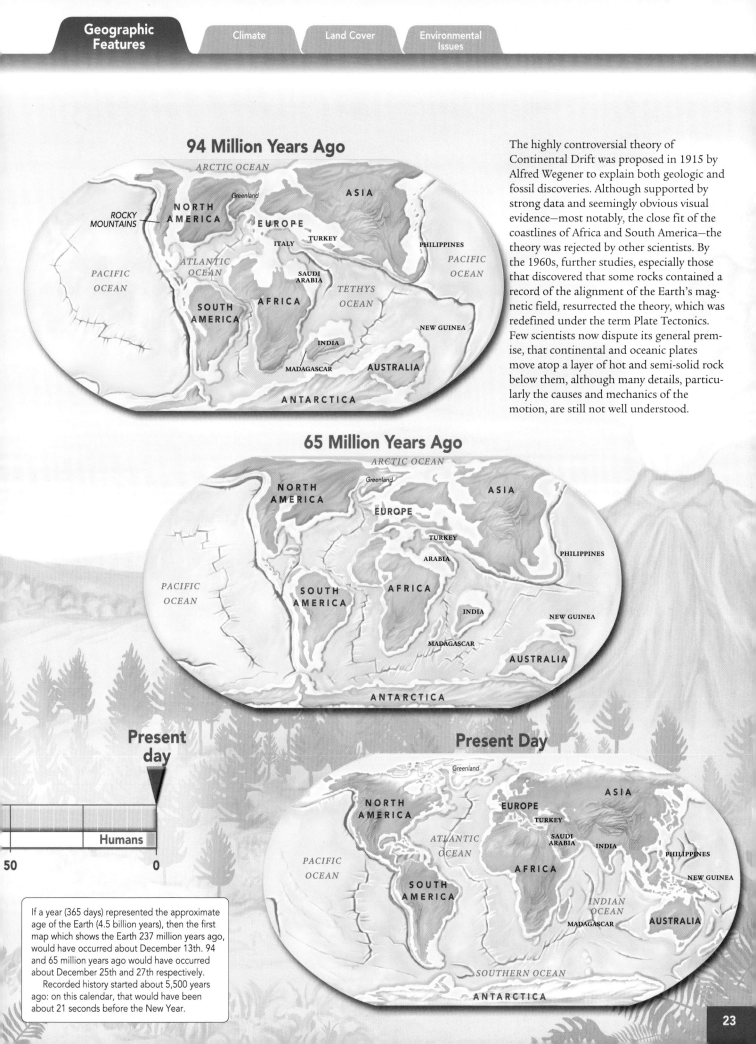

ARCTIC OCEAN

Greenland

ASIA

NORTH AMERICA

ROCKY MOUNTAINS

EUROPE

ITALY

TURKEY

PHILIPPINES

ATLANTIC OCEAN

PACIFIC OCEAN

PACIFIC OCEAN

SAUDI ARABIA

SOUTH AMERICA

AFRICA

TETHYS OCEAN

NEW GUINEA

INDIA

MADAGASCAR

AUSTRALIA

ANTARCTICA

The highly controversial theory of Continental Drift was proposed in 1915 by Alfred Wegener to explain both geologic and fossil discoveries. Although supported by strong data and seemingly obvious visual evidence—most notably, the close fit of the coastlines of Africa and South America—the theory was rejected by other scientists. By the 1960s, further studies, especially those that discovered that some rocks contained a record of the alignment of the Earth's magnetic field, resurrected the theory, which was redefined under the term Plate Tectonics. Few scientists now dispute its general premise, that continental and oceanic plates move atop a layer of hot and semi-solid rock below them, although many details, particularly the causes and mechanics of the motion, are still not well understood.

65 Million Years Ago

ARCTIC OCEAN

Greenland

NORTH AMERICA

ASIA

EUROPE

TURKEY

PHILIPPINES

ARABIA

PACIFIC OCEAN

SOUTH AMERICA

AFRICA

INDIA

NEW GUINEA

MADAGASCAR

AUSTRALIA

ANTARCTICA

Present day

Humans

50   0

Present Day

Greenland

NORTH AMERICA

EUROPE

ASIA

TURKEY

ATLANTIC OCEAN

SAUDI ARABIA

INDIA

PHILIPPINES

PACIFIC OCEAN

AFRICA

NEW GUINEA

SOUTH AMERICA

INDIAN OCEAN

MADAGASCAR

AUSTRALIA

SOUTHERN OCEAN

ANTARCTICA

If a year (365 days) represented the approximate age of the Earth (4.5 billion years), then the first map which shows the Earth 237 million years ago, would have occurred about December 13th. 94 and 65 million years ago would have occurred about December 25th and 27th respectively.

Recorded history started about 5,500 years ago: on this calendar, that would have been about 21 seconds before the New Year.

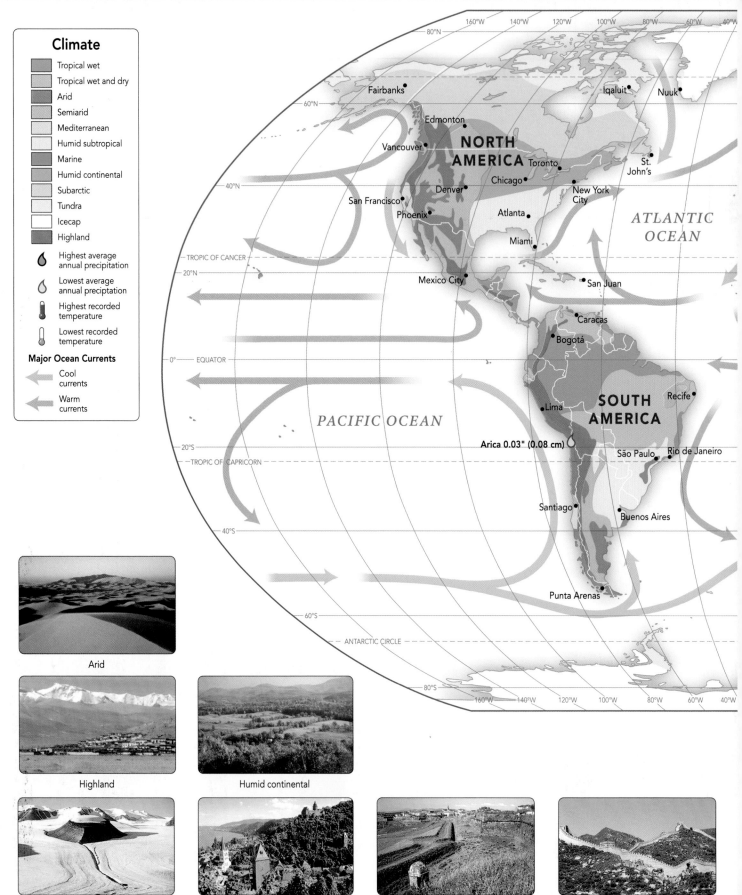

Climate

- Tropical wet
- Tropical wet and dry
- Arid
- Semiarid
- Mediterranean
- Humid subtropical
- Marine
- Humid continental
- Subarctic
- Tundra
- Icecap
- Highland

- Highest average annual precipitation
- Lowest average annual preciptation
- Highest recorded temperature
- Lowest recorded temperature

Major Ocean Currents

- Cool currents
- Warm currents

Fairbanks
Iqaluit
Nuuk
Edmonton
Vancouver
NORTH AMERICA
Toronto
St. John's
Chicago
Denver
New York City
San Francisco
Atlanta
Phoenix
Miami
ATLANTIC OCEAN
Mexico City
San Juan
Caracas
Bogotá
SOUTH AMERICA
Recife
PACIFIC OCEAN
Lima
Arica 0.03" (0.08 cm)
São Paulo
Rio de Janeiro
Santiago
Buenos Aires
Punta Arenas

80°N
60°N
40°N
TROPIC OF CANCER
20°N
EQUATOR 0°
20°S
TROPIC OF CAPRICORN
40°S
60°S
ANTARCTIC CIRCLE
80°S

160°W 140°W 120°W 100°W 80°W 60°W 40°W

Arid

Highland

Humid continental

Icecap

Marine

Mediterranean

Semiarid

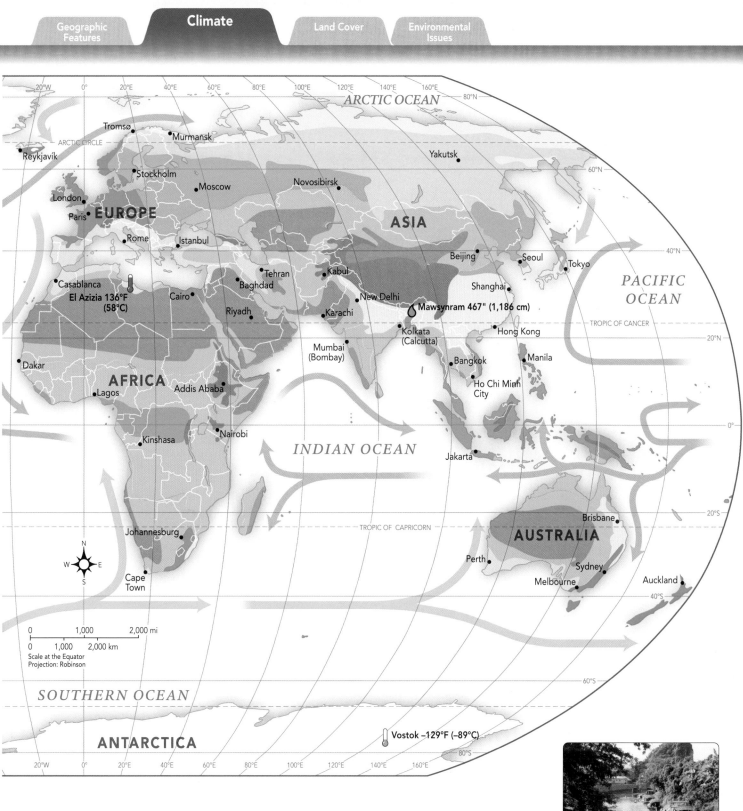

ARCTIC OCEAN

80°N

Tromsø
Murmansk
ARCTIC CIRCLE
Reykjavík
Yakutsk
60°N
Stockholm
London
Moscow
Novosibirsk
EUROPE
Paris
Rome
Istanbul
ASIA
40°N
Beijing
Seoul
Tokyo
PACIFIC OCEAN
Casablanca
Tehran
Kabul
Shanghai
El Azizia 136°F (58°C)
Baghdad
Cairo
New Delhi
Mawsynram 467" (1,186 cm)
Riyadh
Karachi
Hong Kong
TROPIC OF CANCER
Kolkata (Calcutta)
20°N
Dakar
Mumbai (Bombay)
Bangkok
Manila
AFRICA
Addis Ababa
Ho Chi Minh City
Lagos
0°
Kinshasa
Nairobi
INDIAN OCEAN
Jakarta

N
W E
S

AUSTRALIA
20°S
Johannesburg
Brisbane
TROPIC OF CAPRICORN
Perth
Sydney
Cape Town
Melbourne
Auckland
40°S

0   1,000   2,000 mi
0   1,000   2,000 km
Scale at the Equator
Projection: Robinson

SOUTHERN OCEAN
60°S

ANTARCTICA
Vostok −129°F (−89°C)
80°S

Humid subtropical

Subarctic

Tropical wet

Tropical wet and dry

Tundra

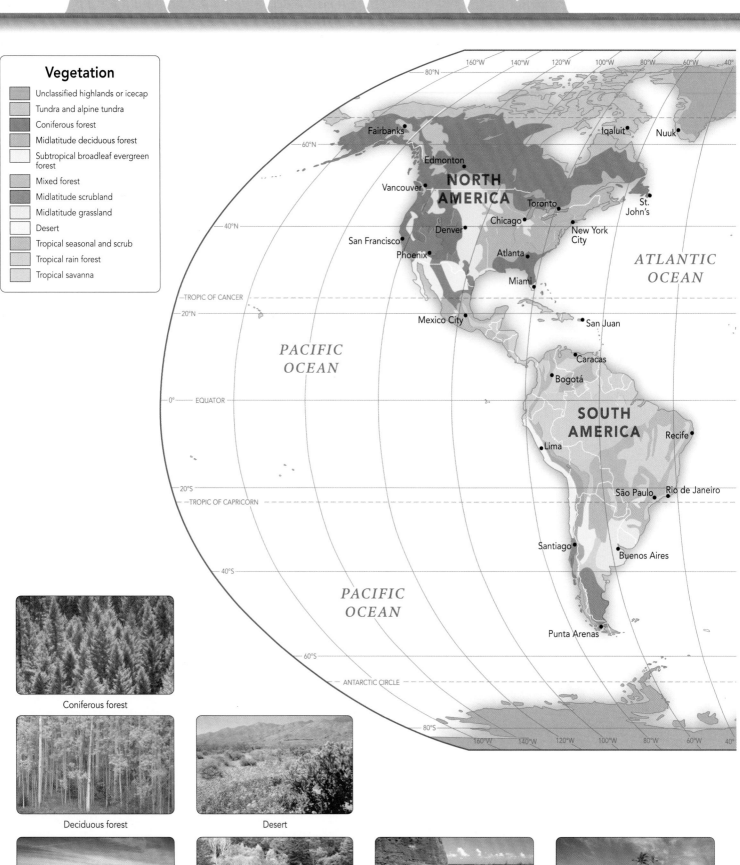

Vegetation

- Unclassified highlands or icecap
- Tundra and alpine tundra
- Coniferous forest
- Midlatitude deciduous forest
- Subtropical broadleaf evergreen forest
- Mixed forest
- Midlatitude scrubland
- Midlatitude grassland
- Desert
- Tropical seasonal and scrub
- Tropical rain forest
- Tropical savanna

Fairbanks · Iqaluit · Nuuk · Edmonton · Vancouver · **NORTH AMERICA** · Toronto · St. John's · Denver · Chicago · New York City · San Francisco · Atlanta · Phoenix · Miami · Mexico City · San Juan · Caracas · Bogotá · **SOUTH AMERICA** · Recife · Lima · São Paulo · Rio de Janeiro · Santiago · Buenos Aires · Punta Arenas

ATLANTIC OCEAN

PACIFIC OCEAN

PACIFIC OCEAN

TROPIC OF CANCER · EQUATOR · TROPIC OF CAPRICORN · ANTARCTIC CIRCLE

Coniferous forest

Deciduous forest

Desert

Midlatitude scrubland

Mixed forest

Subtropical broadleaf evergreen forest

Tropical rain forest

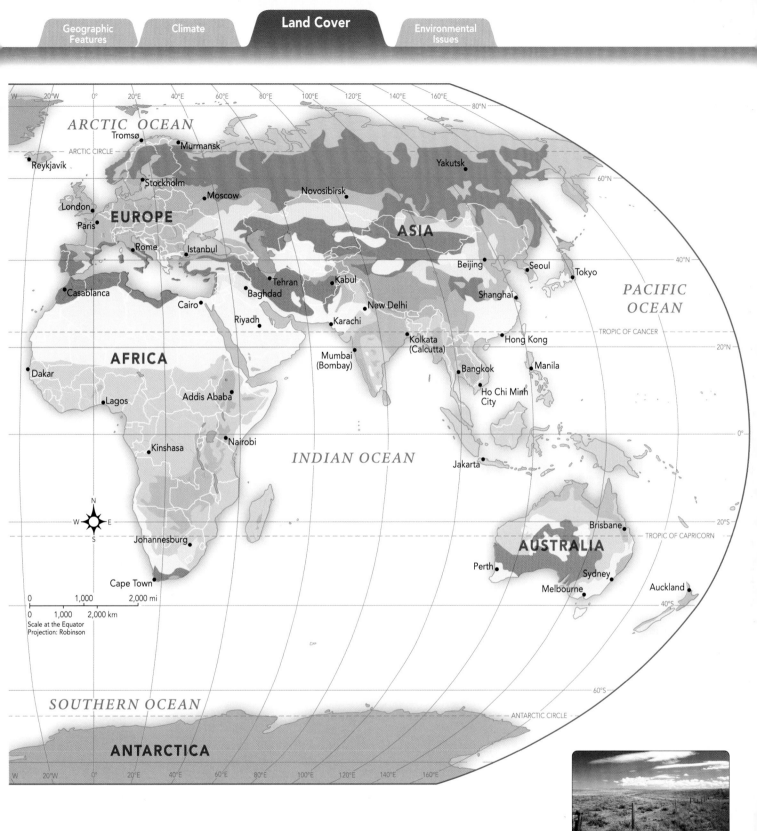

ARCTIC OCEAN

ARCTIC CIRCLE

Tromsø
Murmansk
Reykjavík
Yakutsk

Stockholm
Novosibirsk
London
Moscow
EUROPE
ASIA
Paris
Rome
Istanbul
Beijing
Seoul
Tokyo

PACIFIC OCEAN

Casablanca
Tehran
Kabul
Shanghai
Cairo
Baghdad
Riyadh
New Delhi
Karachi
Hong Kong
TROPIC OF CANCER

Kolkata (Calcutta)
AFRICA
Mumbai (Bombay)
Bangkok
Manila
Dakar
Ho Chi Minh City

Lagos
Addis Ababa
Nairobi
INDIAN OCEAN
Kinshasa
Jakarta

Johannesburg
AUSTRALIA
Brisbane
TROPIC OF CAPRICORN

Perth
Sydney
Cape Town
Melbourne
Auckland

0   1,000   2,000 mi
0   1,000   2,000 km
Scale at the Equator
Projection: Robinson

SOUTHERN OCEAN

ANTARCTIC CIRCLE

ANTARCTICA

Midlatitude grassland

Tropical savanna

Tropical seasonal and scrub

Tundra and alpine tundra

Unclassified highlands or icecap

World Forest Cover

Forests help regulate climate by storing huge amounts of carbon dioxide, while providing habitats for countless animal and plant species. Environmentalists have voiced concern over a long-term decrease in forest cover, as forest lands have been cleared for such purposes as farming, logging, mining, and urban expansion.

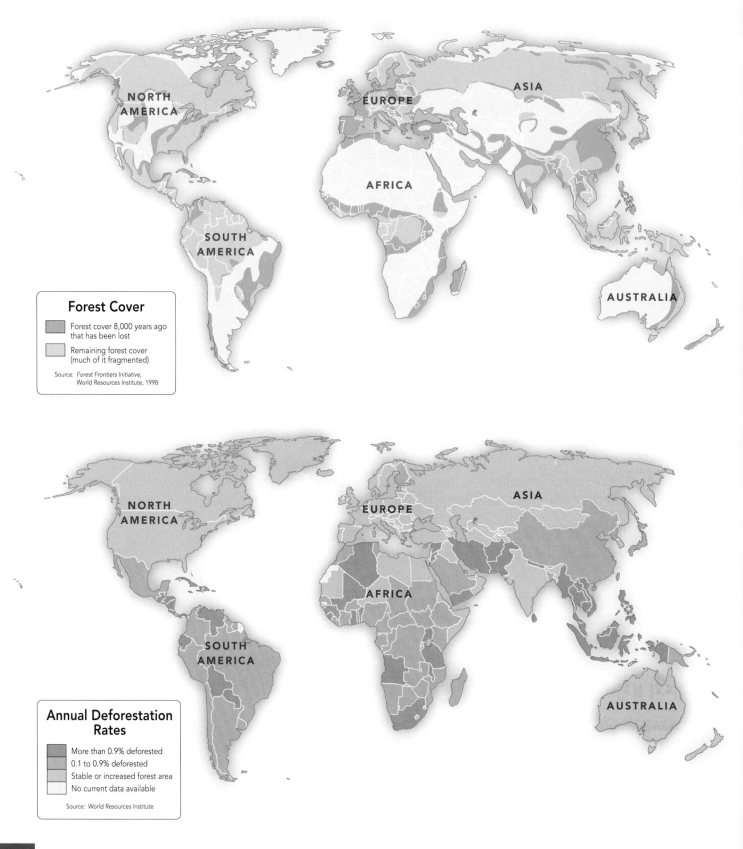

Forest Cover

- Forest cover 8,000 years ago that has been lost
- Remaining forest cover (much of it fragmented)

Source: *Forest Frontiers Initiative,* World Resources Institute, 1998

Annual Deforestation Rates

- More than 0.9% deforested
- 0.1 to 0.9% deforested
- Stable or increased forest area
- No current data available

Source: World Resources Institute

Tropical Rain Forests

Tropical rain forests, found around the Earth within 10 degrees of the Equator, contain more than half of all the world's plants and animal species, besides being home to many indigenous peoples. They are vital to the balance of nature. In the past 40 years alone, about one-fifth of the acreage has been cleared for logging and other purposes. These rain forests, including the major forests pinpointed here, remain under serious threat.

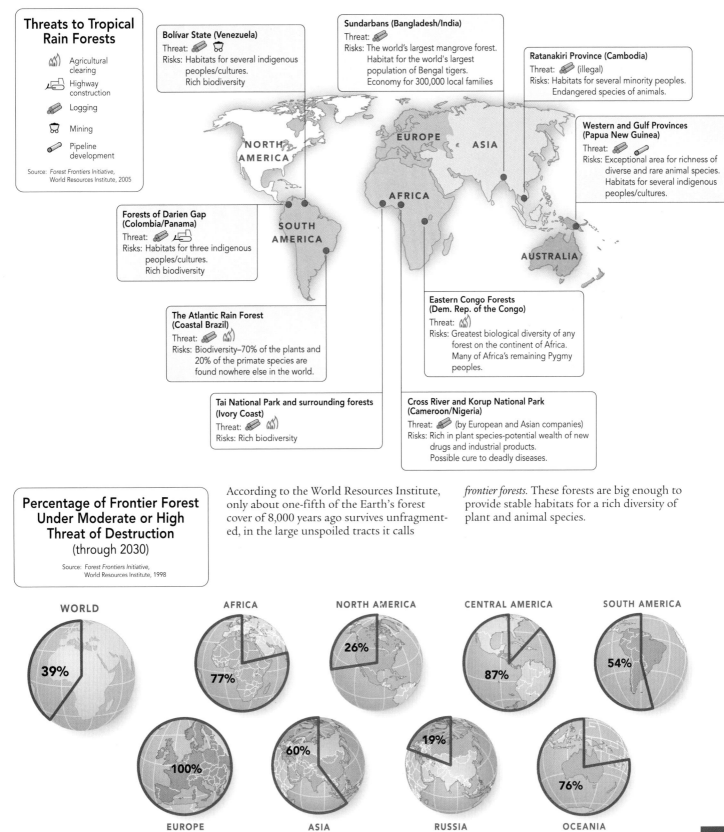

Threats to Tropical Rain Forests

- Agricultural clearing
- Highway construction
- Logging
- Mining
- Pipeline development

Source: *Forest Frontiers Initiative, World Resources Institute, 2005*

Bolívar State (Venezuela)
Threat:
Risks: Habitats for several indigenous peoples/cultures. Rich biodiversity

Sundarbans (Bangladesh/India)
Threat:
Risks: The world's largest mangrove forest. Habitat for the world's largest population of Bengal tigers. Economy for 300,000 local families

Ratanakiri Province (Cambodia)
Threat: (illegal)
Risks: Habitats for several minority peoples. Endangered species of animals.

Western and Gulf Provinces (Papua New Guinea)
Threat:
Risks: Exceptional area for richness of diverse and rare animal species. Habitats for several indigenous peoples/cultures.

Forests of Darien Gap (Colombia/Panama)
Threat:
Risks: Habitats for three indigenous peoples/cultures. Rich biodiversity

The Atlantic Rain Forest (Coastal Brazil)
Threat:
Risks: Biodiversity–70% of the plants and 20% of the primate species are found nowhere else in the world.

Eastern Congo Forests (Dem. Rep. of the Congo)
Threat:
Risks: Greatest biological diversity of any forest on the continent of Africa. Many of Africa's remaining Pygmy peoples.

Tai National Park and surrounding forests (Ivory Coast)
Threat:
Risks: Rich biodiversity

Cross River and Korup National Park (Cameroon/Nigeria)
Threat: (by European and Asian companies)
Risks: Rich in plant species-potential wealth of new drugs and industrial products. Possible cure to deadly diseases.

NORTH AMERICA · SOUTH AMERICA · EUROPE · ASIA · AFRICA · AUSTRALIA

Percentage of Frontier Forest Under Moderate or High Threat of Destruction
(through 2030)

Source: *Forest Frontiers Initiative, World Resources Institute, 1998*

According to the World Resources Institute, only about one-fifth of the Earth's forest cover of 8,000 years ago survives unfragmented, in the large unspoiled tracts it calls *frontier forests*. These forests are big enough to provide stable habitats for a rich diversity of plant and animal species.

WORLD 39%

AFRICA 77%

NORTH AMERICA 26%

CENTRAL AMERICA 87%

SOUTH AMERICA 54%

EUROPE 100%

ASIA 60%

RUSSIA 19%

OCEANIA 76%

29

Population

Population
Issues

Languages/
Literacy/Religions

Land Use/GDP/
Employment

Mining/Energy

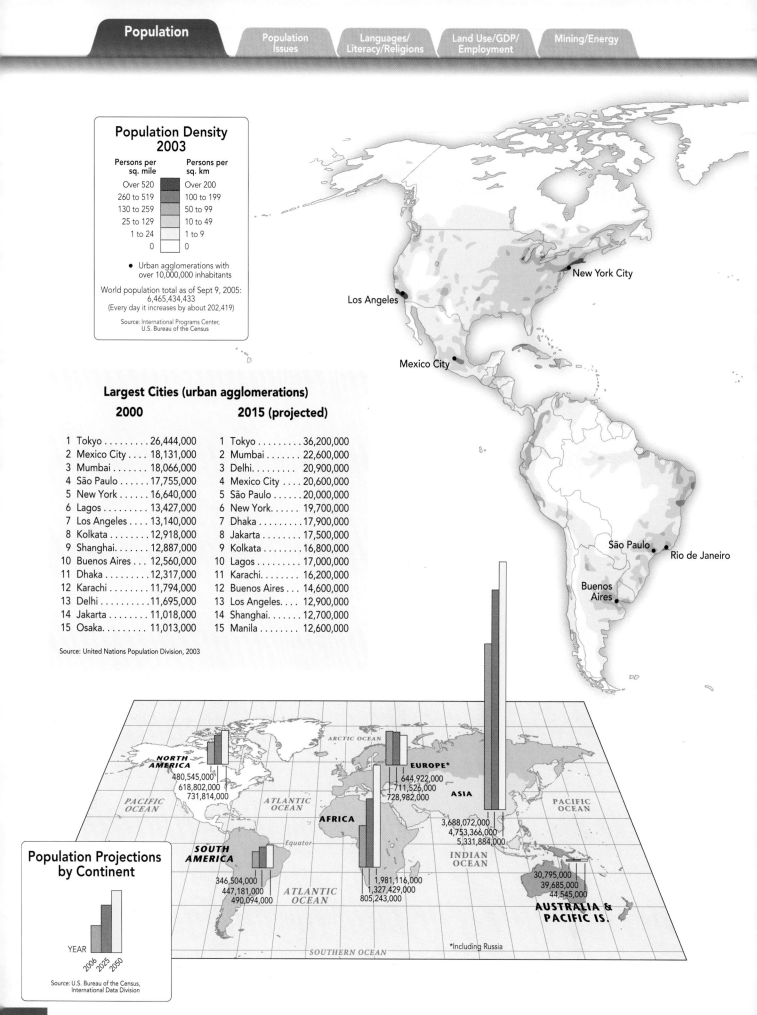

Population Density 2003

Persons per sq. mile		Persons per sq. km
Over 520		Over 200
260 to 519		100 to 199
130 to 259		50 to 99
25 to 129		10 to 49
1 to 24		1 to 9
0		0

• Urban agglomerations with over 10,000,000 inhabitants

World population total as of Sept 9, 2005: 6,465,434,433
(Every day it increases by about 202,419)

Source: International Programs Center, U.S. Bureau of the Census

Largest Cities (urban agglomerations)

	2000		2015 (projected)
1	Tokyo 26,444,000	1	Tokyo 36,200,000
2	Mexico City 18,131,000	2	Mumbai 22,600,000
3	Mumbai 18,066,000	3	Delhi 20,900,000
4	São Paulo 17,755,000	4	Mexico City 20,600,000
5	New York 16,640,000	5	São Paulo 20,000,000
6	Lagos 13,427,000	6	New York 19,700,000
7	Los Angeles 13,140,000	7	Dhaka 17,900,000
8	Kolkata 12,918,000	8	Jakarta 17,500,000
9	Shanghai. 12,887,000	9	Kolkata 16,800,000
10	Buenos Aires . . . 12,560,000	10	Lagos 17,000,000
11	Dhaka 12,317,000	11	Karachi. 16,200,000
12	Karachi 11,794,000	12	Buenos Aires . . . 14,600,000
13	Delhi 11,695,000	13	Los Angeles. . . . 12,900,000
14	Jakarta 11,018,000	14	Shanghai. 12,700,000
15	Osaka. 11,013,000	15	Manila 12,600,000

Source: United Nations Population Division, 2003

New York City

Los Angeles

Mexico City

São Paulo

Rio de Janeiro

Buenos Aires

Population Projections by Continent

YEAR

2006 2025 2050

Source: U.S. Bureau of the Census, International Data Division

ARCTIC OCEAN

NORTH AMERICA
480,545,000
618,802,000
731,814,000

EUROPE*
644,922,000
711,526,000
728,982,000

ASIA
3,688,072,000
4,753,366,000
5,331,884,000

PACIFIC OCEAN

ATLANTIC OCEAN

AFRICA
1,981,116,000
1,327,429,000
805,243,000

SOUTH AMERICA
346,504,000
447,181,000
490,094,000

Equator

ATLANTIC OCEAN

INDIAN OCEAN

PACIFIC OCEAN

AUSTRALIA & PACIFIC IS.
30,795,000
39,685,000
44,545,000

*Including Russia

SOUTHERN OCEAN

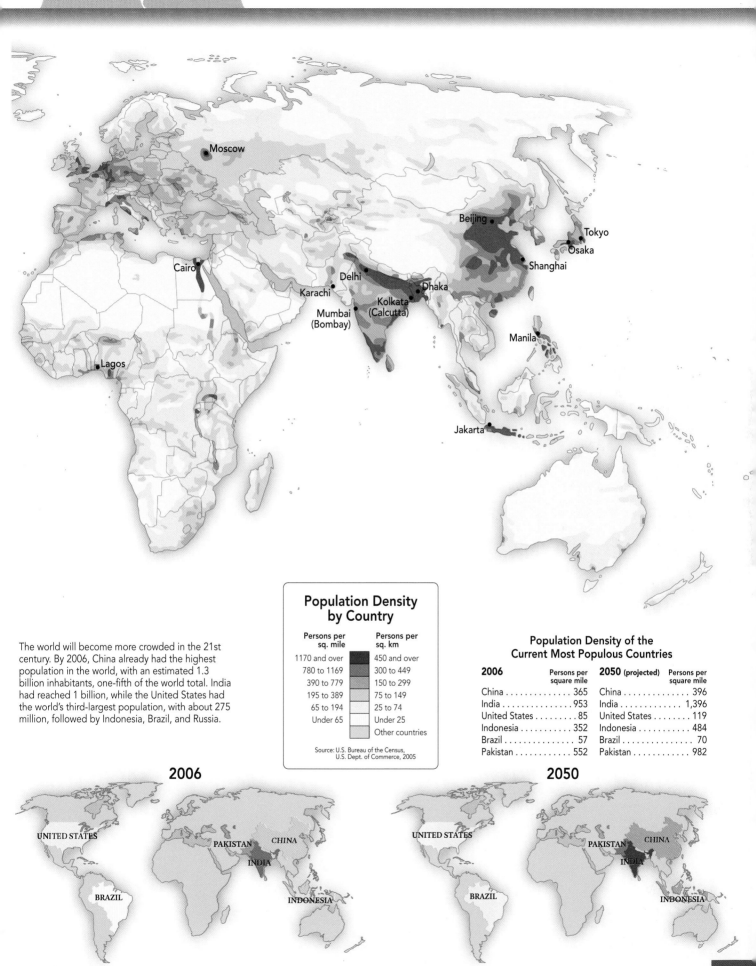

Population Density by Country

Persons per sq. mile	Persons per sq. km
1170 and over	450 and over
780 to 1169	300 to 449
390 to 779	150 to 299
195 to 389	75 to 149
65 to 194	25 to 74
Under 65	Under 25
	Other countries

Source: U.S. Bureau of the Census,
U.S. Dept. of Commerce, 2005

The world will become more crowded in the 21st century. By 2006, China already had the highest population in the world, with an estimated 1.3 billion inhabitants, one-fifth of the world total. India had reached 1 billion, while the United States had the world's third-largest population, with about 275 million, followed by Indonesia, Brazil, and Russia.

Population Density of the Current Most Populous Countries

2006	Persons per square mile	2050 (projected)	Persons per square mile
China	365	China	396
India	953	India	1,396
United States	85	United States	119
Indonesia	352	Indonesia	484
Brazil	57	Brazil	70
Pakistan	552	Pakistan	982

2006

2050

Population

Population
Issues

Languages/
Literacy/Religions

Land Use/GDP/
Employment

Mining/Energy

Life Expectancy

Life expectancy at birth is a common measure of the number of years a person may expect to live. There are many factors, such as nutrition, sanitation, health and medical services, that contribute to helping people live longer.

As some of the above factors improve in the develop-ing countries, life expectancy there should increase. But most of sub-Saharan Africa will have less than average life expectancies.

Although it is not included here, females almost always have a longer life expectancy than males.

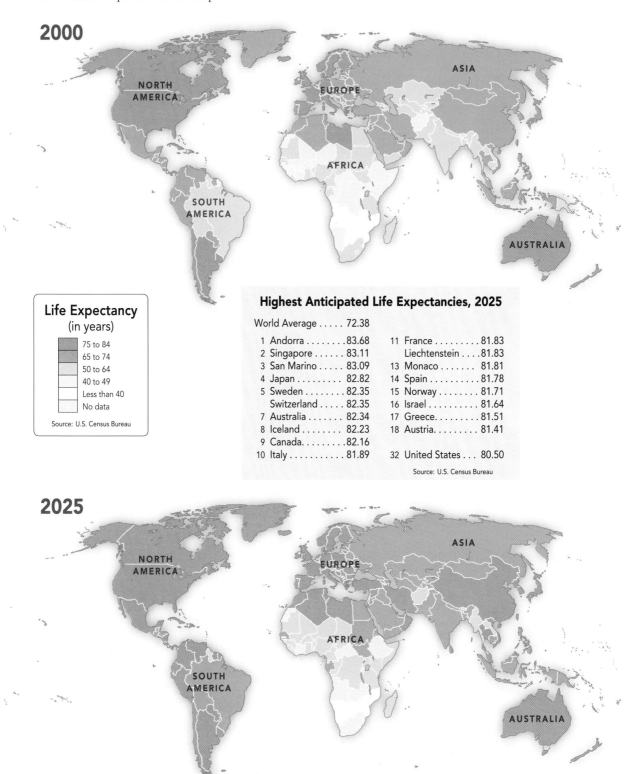

2000

2025

Life Expectancy
(in years)

	75 to 84
	65 to 74
	50 to 64
	40 to 49
	Less than 40
	No data

Source: U.S. Census Bureau

Highest Anticipated Life Expectancies, 2025

World Average 72.38

1	Andorra 83.68	11	France 81.83
2	Singapore 83.11		Liechtenstein 81.83
3	San Marino 83.09	13	Monaco 81.81
4	Japan 82.82	14	Spain 81.78
5	Sweden 82.35	15	Norway 81.71
	Switzerland 82.35	16	Israel 81.64
7	Australia 82.34	17	Greece 81.51
8	Iceland 82.23	18	Austria 81.41
9	Canada 82.16		
10	Italy 81.89	32	United States . . . 80.50

Source: U.S. Census Bureau

Youthful Population

A country with a youthful population often reflects a high birthrate and a short life expectancy. The youthful component of a country's population should be the healthiest and the most energetic. In countries where there is a good system of education, the standards of living can only benefit from a large, educated youthful population. Furthermore, large numbers of young workers offer a means for providing financial and social support for the older members of the population. Unfortunately, a country's economic and physical resources may not be able to absorb a ballooning youthful population. A lack of opportunity in rural regions encourages migration to over-crowded cities where, in turn, a lack of jobs or space in schools leads to swelling numbers of unemployed.

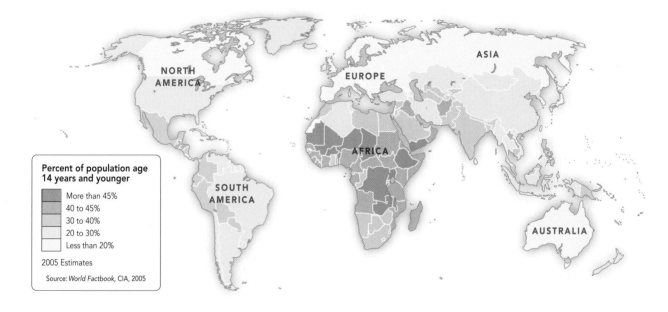

Percent of population age 14 years and younger

- More than 45%
- 40 to 45%
- 30 to 40%
- 20 to 30%
- Less than 20%

2005 Estimates

Source: *World Factbook*, CIA, 2005

Food and Nutrition

There has been a general trend towards better nutrition, but sub-Saharan Africa remains a problem area: increasing numbers of people will be suffering from undernutrition.

On a worldwide basis, the food supply seems adequate. Unfortunately the availability of food and the distribution of people don't always match up.

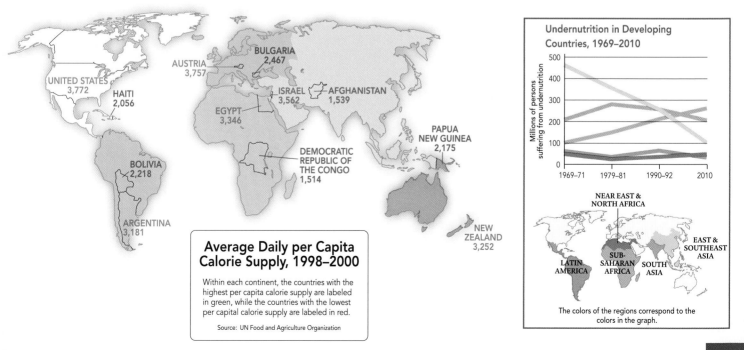

UNITED STATES 3,772
HAITI 2,056
BOLIVIA 2,218
ARGENTINA 3,181
AUSTRIA 3,757
BULGARIA 2,467
ISRAEL 3,562
AFGHANISTAN 1,539
EGYPT 3,346
DEMOCRATIC REPUBLIC OF THE CONGO 1,514
PAPUA NEW GUINEA 2,175
NEW ZEALAND 3,252

Average Daily per Capita Calorie Supply, 1998–2000

Within each continent, the countries with the highest per capita calorie supply are labeled in green, while the countries with the lowest per capital calorie supply are labeled in red.

Source: UN Food and Agriculture Organization

Undernutrition in Developing Countries, 1969–2010

Millions of persons suffering from undernutrition

500
400
300
200
100
0

1969–71   1979–81   1990–92   2010

NEAR EAST & NORTH AFRICA
LATIN AMERICA
SUB-SAHARAN AFRICA
SOUTH ASIA
EAST & SOUTHEAST ASIA

The colors of the regions correspond to the colors in the graph.

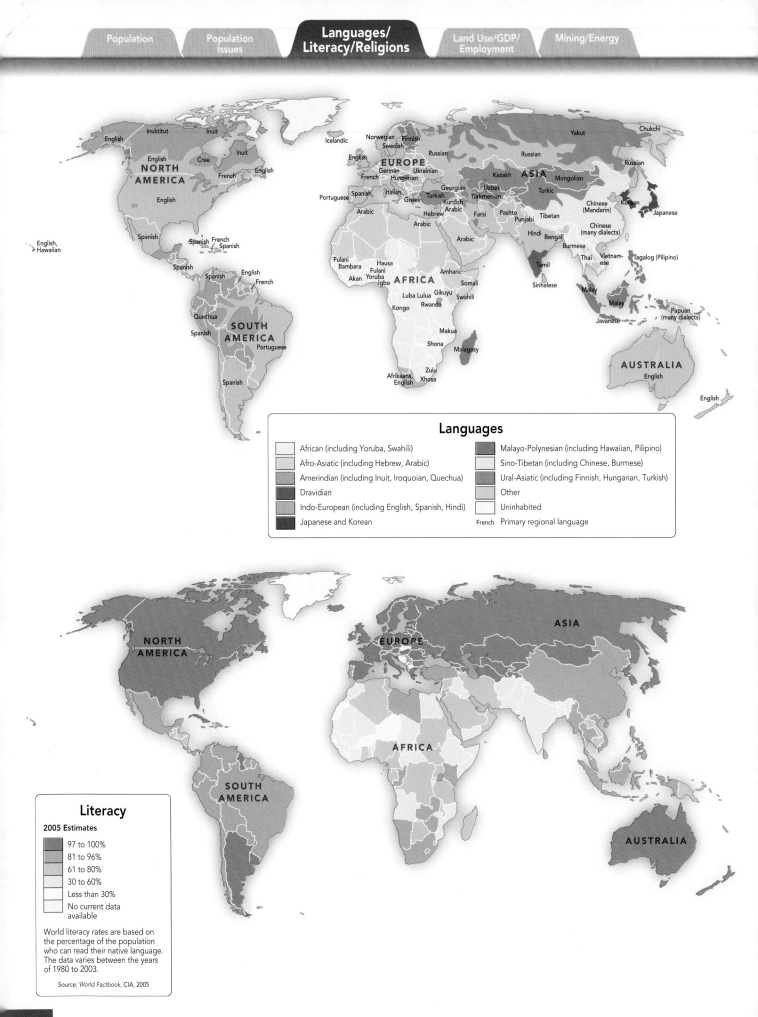

Languages

African (including Yoruba, Swahili)	Malayo-Polynesian (including Hawaiian, Pilipino)
Afro-Asiatic (including Hebrew, Arabic)	Sino-Tibetan (including Chinese, Burmese)
Amerindian (including Inuit, Iroquoian, Quechua)	Ural-Asiatic (including Finnish, Hungarian, Turkish)
Dravidian	Other
Indo-European (including English, Spanish, Hindi)	Uninhabited
Japanese and Korean	French Primary regional language

Literacy

2005 Estimates

- 97 to 100%
- 81 to 96%
- 61 to 80%
- 30 to 60%
- Less than 30%
- No current data available

World literacy rates are based on the percentage of the population who can read their native language. The data varies between the years of 1980 to 2003.

Source: *World Factbook*, CIA, 2005

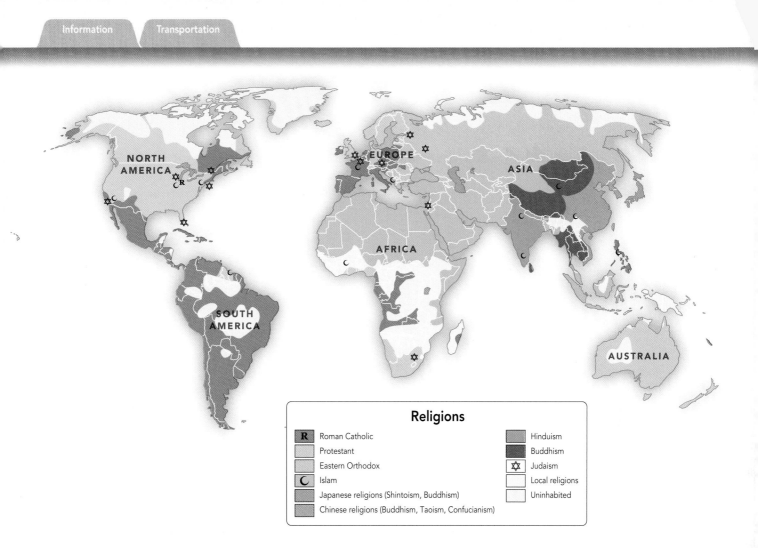

NORTH
AMERICA

EUROPE

ASIA

AFRICA

SOUTH
AMERICA

AUSTRALIA

Religions

R Roman Catholic	Hinduism
Protestant	Buddhism
Eastern Orthodox	☆ Judaism
☪ Islam	Local religions
Japanese religions (Shintoism, Buddhism)	Uninhabited
Chinese religions (Buddhism, Taoism, Confucianism)	

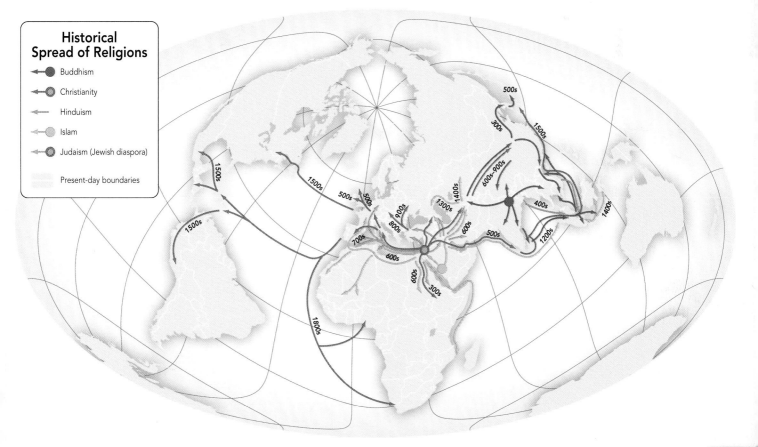

Historical
Spread of Religions

← Buddhism	
← Christianity	
← Hinduism	
← Islam	
← Judaism (Jewish diaspora)	
Present-day boundaries	

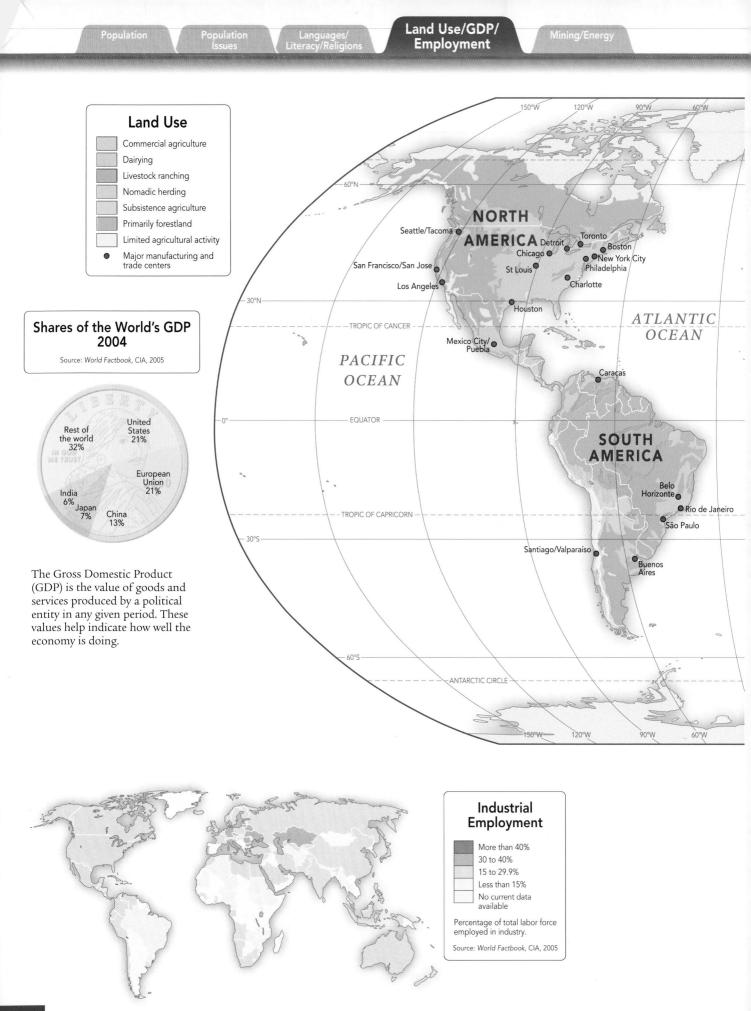

Land Use

- Commercial agriculture
- Dairying
- Livestock ranching
- Nomadic herding
- Subsistence agriculture
- Primarily forestland
- Limited agricultural activity
- ● Major manufacturing and trade centers

Shares of the World's GDP 2004

Source: *World Factbook*, CIA, 2005

Rest of the world 32%
United States 21%
European Union 21%
India 6%
Japan 7%
China 13%

The Gross Domestic Product (GDP) is the value of goods and services produced by a political entity in any given period. These values help indicate how well the economy is doing.

Industrial Employment

- More than 40%
- 30 to 40%
- 15 to 29.9%
- Less than 15%
- No current data available

Percentage of total labor force employed in industry.

Source: *World Factbook*, CIA, 2005

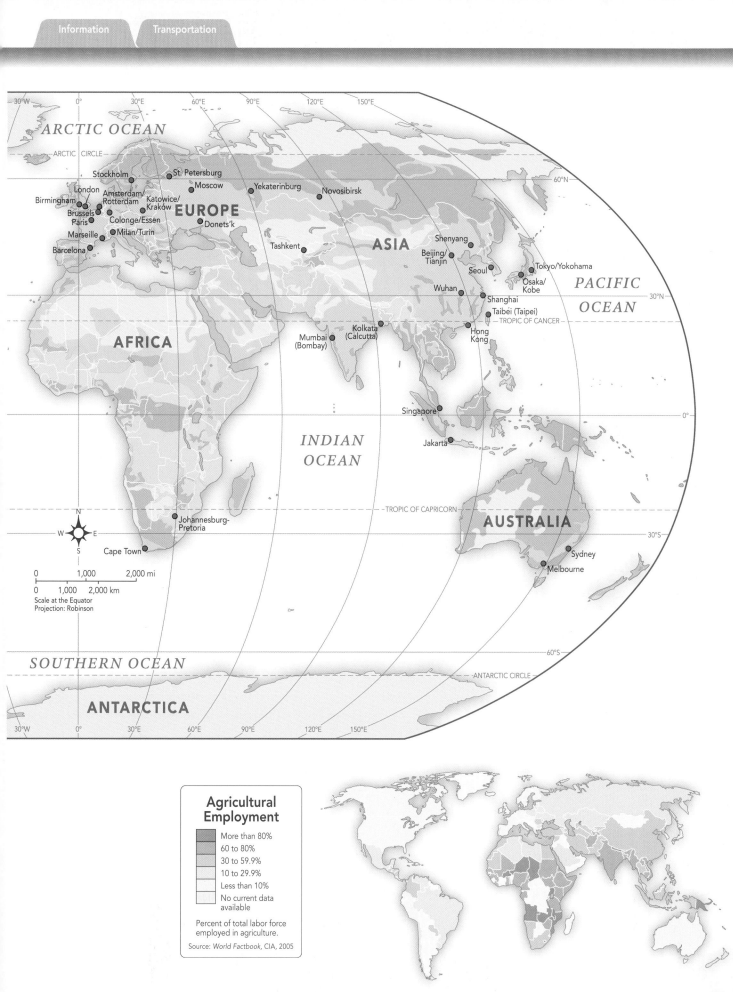

ARCTIC OCEAN

ARCTIC CIRCLE

Stockholm
St. Petersburg
London
Moscow
Birmingham
Amsterdam/
Rotterdam
Yekaterinburg
Novosibirsk
Brussels
Katowice/
Kraków
EUROPE
Paris
Colonge/Essen
Donets'k
Marseille
Milan/Turin
Barcelona
Tashkent
ASIA
Shenyang
Beijing/
Tianjin
Seoul
Tokyo/Yokohama
Osaka/
Kobe
PACIFIC
OCEAN
Wuhan
Shanghai
Taibéi (Taipei)
TROPIC OF CANCER
AFRICA
Mumbai
(Bombay)
Kolkata
(Calcutta)
Hong
Kong

Singapore

INDIAN
OCEAN

Jakarta

AUSTRALIA

TROPIC OF CAPRICORN

Johannesburg-
Pretoria

N
W   E
S

Cape Town

Sydney
Melbourne

0   1,000   2,000 mi
0   1,000   2,000 km
Scale at the Equator
Projection: Robinson

SOUTHERN OCEAN

ANTARCTIC CIRCLE

ANTARCTICA

Agricultural Employment

- More than 80%
- 60 to 80%
- 30 to 59.9%
- 10 to 29.9%
- Less than 10%
- No current data available

Percent of total labor force employed in agriculture.

Source: *World Factbook*, CIA, 2005

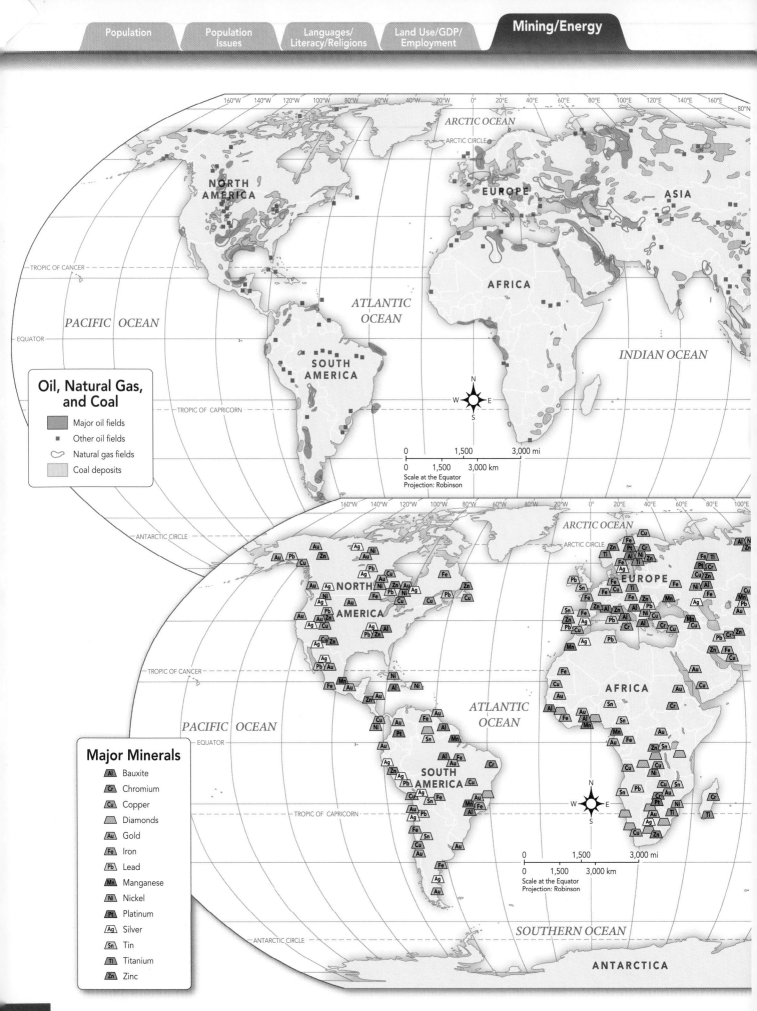

Oil, Natural Gas, and Coal

- Major oil fields
- Other oil fields
- Natural gas fields
- Coal deposits

Major Minerals

- Al — Bauxite
- Cr — Chromium
- Cu — Copper
- Diamonds
- Au — Gold
- Fe — Iron
- Pb — Lead
- Mn — Manganese
- Ni — Nickel
- Pt — Platinum
- Ag — Silver
- Sn — Tin
- Ti — Titanium
- Zn — Zinc

0   1,500   3,000 mi
0 1,500 3,000 km
Scale at the Equator
Projection: Robinson

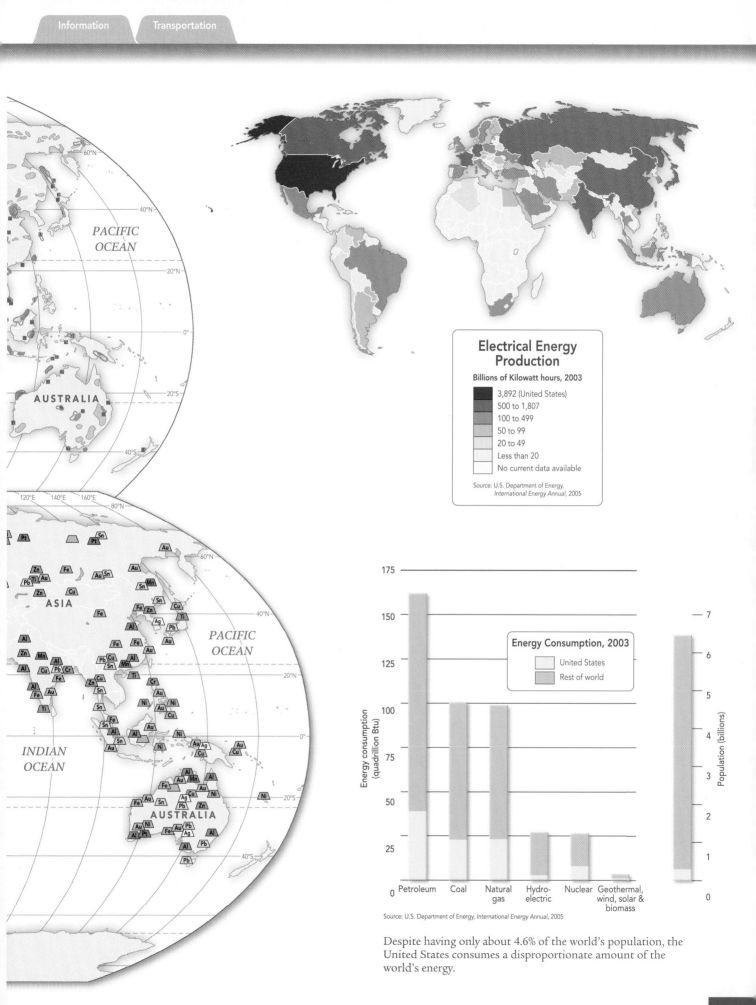

PACIFIC
OCEAN

AUSTRALIA

Electrical Energy Production

Billions of Kilowatt hours, 2003

- 3,892 (United States)
- 500 to 1,807
- 100 to 499
- 50 to 99
- 20 to 49
- Less than 20
- No current data available

Source: U.S. Department of Energy,
International Energy Annual, 2005

PACIFIC
OCEAN

ASIA

INDIAN
OCEAN

AUSTRALIA

Energy Consumption, 2003

- United States
- Rest of world

Energy consumption (quadrillion Btu)

Population (billions)

Petroleum Coal Natural gas Hydro-electric Nuclear Geothermal, wind, solar & biomass

Source: U.S. Department of Energy, *International Energy Annual*, 2005

Despite having only about 4.6% of the world's population, the United States consumes a disproportionate amount of the world's energy.

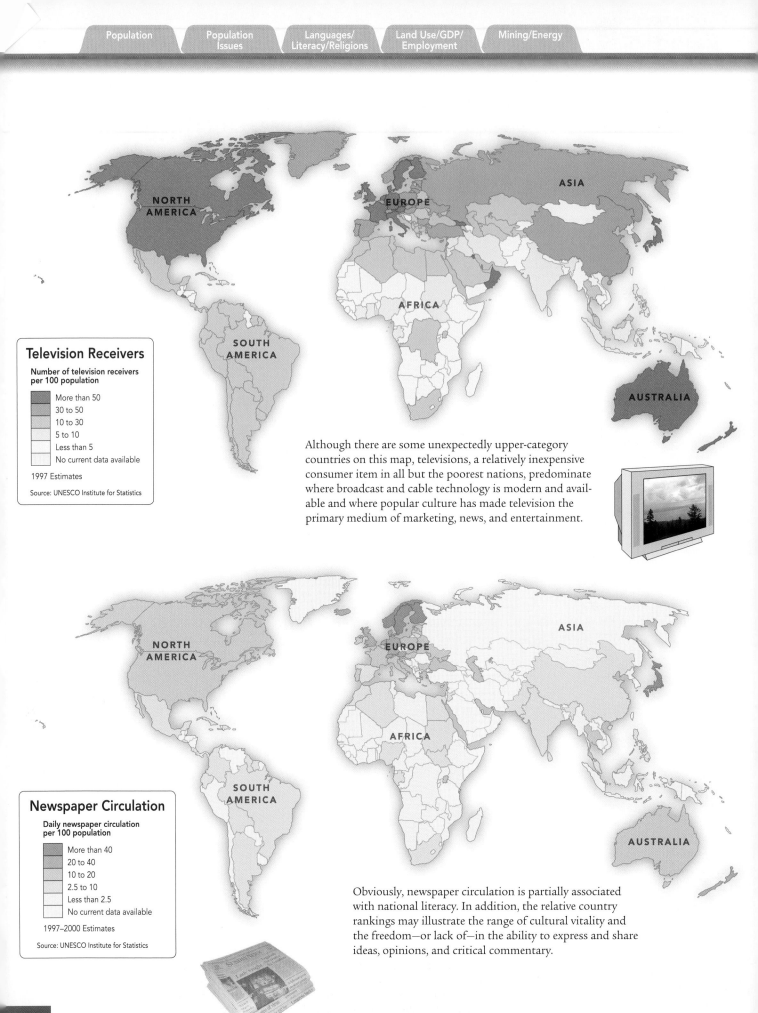

Television Receivers

Number of television receivers per 100 population

- More than 50
- 30 to 50
- 10 to 30
- 5 to 10
- Less than 5
- No current data available

1997 Estimates

Source: UNESCO Institute for Statistics

Although there are some unexpectedly upper-category countries on this map, televisions, a relatively inexpensive consumer item in all but the poorest nations, predominate where broadcast and cable technology is modern and available and where popular culture has made television the primary medium of marketing, news, and entertainment.

Newspaper Circulation

Daily newspaper circulation per 100 population

- More than 40
- 20 to 40
- 10 to 20
- 2.5 to 10
- Less than 2.5
- No current data available

1997–2000 Estimates

Source: UNESCO Institute for Statistics

Obviously, newspaper circulation is partially associated with national literacy. In addition, the relative country rankings may illustrate the range of cultural vitality and the freedom—or lack of—in the ability to express and share ideas, opinions, and critical commentary.

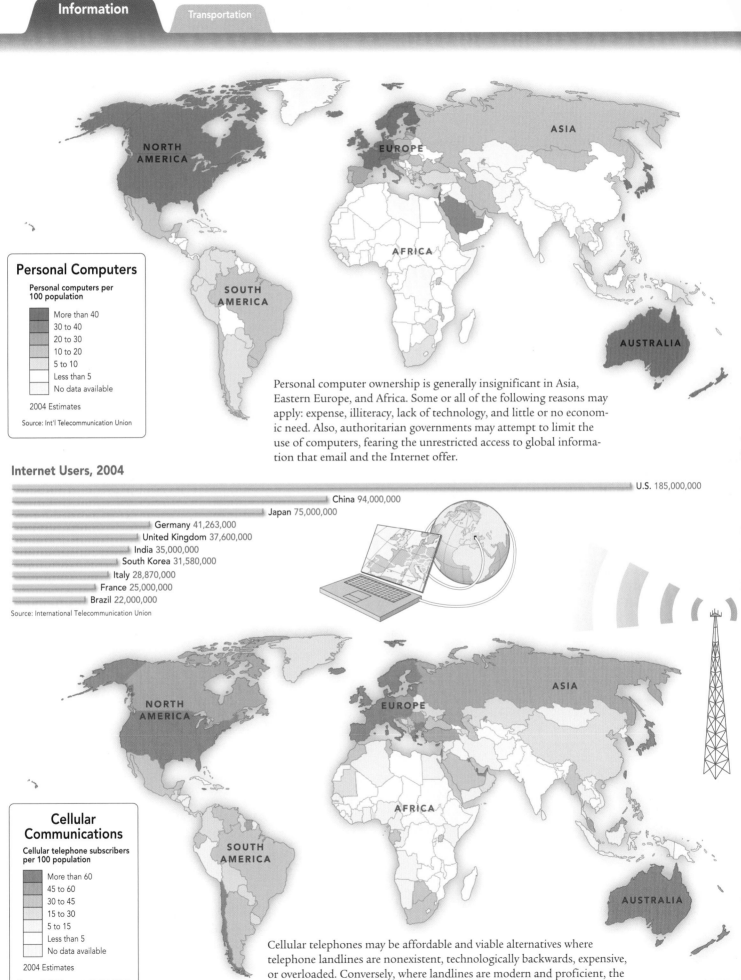

Personal Computers

Personal computers per 100 population

	More than 40
	30 to 40
	20 to 30
	10 to 20
	5 to 10
	Less than 5
	No data available

2004 Estimates

Source: Int'l Telecommunication Union

Personal computer ownership is generally insignificant in Asia, Eastern Europe, and Africa. Some or all of the following reasons may apply: expense, illiteracy, lack of technology, and little or no economic need. Also, authoritarian governments may attempt to limit the use of computers, fearing the unrestricted access to global information that email and the Internet offer.

Internet Users, 2004

- U.S. 185,000,000
- China 94,000,000
- Japan 75,000,000
- Germany 41,263,000
- United Kingdom 37,600,000
- India 35,000,000
- South Korea 31,580,000
- Italy 28,870,000
- France 25,000,000
- Brazil 22,000,000

Source: International Telecommunication Union

Cellular Communications

Cellular telephone subscribers per 100 population

	More than 60
	45 to 60
	30 to 45
	15 to 30
	5 to 15
	Less than 5
	No data available

2004 Estimates

Source: Int'l Telecommunication Union

Cellular telephones may be affordable and viable alternatives where telephone landlines are nonexistent, technologically backwards, expensive, or overloaded. Conversely, where landlines are modern and proficient, the demand for cellular telephones may be less than expected.

Time Zones

Non-standard times

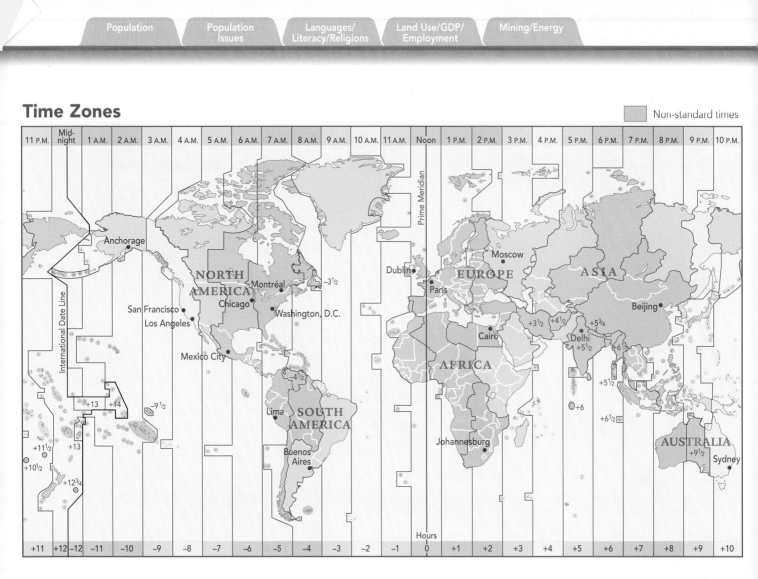

| 11 P.M. | Mid-night | 1 A.M. | 2 A.M. | 3 A.M. | 4 A.M. | 5 A.M. | 6 A.M. | 7 A.M. | 8 A.M. | 9 A.M. | 10 A.M. | 11 A.M. | Noon | 1 P.M. | 2 P.M. | 3 P.M. | 4 P.M. | 5 P.M. | 6 P.M. | 7 P.M. | 8 P.M. | 9 P.M. | 10 P.M. |

Prime Meridian

International Date Line

Anchorage

NORTH AMERICA

Montréal

San Francisco
Los Angeles
Chicago
Washington, D.C.

Mexico City

−3½

Dublin

Moscow

EUROPE

Paris

ASIA

Beijing

+3½ +4½ +5¾

Cairo

Delhi
+5½

+6¼

−4½

AFRICA

Lima

SOUTH AMERICA

+5½

+13 +14

−9½

+6

+6½

+11½
+10½
+13

+12¾

Buenos Aires

Johannesburg

AUSTRALIA
+9½
Sydney

| Hours |
| +11 | +12 | −12 | −11 | −10 | −9 | −8 | −7 | −6 | −5 | −4 | −3 | −2 | −1 | 0 | +1 | +2 | +3 | +4 | +5 | +6 | +7 | +8 | +9 | +10 |

The World is divided into 24 time zones, beginning at the Prime Meridian, which runs through Greenwich, England. The twelve zones east and twelve zones west of the Prime Meridian meet halfway around the globe at the International Date Line.

Traveling in an easterly direction, the time of day moves ahead one hour for each zone crossed. Traveling west, time falls behind one hour per zone. At the International Date Line a traveler gains one day crossing it in an easterly direction, and loses one day traveling west.

Note that the times shown are "standard time." Adjustments are necessary when "daylight saving time" is used.

Average Speeds of Some Passenger Transportation

Walking 3–4 mph/5-6 kph

Bicycle 10 mph/16 kph

Ocean liner, *Queen Elizabeth II* 33 mph/53 kph

Intercity bus, Greyhound; U.S. 54 mph/87 kph

Air cushion vehicle, United Kingdom 69 mph/111kph

Electric train, Amtrak *Acela Express;* Eastern U.S. 150 mph/241 kph (top speed)

High-speed train, *Shinkansen* (Bullet Train); Japan 164 mph/263 kph (average speed between stations)

Jet airliner, Boeing 737 500 mph/805 kph

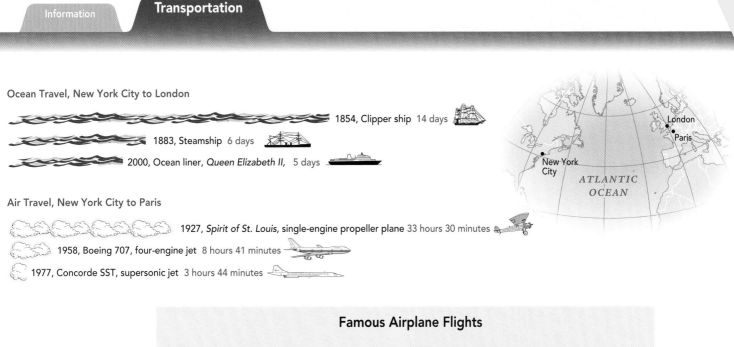

Ocean Travel, New York City to London

1854, Clipper ship 14 days

1883, Steamship 6 days

2000, Ocean liner, *Queen Elizabeth II*, 5 days

Air Travel, New York City to Paris

1927, *Spirit of St. Louis*, single-engine propeller plane 33 hours 30 minutes

1958, Boeing 707, four-engine jet 8 hours 41 minutes

1977, Concorde SST, supersonic jet 3 hours 44 minutes

London
Paris
New York City
ATLANTIC OCEAN

Famous Airplane Flights

1903
Orville and Wilbur Wright made the first engine-powered flight in a heavier-than-air craft at Kitty Hawk, NC. The flight lasted less than 12 seconds.

1908
Glenn Curtiss made the first official flight of more than 1 kilometer (0.62 miles).

1926
Floyd Bennett (pilot) and Richard E. Byrd (navigator) claimed to have circled the North Pole.

1927
Charles A. Lindbergh made the first solo, nonstop, trans-atlantic flight. He flew from Garden City, NY to Paris in 33 hours 30 minutes.

1929
Richard E. Byrd established an Antarctic base at Little America. On November 28 and 29, Byrd and his pilot, Bernt Balchen, left the base and flew to the South Pole.

1932
Amelia Earhart was the first woman to fly across the Atlantic Ocean. She flew from Harbour Grace, Newfoundland to Northern Ireland, a distance of 2,026 miles (3,260 kilometers) in 15 hours 18 minutes.

1933
Wiley Post made the first solo, round-the-world flight. He flew from Floyd Bennett Field in Brooklyn, NY and covered 15,596 miles (25,099 kilometers) in 7 days 18 hours 49 minutes.

1949
An Air Force crew made the first nonstop, round-the-world flight. Using a B-50A bomber, they traveled 23,452 miles (37,742 kilometers) in 3 days 22 hours 1 minute.

1992
French pilots flew the supersonic Concorde around the world, east-to-west, in a record setting 32 hours 49 minutes 3 seconds.

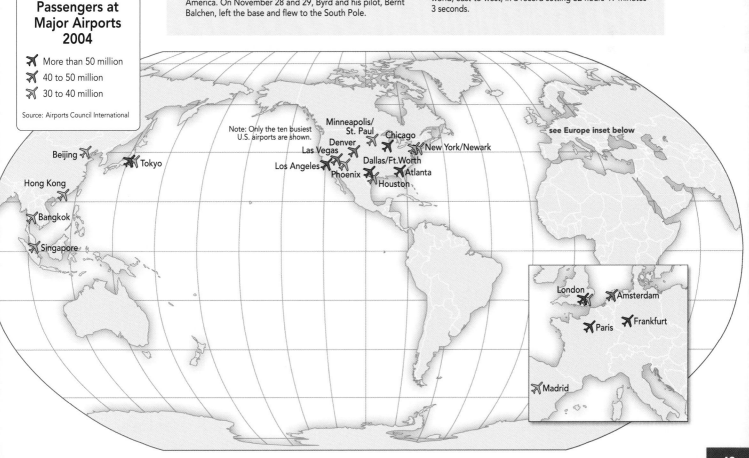

Passengers at Major Airports 2004

✈ More than 50 million

✈ 40 to 50 million

✈ 30 to 40 million

Source: Airports Council International

Note: Only the ten busiest U.S. airports are shown.

Beijing
Tokyo
Hong Kong
Bangkok
Singapore
Minneapolis/ St. Paul
Chicago
Las Vegas
New York/Newark
Denver
Los Angeles
Dallas/Ft.Worth
Phoenix
Atlanta
Houston
see Europe inset below

London
Amsterdam
Paris
Frankfurt
Madrid

North America

Legend

- International boundary
- State or provincial boundary
- ⊛ National capital

Symbol and label sizes indicate relative sizes of cities:

- ● **New York**
- ● Baltimore
- • Charlotte

Facts

- Area: 8,260,174 square miles (21,393,762 square kilometers)
- Highest Point: Denali, United States, 20,310 ft. (6,190 m)
- Lowest Point: Death Valley, United States, 282 ft. (86 m) below sea level
- Longest River: Mississippi-Missouri, 3,877 mi. (6,238 km)
- Largest Lake: Lake Superior, United States/ Canada, 31,700 sq. mi. (82,103 sq. km)
- Largest Country: Canada, 3,851,809 sq. mi. (9,976,185 sq. km)
- Largest Urban Concentration: Mexico City, Mexico, and New York City, United States [A]

Source and notes:
[A] imprecise data prevents selecting one over the other—common estimates for both are 18 million plus; high estimates for both are around 22 million

Nations of the Lesser Antilles

Country	Capital	Country	Capital
Antigua and Barbuda	St. John's	St. Vincent and the Grenadines	Kingstown
St. Kitts and Nevis	Basseterre	Grenada	St. George's
Dominica	Roseau	Trinidad and Tobago	Port-of-Spain
St. Lucia	Castries		
Barbados	Bridgetown		

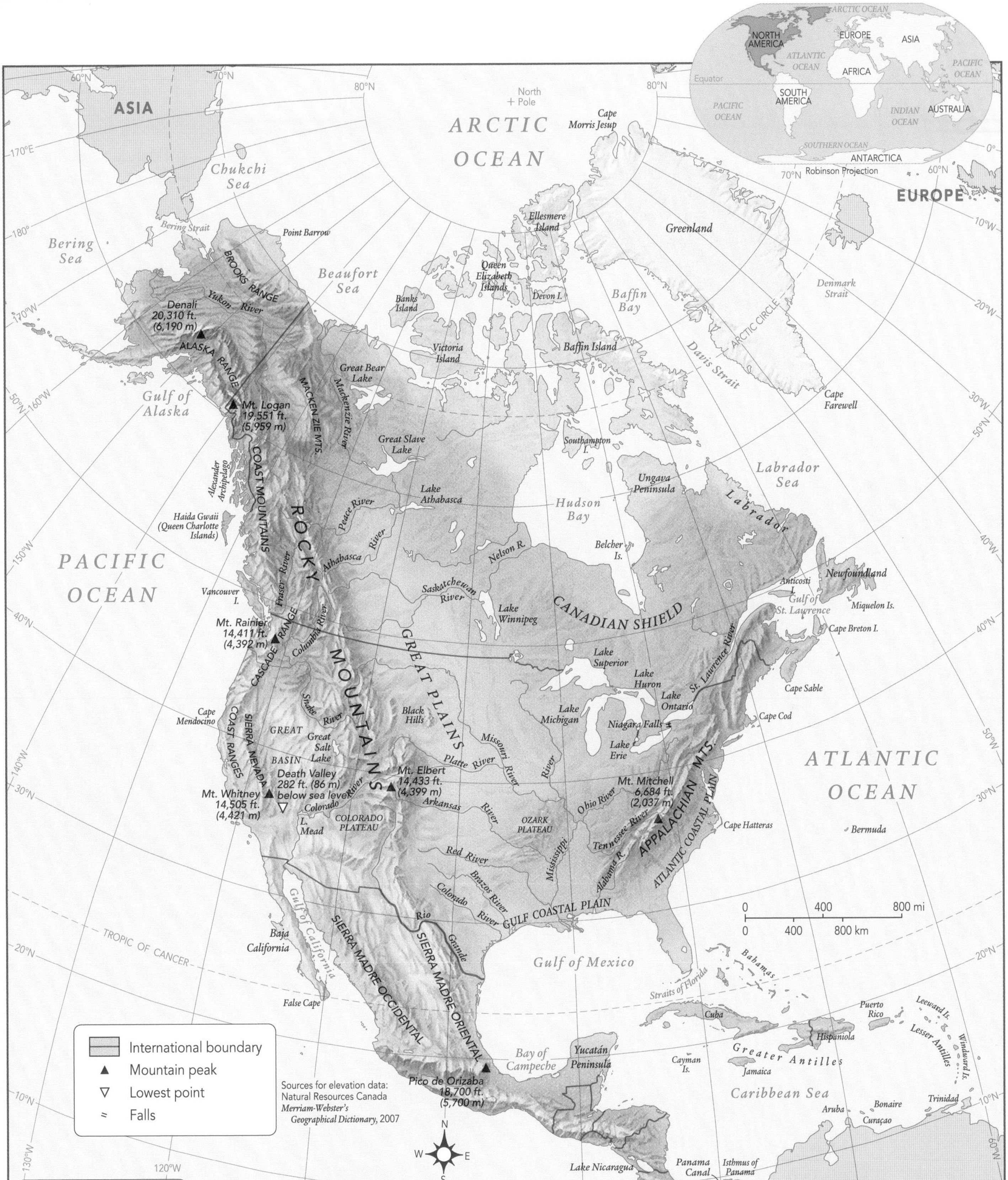
NORTH AMERICA
EUROPE
ASIA
ATLANTIC OCEAN
AFRICA
PACIFIC OCEAN
SOUTH AMERICA
INDIAN OCEAN
AUSTRALIA
ARCTIC OCEAN
Equator
SOUTHERN OCEAN
ANTARCTICA
Robinson Projection
ASIA
ARCTIC OCEAN
North Pole
Cape Morris Jesup
Chukchi Sea
Bering Sea
Bering Strait
Point Barrow
Beaufort Sea
BROOKS RANGE
Yukon River
Denali 20,310 ft. (6,190 m)
ALASKA RANGE
Mt. Logan 19,551 ft. (5,959 m)
Gulf of Alaska
MACKENZIE MTS.
Mackenzie River
Great Bear Lake
Great Slave Lake
Banks Island
Victoria Island
Ellesmere Island
Queen Elizabeth Islands
Devon I.
Baffin Bay
Baffin Island
Greenland
Denmark Strait
ARCTIC CIRCLE
Davis Strait
Cape Farewell
EUROPE
Southampton I.
Ungava Peninsula
Labrador Sea
Labrador
Hudson Bay
Belcher Is.
Alexander Archipelago
COAST MOUNTAINS
Haida Gwaii (Queen Charlotte Islands)
ROCKY MOUNTAINS
Peace River
Lake Athabasca
Athabasca River
Nelson R.
Fraser River
PACIFIC OCEAN
Vancouver I.
Saskatchewan River
Lake Winnipeg
CANADIAN SHIELD
Anticosti I.
Newfoundland
Gulf of St. Lawrence
Miquelon Is.
Cape Breton I.
Mt. Rainier 14,411 ft. (4,392 m)
CASCADE RANGE
Columbia River
GREAT PLAINS
Lake Superior
Lake Huron
Lake Ontario
St. Lawrence River
Cape Sable
Cape Cod
Cape Mendocino
COAST RANGES
SIERRA NEVADA
Snake River
GREAT BASIN
Great Salt Lake
Black Hills
Lake Michigan
Niagara Falls
Lake Erie
Missouri River
Platte River
Mt. Elbert 14,433 ft. (4,399 m)
Death Valley 282 ft. (86 m) below sea level
Mt. Whitney 14,505 ft. (4,421 m)
Colorado River
L. Mead
COLORADO PLATEAU
Arkansas River
OZARK PLATEAU
Mississippi River
Ohio River
Mt. Mitchell 6,684 ft. (2,037 m)
APPALACHIAN MTS.
Tennessee River
Alabama R.
ATLANTIC COASTAL PLAIN
ATLANTIC OCEAN
Cape Hatteras
Bermuda
Red River
Brazos River
Colorado River
GULF COASTAL PLAIN
Rio Grande
Baja California
Gulf of California
SIERRA MADRE OCCIDENTAL
SIERRA MADRE ORIENTAL
TROPIC OF CANCER
Gulf of Mexico
Bahamas
Straits of Florida
False Cape
Cuba
Puerto Rico
Leeward Is.
Hispaniola
Lesser Antilles
Windward Is.
Bay of Campeche
Yucatán Peninsula
Cayman Is.
Greater Antilles
Jamaica
Pico de Orizaba 18,700 ft. (5,700 m)
Caribbean Sea
Trinidad
Aruba
Bonaire
Curaçao
Lake Nicaragua
Panama Canal
Isthmus of Panama
SOUTH AMERICA
0 400 800 mi
0 400 800 km
International boundary
Mountain peak
Lowest point
Falls
Sources for elevation data:
Natural Resources Canada
Merriam-Webster's Geographical Dictionary, 2007
N
W
E
S
60°N
70°N
80°N
170°E
180°
170°W
160°W
150°W
140°W
130°W
120°W
110°W
100°W
90°W
80°W
70°W
60°W
10°W
20°W
30°W
0°
50°N
40°N
30°N
20°N
10°N

Elevation Profile

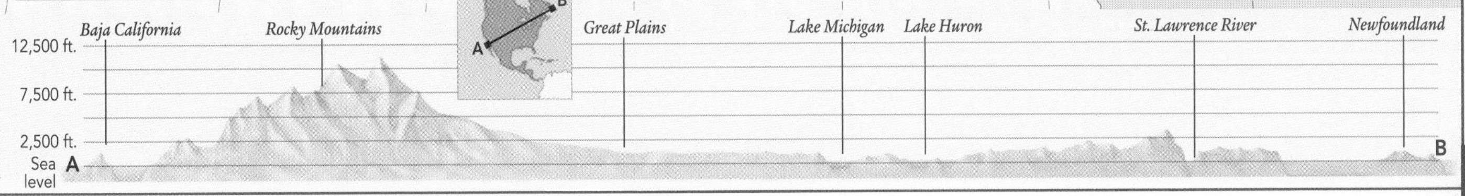
A
B
Baja California
Rocky Mountains
Great Plains
Lake Michigan
Lake Huron
St. Lawrence River
Newfoundland
12,500 ft.
7,500 ft.
2,500 ft.
Sea level

Major Metropolitan Areas

Antigua & Barbuda
St. John's — 22,000

Bahamas
Nassau — 211,000

Barbados
Bridgetown — 6,000

Belize
Belize City — 49,000
Belmopan — 8,000

Canada
Toronto — 4,683,000
Montréal — 3,426,000
Vancouver — 1,987,000
Ottawa — 1,064,000
Calgary — 951,000
Edmonton — 938,000
Québec — 683,000
Winnipeg — 671,000
Hamilton — 662,000

Costa Rica
San José — 1,305,000

Cuba
Havana — 2,192,000

Dominica
Roseau — 16,000

Dominican Republic
Santo Domingo — 2,677,000

El Salvador
San Salvador — 1,909,000

Grenada
St. George's — 5,000

Guatemala
Guatemala City — 1,007,000

Haiti
Port-au-Prince — 991,000

Honduras
Tegucigalpa — 835,000

Jamaica
Kingston — 578,000

Mexico
Mexico City — 16,203,000
Guadalajara — 3,349,000
Monterrey — 3,131,000
Puebla — 1,272,000
Ciudad Juárez — 1,187,000
Tijuana — 1,149,000
León — 1,021,000

Nicaragua
Managua — 1,148,000

Panama
Panama City — 1,002,000

Puerto Rico
San Juan — 2,450,000

St. Kitts & Nevis
Basseterre — 13,000

St. Lucia
Castries — 11,000

St. Vincent & Grenadines
Kingstown — 15,000

Trinidad & Tobago
Port of Spain — 48,000

United States
New York-Newark — 21,200,000
Los Angeles — 16,374,000
Chicago — 9,158,000
Washington-Baltimore — 7,608,000
San Francisco-Oakland-San Jose — 7,039,000
Philadelphia — 6,188,000
Boston — 5,819,000
Detroit — 5,456,000
Dallas-Ft. Worth — 5,222,000
Houston — 4,670,000
Atlanta — 4,112,000
Miami — 3,876,000
Seattle-Tacoma — 3,555,000
Phoenix — 3,252,000
Minneapolis-St. Paul — 2,969,000
Cleveland-Akron — 2,946,000
San Diego — 2,814,000
St. Louis — 2,604,000
Denver — 2,582,000
Tampa-St. Petersburg — 2,396,000
Pittsburgh — 2,359,000
Portland — 2,265,000
Cincinnati — 1,979,000
Sacramento — 1,797,000
Kansas City — 1,776,000
Milwaukee — 1,690,000

International comparability of population data is limited by varying census methods. Where metropolitan population is unavailable, core city population is shown.

Population

Persons per sq. mile	Persons per sq. km
Over 520	Over 200
260 to 519	100 to 199
130 to 259	50 to 99
25 to 129	10 to 49
1 to 24	1 to 9
0	0

Major metropolitan areas
- Over 2 million
- 1 million to 2 million
- Under 1 million

Estimated 2005 Population (in millions)

United States 296
Mexico 106
Canada 33
Guatemala 12
Cuba 11
All others 54

Source: U.S. Census Bureau

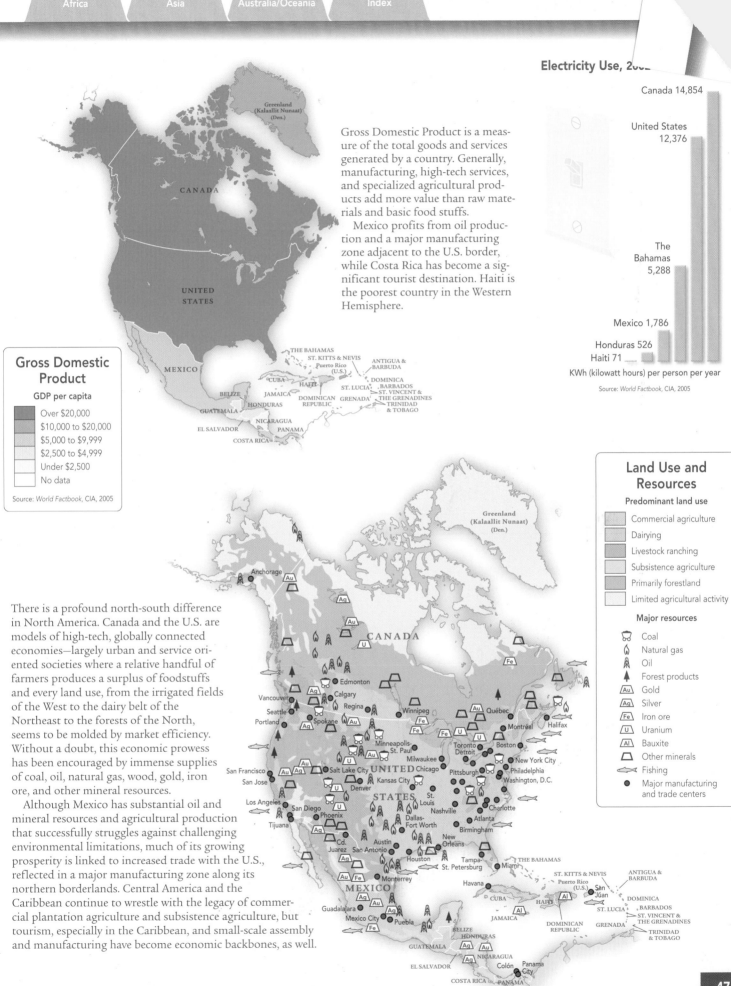

Electricity Use, 2005

Canada 14,854

United States 12,376

The Bahamas 5,288

Mexico 1,786

Honduras 526

Haiti 71

KWh (kilowatt hours) per person per year

Source: *World Factbook*, CIA, 2005

Gross Domestic Product is a measure of the total goods and services generated by a country. Generally, manufacturing, high-tech services, and specialized agricultural products add more value than raw materials and basic food stuffs.

Mexico profits from oil production and a major manufacturing zone adjacent to the U.S. border, while Costa Rica has become a significant tourist destination. Haiti is the poorest country in the Western Hemisphere.

Gross Domestic Product

GDP per capita

Over $20,000
$10,000 to $20,000
$5,000 to $9,999
$2,500 to $4,999
Under $2,500
No data

Source: *World Factbook*, CIA, 2005

Land Use and Resources

Predominant land use

Commercial agriculture
Dairying
Livestock ranching
Subsistence agriculture
Primarily forestland
Limited agricultural activity

Major resources

Coal
Natural gas
Oil
Forest products
Au Gold
Ag Silver
Fe Iron ore
U Uranium
Al Bauxite
Other minerals
Fishing
● Major manufacturing and trade centers

There is a profound north-south difference in North America. Canada and the U.S. are models of high-tech, globally connected economies—largely urban and service oriented societies where a relative handful of farmers produces a surplus of foodstuffs and every land use, from the irrigated fields of the West to the dairy belt of the Northeast to the forests of the North, seems to be molded by market efficiency. Without a doubt, this economic prowess has been encouraged by immense supplies of coal, oil, natural gas, wood, gold, iron ore, and other mineral resources.

Although Mexico has substantial oil and mineral resources and agricultural production that successfully struggles against challenging environmental limitations, much of its growing prosperity is linked to increased trade with the U.S., reflected in a major manufacturing zone along its northern borderlands. Central America and the Caribbean continue to wrestle with the legacy of commercial plantation agriculture and subsistence agriculture, but tourism, especially in the Caribbean, and small-scale assembly and manufacturing have become economic backbones, as well.

47

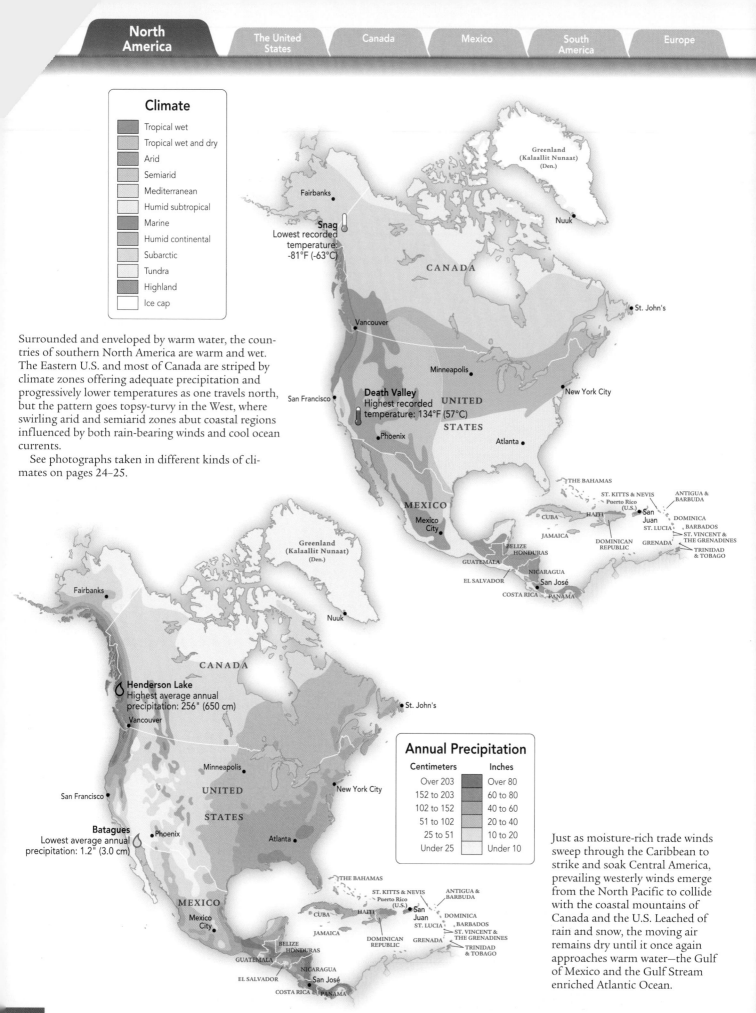

Climate

- Tropical wet
- Tropical wet and dry
- Arid
- Semiarid
- Mediterranean
- Humid subtropical
- Marine
- Humid continental
- Subarctic
- Tundra
- Highland
- Ice cap

Surrounded and enveloped by warm water, the countries of southern North America are warm and wet. The Eastern U.S. and most of Canada are striped by climate zones offering adequate precipitation and progressively lower temperatures as one travels north, but the pattern goes topsy-turvy in the West, where swirling arid and semiarid zones abut coastal regions influenced by both rain-bearing winds and cool ocean currents.

See photographs taken in different kinds of climates on pages 24–25.

Snag Lowest recorded temperature: -81°F (-63°C)

Death Valley Highest recorded temperature: 134°F (57°C)

Henderson Lake Highest average annual precipitation: 256" (650 cm)

Batagues Lowest average annual precipitation: 1.2" (3.0 cm)

Annual Precipitation

Centimeters	Inches
Over 203	Over 80
152 to 203	60 to 80
102 to 152	40 to 60
51 to 102	20 to 40
25 to 51	10 to 20
Under 25	Under 10

Just as moisture-rich trade winds sweep through the Caribbean to strike and soak Central America, prevailing westerly winds emerge from the North Pacific to collide with the coastal mountains of Canada and the U.S. Leached of rain and snow, the moving air remains dry until it once again approaches warm water—the Gulf of Mexico and the Gulf Stream enriched Atlantic Ocean.

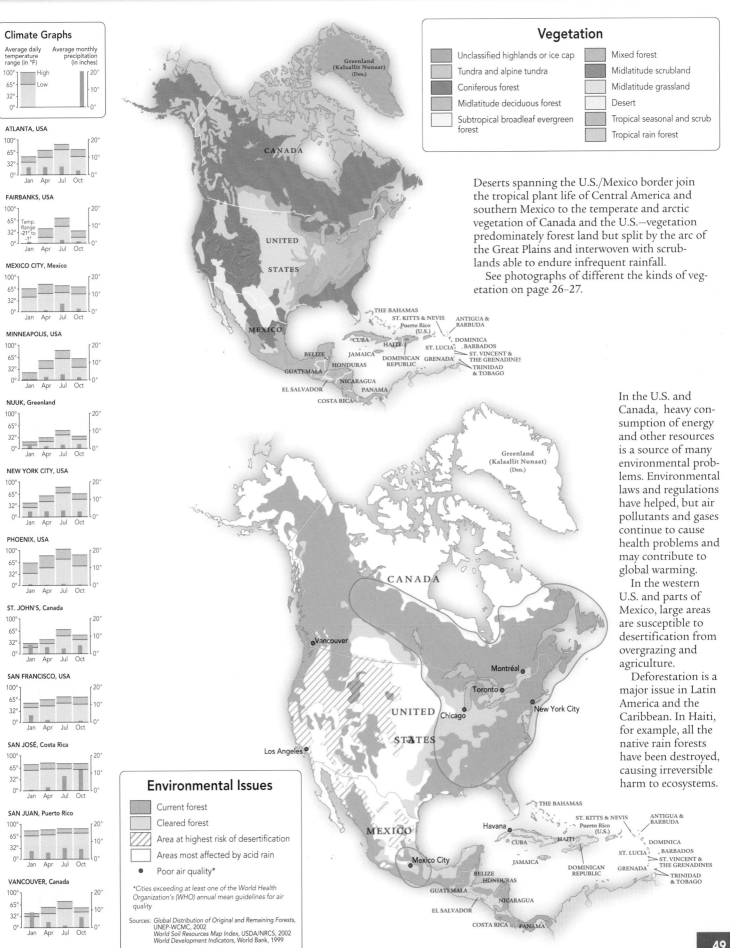

Climate Graphs

Average daily temperature range (in °F) | Average monthly precipitation (in inches)

100° High
65° Low
32°
0°
20°
10°
0°

ATLANTA, USA

FAIRBANKS, USA

MEXICO CITY, Mexico

MINNEAPOLIS, USA

NUUK, Greenland

NEW YORK CITY, USA

PHOENIX, USA

ST. JOHN'S, Canada

SAN FRANCISCO, USA

SAN JOSÉ, Costa Rica

SAN JUAN, Puerto Rico

VANCOUVER, Canada

Vegetation

- Unclassified highlands or ice cap
- Tundra and alpine tundra
- Coniferous forest
- Midlatitude deciduous forest
- Subtropical broadleaf evergreen forest
- Mixed forest
- Midlatitude scrubland
- Midlatitude grassland
- Desert
- Tropical seasonal and scrub
- Tropical rain forest

Deserts spanning the U.S./Mexico border join the tropical plant life of Central America and southern Mexico to the temperate and arctic vegetation of Canada and the U.S.—vegetation predominately forest land but split by the arc of the Great Plains and interwoven with scrublands able to endure infrequent rainfall.

See photographs of different the kinds of vegetation on page 26–27.

In the U.S. and Canada, heavy consumption of energy and other resources is a source of many environmental problems. Environmental laws and regulations have helped, but air pollutants and gases continue to cause health problems and may contribute to global warming.

In the western U.S. and parts of Mexico, large areas are susceptible to desertification from overgrazing and agriculture.

Deforestation is a major issue in Latin America and the Caribbean. In Haiti, for example, all the native rain forests have been destroyed, causing irreversible harm to ecosystems.

Environmental Issues

- Current forest
- Cleared forest
- Area at highest risk of desertification
- Areas most affected by acid rain
- Poor air quality*

*Cities exceeding at least one of the World Health Organization's (WHO) annual mean guidelines for air quality

Sources: Global Distribution of Original and Remaining Forests, UNEP-WCMC, 2002
World Soil Resources Map Index, USDA/NRCS, 2002
World Development Indicators, World Bank, 1999

49

United States

United States

Alabama

Alaska

Arizona

Arkansas

California

Hawaii

Idaho

Iowa

Kansas

Maine

Maryland

Minnesota

Mississippi

Nebraska

Nevada

New Mexico

New York

Ohio

Oklahoma

Rhode Island

South Carolina

South Dakota

Tennessee

Texas

Utah

Colorado

Connecticut

Delaware

District of Columbia

Florida

Georgia

Illinois

Indiana

Kentucky

Louisiana

Massachusetts

Michigan

Missouri

Montana

New Hampshire

New Jersey

North Carolina

North Dakota

Oregon

Pennsylvania

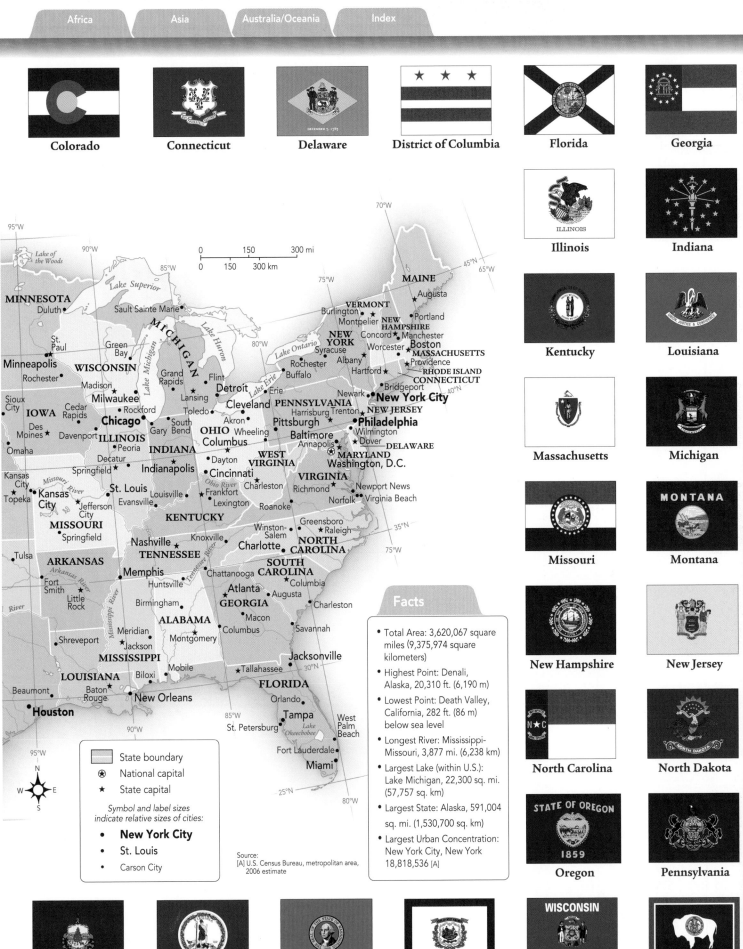

Facts

- Total Area: 3,620,067 square miles (9,375,974 square kilometers)
- Highest Point: Denali, Alaska, 20,310 ft. (6,190 m)
- Lowest Point: Death Valley, California, 282 ft. (86 m) below sea level
- Longest River: Mississippi-Missouri, 3,877 mi. (6,238 km)
- Largest Lake (within U.S.): Lake Michigan, 22,300 sq. mi. (57,757 sq. km)
- Largest State: Alaska, 591,004 sq. mi. (1,530,700 sq. km)
- Largest Urban Concentration: New York City, New York 18,818,536 [A]

Source:
[A] U.S. Census Bureau, metropolitan area, 2006 estimate

State boundary
⊛ National capital
★ State capital

Symbol and label sizes indicate relative sizes of cities:

• **New York City**
• St. Louis
· Carson City

Vermont

Virginia

Washington

West Virginia

Wisconsin

Wyoming

State	2010 Population and Rank		Capital	Largest City	Abbreviation		Nickname
					Traditional	Postal Service	
Alabama	4,779,736	23rd	Montgomery	Birmingham	ALA.	AL	Heart of Dixie
Alaska	710,231	47th	Juneau	Anchorage	(none)	AK	The Last Frontier
Arizona	6,392,017	16th	Phoenix	Phoenix	ARIZ.	AZ	Grand Canyon State
Arkansas	2,915,918	32nd	Litttle Rock	Little Rock	ARK.	AR	Land of Opportunity
California	37,253,956	1st	Sacramento	Los Angeles	CALIF.	CA	Golden State
Colorado	5,029,196	22nd	Denver	Denver	COLO.	CO	Centennial State
Connecticut	3,574,097	29th	Hartford	Bridgeport	CONN.	CT	Constitution State, Nutmeg State
Delaware	897,934	45th	Dover	Wilmington	DEL.	DE	First State, Diamond State
Florida	18,801,310	4th	Tallahassee	Jacksonville	FLA.	FL	Sunshine State
Georgia	9,687,653	9th	Atlanta	Atlanta	GA.	GA	Empire State of the South, Peach State
Hawaii	1,360,301	40th	Honolulu	Honolulu	(none)	HI	Aloha State
Idaho	1,567,582	39th	Boise	Boise	IDA.	ID	Gem State
Illinois	12,830,632	5th	Springfield	Chicago	ILL.	IL	Prairie State
Indiana	6,483,802	15th	Indianapolis	Indianapolis	IND.	IN	Hoosier State
Iowa	3,046,355	30th	Des Moines	Des Moines	(none)	IA	Hawkeye State
Kansas	2,853,118	33rd	Topeka	Wichita	KANS.	KS	Sunflower State
Kentucky	4,339,367	26th	Frankfort	Louisville	KY. or KEN.	KY	Bluegrass State
Louisiana	4,533,372	25th	Baton Rouge	New Orleans	LA.	LA	Pelican State
Maine	1,328,361	41st	Augusta	Portland	(none)	ME	Pine Tree State
Maryland	5,773,552	19th	Annapolis	Baltimore	MD.	MD	Old Line State, Free State
Massachusetts	6,547,629	14th	Boston	Boston	MASS.	MA	Bay State, Old Colony
Michigan	9,883,640	8th	Lansing	Detroit	MICH.	MI	Wolverine State
Minnesota	5,303,925	21st	St. Paul	Minneapolis	MINN.	MN	North Star State, Gopher State
Mississippi	2,967,297	31st	Jackson	Jackson	MISS.	MS	Magnolia State
Missouri	5,988,927	18th	Jefferson City	Kansas City	MO.	MO	Show Me State

State	2010 Population and Rank		Capital	Largest City	Abbreviation		Nickname
					Traditional	Postal Service	
Montana	989,415	44th	Helena	Billings	MONT.	MT	Treasure State
Nebraska	1,826,341	38th	Lincoln	Omaha	NEBR.	NE	Cornhusker State
Nevada	2,700,551	35th	Carson City	Las Vegas	NEV.	NV	Silver State
New Hampshire	1,316,470	42nd	Concord	Manchester	N.H.	NH	Granite State
New Jersey	8,791,894	11th	Trenton	Newark	N.J.	NJ	Garden State
New Mexico	2,059,179	36th	Santa Fe	Albuquerque	N. MEX. or N.M.	NM	Land of Enchantment
New York	19,378,102	3rd	Albany	New York City	N.Y.	NY	Empire State
North Carolina	9,535,483	10th	Raleigh	Charlotte	N.C.	NC	Tar Heel State
North Dakota	672,591	48th	Bismarck	Fargo	N. DAK. or N.D.	ND	Peace Garden State, Flickertail State
Ohio	11,536,504	7th	Columbus	Columbus	(none)	OH	Buckeye State
Oklahoma	3,751,351	28th	Oklahoma City	Oklahoma City	OKLA.	OK	Sooner State
Oregon	3,831,074	27th	Salem	Portland	ORE.	OR	Beaver State
Pennsylvania	12,702,379	6th	Harrisburg	Philadelphia	PA. or PENN.	PA	Keystone State
Rhode Island	1,052,567	43rd	Providence	Providence	R.I.	RI	Ocean State
South Carolina	4,625,364	24th	Columbia	Columbia	S.C.	SC	Palmetto State
South Dakota	814,180	46th	Pierre	Sioux Falls	S. DAK. or S.D.	SD	Mt. Rushmore State
Tennessee	6,346,105	17th	Nashville	Memphis	TENN.	TN	Volunteer State
Texas	25,145,561	2nd	Austin	Houston	TEX.	TX	Lone Star State
Utah	2,763,885	34th	Salt Lake City	Salt Lake City	(none)	UT	Beehive State
Vermont	625,741	49th	Montpelier	Burlington	VT.	VT	Green Mountain State
Virginia	8,001,024	12th	Richmond	Virginia Beach	VA.	VA	Old Dominion
Washington	6,724,540	13th	Olympia	Seattle	WASH.	WA	Evergreen State
West Virginia	1,852,994	37th	Charleston	Charleston	W. VA.	WV	Mountain State
Wisconsin	5,686,986	20th	Madison	Milwaukee	WIS.	WI	Badger State
Wyoming	563,626	50th	Cheyenne	Cheyenne	WYO.	WY	Equality State

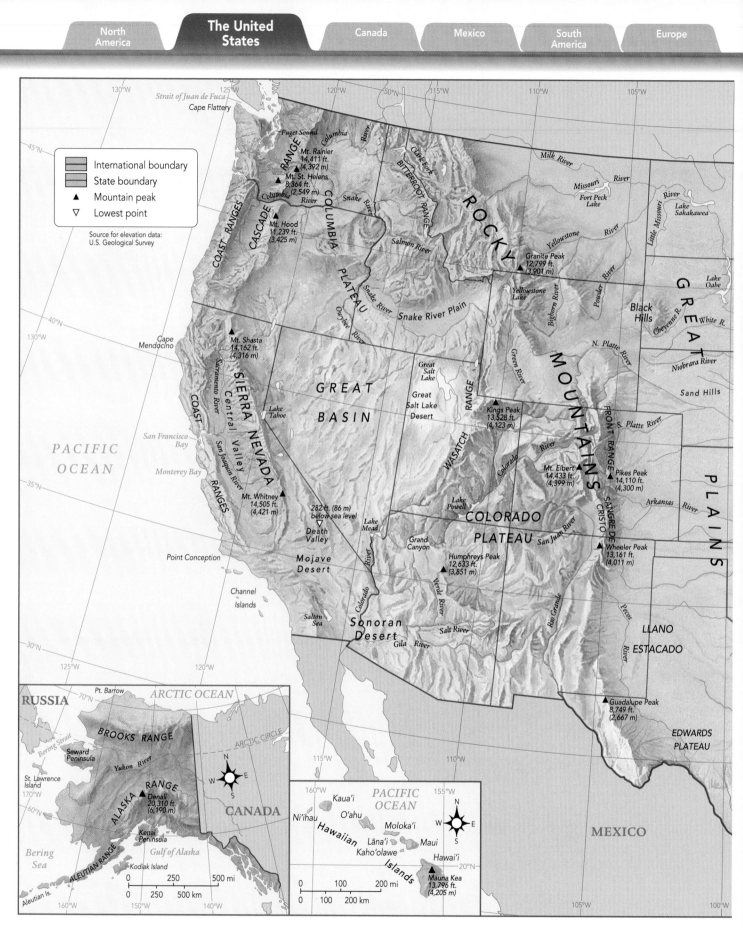

Legend

International boundary
State boundary
▲ Mountain peak
▽ Lowest point

Source for elevation data:
U.S. Geological Survey

Strait of Juan de Fuca
Cape Flattery
Puget Sound
Mt. Rainier 14,411 ft. (4,392 m)
Mt. St. Helens 8,364 ft. (2,549 m)
Columbia River
Mt. Hood 11,239 ft. (3,425 m)
COAST RANGES
CASCADE RANGE
COLUMBIA PLATEAU
BITTERROOT RANGE
Clark Fork
Snake River
Salmon River
ROCKY
Milk River
Missouri River
Fort Peck Lake
Little Missouri River
Lake Sakakawea
Yellowstone River
Granite Peak 12,799 ft. (3,901 m)
Yellowstone Lake
Bighorn River
Powder River
Lake Oahe
GREAT
Black Hills
Cheyenne R.
White R.
N. Platte River
Niobrara River
Sand Hills

Cape Mendocino
Mt. Shasta 14,162 ft. (4,316 m)
Sacramento River
SIERRA NEVADA
Central Valley
Lake Tahoe
GREAT BASIN
Great Salt Lake
Great Salt Lake Desert
WASATCH RANGE
Kings Peak 13,528 ft. (4,123 m)
Green River
MOUNTAINS
FRONT RANGE
S. Platte River

PACIFIC OCEAN

San Francisco Bay
Monterey Bay
COAST
San Joaquin River
RANGES
Mt. Whitney 14,505 ft. (4,421 m)
282 ft. (86 m) below sea level ▽ Death Valley
Lake Mead
Colorado River
Lake Powell
COLORADO PLATEAU
San Juan River
Colorado River
Mt. Elbert 14,433 ft. (4,399 m)
Pikes Peak 14,110 ft. (4,300 m)
Arkansas River
SANGRE DE CRISTO
GREAT PLAINS

Point Conception
Channel Islands
Mojave Desert
Grand Canyon
Humphreys Peak 12,633 ft. (3,851 m)
Verde River
Wheeler Peak 13,161 ft. (4,011 m)
Salton Sea
Sonoran Desert
Colorado River
Salt River
Gila River
Rio Grande
Pecos River
LLANO ESTACADO

Guadalupe Peak 8,749 ft. (2,667 m)
EDWARDS PLATEAU

Alaska inset

RUSSIA
Pt. Barrow
ARCTIC OCEAN
Bering Strait
BROOKS RANGE
Seward Peninsula
Yukon River
ARCTIC CIRCLE
St. Lawrence Island
ALASKA RANGE
Denali 20,310 ft. (6,190 m)
CANADA
Kenai Peninsula
Bering Sea
ALEUTIAN RANGE
Gulf of Alaska
Kodiak Island
Aleutian Is.
N W E S

0   250   500 mi
0   250   500 km

Hawaii inset

PACIFIC OCEAN
Kaua'i
Ni'ihau
O'ahu
Moloka'i
Lāna'i
Maui
Kaho'olawe
Hawaiian Islands
Hawai'i
Mauna Kea 13,796 ft. (4,205 m)
N W E S

0   100   200 mi
0   100   200 km

MEXICO

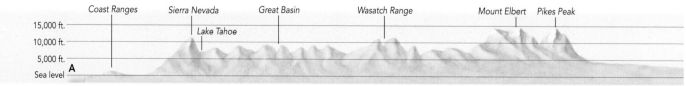

Coast Ranges | Sierra Nevada | Great Basin | Wasatch Range | Mount Elbert | Pikes Peak
15,000 ft.
Lake Tahoe
10,000 ft.
5,000 ft.
Sea level A

CANADA

Lake of the Woods

Isle Royale

Lake Superior

Upper Peninsula

MESABI RANGE

Red River of the North

Minnesota River

St. Croix River

Mississippi

Wisconsin River

Lake Michigan

Lake Huron

Lower Peninsula

Grand River

Lake St. Clair

Lake Erie

Lake Ontario

Genesee R.

ADIRONDACK MTS.

St. Lawrence River

GREEN MTS.

WHITE MTS.

Mt. Washington 6,288 ft. (1,917 m)

Saint John River

Penobscot River

Quoddy Head

Gulf of Maine

Lake Champlain

Merrimack R.

Connecticut River

Cape Cod

Long Island Sound

Long Island

James River

Des Moines River

Iowa River

Cedar River

Rock

River

Illinois River

CENTRAL LOWLAND

White River

Scioto River

Allegheny R.

ALLEGHENY PLATEAU

Susquehanna River

Potomac River

Hudson River

Delaware River

Delaware Bay

40°N

70°W

Loup R.

Platte River

Missouri

Kansas River

River

Republican River

Smoky Hill R.

FLINT HILLS

Lake of the Ozarks

Kaskaskia River

Wabash

Green River

Ohio River

Kentucky R.

Cumberland River

Tennessee River

ALLEGHENY MOUNTAINS

APPALACHIAN

MOUNTAINS

BLUE RIDGE

Roanoke River

James River

PIEDMONT

Chesapeake Bay

Cape Hatteras

35°N

OZARK PLATEAU

BOSTON MTS.

White River

Mississippi River

Red

OUACHITA MOUNTAINS

Cimarron River

Canadian River

Arkansas River

Ouachita

CUMBERLAND PLATEAU

Mt. Mitchell 6,684 ft. (2,037 m)

Pee Dee R.

Savannah River

Oconee River

Ocmulgee River

Cape Fear

ATLANTIC COASTAL PLAIN

ATLANTIC OCEAN

Brazos River

Trinity River

Colorado River

Sabine River

Mississippi River

Yazoo River

Tombigbee River

Alabama River

Pearl River

Chattahoochee

Flint River

Apalachicola River

Altamaha River

St. Johns River

30°N

GULF

COASTAL

PLAIN

Lake Pontchartrain

Mobile Bay

Cape Canaveral

Nueces River

Galveston Bay

Mississippi Delta

Tampa Bay

Lake Okeechobee

THE BAHAMAS

25°N

Padre Island

Rio Grande

Gulf of Mexico

N
W E
S

0   150   300 mi
0   150   300 km

Florida Keys

Straits of Florida

95°W   90°W   85°W   80°W   75°W

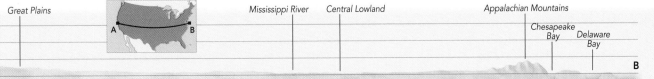

Great Plains | Mississippi River | Central Lowland | Appalachian Mountains | Chesapeake Bay | Delaware Bay

A   B

B

State	Total Area and Rank		Highest Point		Temperature °F		Annual Precipitation	
					Highest Recorded	Lowest Recorded	Highest Recorded	Lowest Recorded
Alabama	52,419 sq mi 135,765 sq km	30th	Cheaha Mtn.	2,407 ft 734 m	112°	−27°	106.57"	22.00"
Alaska	591,004 sq mi 1,530,700 sq km	1st	Denali	20,310 ft 6,190 m	100°	−80°	332.29"	1.61"
Arizona	113,998 sq mi 295,254 sq km	6th	Humphreys Peak	12,633 ft 3,851 m	128°	−40°	58.92"	0.07"
Arkansas	53,179 sq mi 137,732 sq km	29th	Magazine Mtn.	2,753 ft 839 m	120°	−29°	98.55"	19.11"
California	163,696 sq mi 423,970 sq km	3rd	Mt. Whitney	14,505 ft 4,421 m	134°	−45°	153.54"	0.00"
Colorado	104,094 sq mi 269,601 sq km	8th	Mt. Elbert	14,433 ft 4,399 m	118°	−61°	92.84"	1.69"
Connecticut	5,543 sq mi 14,357 sq km	48th	Mt. Frissell on south slope at state line	2,380 ft 725 m	105°	−32°	78.53"	23.60"
Delaware	2,489 sq mi 6,447 sq km	49th	On Ebright Road at DE-PA border	448 ft 137 m	110°	−17°	72.75"	21.38"
Florida	65,755 sq mi 170,304 sq km	22nd	Britton Hill	345 ft 105 m	109°	−2°	112.43"	21.16"
Georgia	59,425 sq mi 153,909 sq km	24th	Brasstown Bald	4,784 ft 1,458 m	112°	−17°	112.16"	17.14"
Hawaii	10,931 sq mi 28,311 sq km	43rd	Pu'u Wekiu, Mauna Kea	13,796 ft 4,205 m	100°	12°	704.83"	0.19"
Idaho	83,570 sq mi 216,446 sq km	14th	Borah Peak	12,662 ft 3,859 m	118°	−60°	81.05"	2.09"
Illinois	57,914 sq mi 149,998 sq km	25th	Charles Mound	1,235 ft 376 m	117°	−35°	74.58"	16.59"
Indiana	36,418 sq mi 94,321 sq km	38th	Hoosier Hill	1,257 ft 383 m	116°	−35°	97.38"	18.67"
Iowa	56,272 sq mi 145,743 sq km	26th	Hawkeye Point	1,670 ft 509 m	118°	−47°	74.50"	12.11"
Kansas	82,277 sq mi 213,096 sq km	15th	Mt. Sunflower	4,039 ft 1,231 m	121°	−40°	67.02"	4.77"
Kentucky	40,409 sq mi 104,659 sq km	37th	Black Mtn.	4,145 ft 1,263 m	114°	−34°	79.68"	14.51"
Louisiana	51,840 sq mi 134,264 sq km	31st	Driskill Mtn.	535 ft 163 m	114°	−16°	113.74"	26.44"
Maine	35,385 sq mi 91,646 sq km	39th	Mt. Katahdin	5,268 ft 1,606 m	105°	−48°	75.64"	23.06"
Maryland	12,407 sq mi 32,133 sq km	42nd	Hoye Crest (point on Backbone Mtn.	3,360 ft 1,024 m	109°	−40°	72.59"	17.76"
Massachusetts	10,555 sq mi 27,336 sq km	44th	Mt. Greylock	3,491 ft 1,064 m	107°	−35°	72.19"	21.76"
Michigan	96,716 sq mi 250,494 sq km	11th	Mt. Arvon	1,979 ft 603 m	112°	−51°	64.01"	15.64"
Minnesota	86,939 sq mi 225,171 sq km	12th	Eagle Mtn.	2,301 ft 701 m	114°	−59°	51.53"	7.81"
Mississippi	48,430 sq mi 125,434 sq km	32nd	Woodall Mtn.	806 ft 246 m	115°	−19°	104.36"	25.97"
Missouri	69,704 sq mi 180,533 sq km	21st	Taum Sauk Mtn.	1,772 ft 540 m	118°	−40°	92.77"	16.14"

State	Total Area and Rank		Highest Point		Temperature °F		Annual Precipitation	
					Highest Recorded	Lowest Recorded	Highest Recorded	Lowest Recorded
Montana	147,042 sq mi 380,838 sq km	4th	Granite Peak	12,799 ft 3,901 m	117°	−70°	55.51"	2.97"
Nebraska	77,354 sq mi 200,345 sq km	16th	Panorama Point	5,424 ft 1,653 m	118°	−47°	64.52"	6.30"
Nevada	110,567 sq mi 286,368 sq km	7th	Boundary Peak	13,140 ft 4,005 m	125°	−50°	59.03"	Trace
New Hampshire	9,350 sq mi 24,216 sq km	46th	Mt. Washington	6,288 ft 1,917 m	106°	−46°	130.14"	22.31"
New Jersey	8,721 sq mi 22,588 sq km	47th	High Point	1,803 ft 550 m	110°	−34°	85.99"	19.85"
New Mexico	121,589 sq mi 314,915 sq km	5th	Wheeler Peak	13,161 ft 4,011 m	122°	−50°	62.45"	1.00"
New York	54,556 sq mi 141,299 sq km	27th	Mt. Marcy	5,344 ft 1,629 m	108°	−52°	82.06"	17.64"
North Carolina	53,819 sq mi 139,389 sq km	28th	Mt. Mitchell	6,684 ft 2,037 m	110°	−34°	129.60"	22.69"
North Dakota	70,700 sq mi 183,112 sq km	19th	White Butte	3,506 ft 1,069 m	121°	−60°	37.98"	4.02"
Ohio	44,825 sq mi 116,096 sq km	34th	Campbell Hill	1,550 ft 472 m	113°	−39°	70.82"	16.96"
Oklahoma	69,898 sq mi 181,036 sq km	20th	Black Mesa	4,973 ft 1,516 m	120°	−27°	84.47"	6.53"
Oregon	98,381 sq mi 254,805 sq km	9th	Mt. Hood	11,239 ft 3,426 m	119°	−54°	168.88"	3.33"
Pennsylvania	46,055 sq mi 119,283 sq km	33rd	Mt. Davis	3,213 ft 979 m	111°	−42°	81.64"	15.71"
Rhode Island	1,545 sq mi 4,002 sq km	50th	Jerimoth Hill	812 ft 247 m	104°	−23°	70.21"	24.08"
South Carolina	32,020 sq mi 82,932 sq km	40th	Sassafras Mtn.	3,560 ft 1,085 m	111°	−19°	101.65"	20.73"
South Dakota	77,116 sq mi 199,731 sq km	17th	Harney Peak	7,242 ft 2,207 m	120°	−58°	48.42"	2.89"
Tennessee	42,143 sq mi 109,151 sq km	36th	Clingmans Dome	6,643 ft 2,025 m	113°	−32°	114.88"	25.23"
Texas	268,581 sq mi 695,621 sq km	2nd	Guadalupe Peak	8,749 ft 2,667 m	120°	−23°	109.38"	1.64"
Utah	84,899 sq mi 219,887 sq km	13th	Kings Peak	13,528 ft 4,123 m	117°	−69°	108.54"	1.34"
Vermont	9,614 sq mi 24,901 sq km	45th	Mt. Mansfield	4,393 ft 1,339 m	105°	−50°	92.88"	22.98"
Virginia	42,774 sq mi 110,785 sq km	35th	Mt. Rogers	5,729 ft 1,746 m	110°	−30°	81.78"	12.52"
Washington	71,300 sq mi 184,665 sq km	18th	Mt. Rainier	14,411 ft 4,392 m	118°	−48°	184.56"	2.61"
West Virginia	24,230 sq mi 62,755 sq km	41st	Spruce Knob	4,863 ft 1,482 m	112°	−37°	94.01"	9.50"
Wisconsin	65,498 sq mi 169,639 sq km	23rd	Timms Hill	1,951 ft 595 m	114°	−54°	62.07"	12.00"
Wyoming	97,814 sq mi 253,336 sq km	10th	Gannett Peak	13,804 ft 4,207 m	114°	−63°	55.46"	1.28"

Divide

DIVIDE: *The boundary or high ground between river systems.* Streams on one side of the divide flow in a different direction and into a different drainage basin from the streams on the other side. A continental divide is the boundary that separates the rivers flowing toward opposite sides of a continent.

In North America a continental divide called the **Great Divide** runs along the crest of the Rocky Mountains, dividing rivers that flow to the Gulf of Mexico and the Atlantic Ocean from those that flow into the Pacific Ocean. Another much lower divide separates those rivers that flow north through Hudson Bay to the Arctic Ocean. Triple Divide Peak in Montana is located on both these divides. Water from one side of this mountain flows east to the Atlantic or Gulf of Mexico; from another side water flows west to the Pacific; and from the north face, water flows to the Arctic Ocean.

Earthquakes

- ■ Major earthquake
- • Other earthquake

The major earthquakes that have occurred in California are distributed along the major fault lines depicted on the California map to the right.

Fall Line

FALL LINE: *A geologic feature where uplands meet lowlands and a series of waterfalls and rapids occur.* Fall lines are formed where a region of hard rock borders softer rock, and the softer rock has eroded away. The erosion creates a ledge that water flows over.

A major fall line exists in the eastern United States. It marks the boundary between the Coastal Plain and the Piedmont and runs between New York and Alabama. Cities have grown into industrial and commercial hubs around each waterfall on the fall line for two reasons. First, the energy of the falling water can be captured and used by industry. Second, the fall line is often the farthest point reachable by ships carrying goods up river, which means that goods are transferred to land-based transport at that point. Some fall line cities on the East Coast include Trenton, Philadelphia, Baltimore, Washington, D.C., Richmond, Petersburg, Columbia, Macon, and Montgomery. If you draw a line on a map connecting these city dots, you will have drawn the Eastern Fall Line.

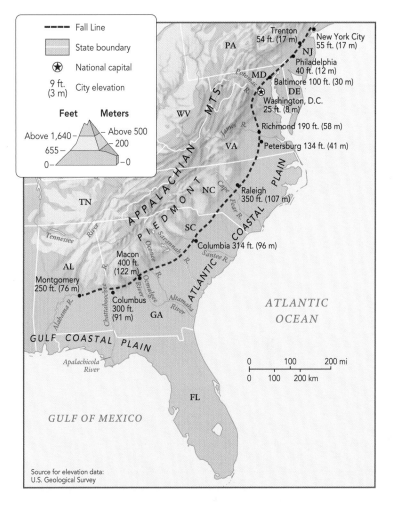

Fault

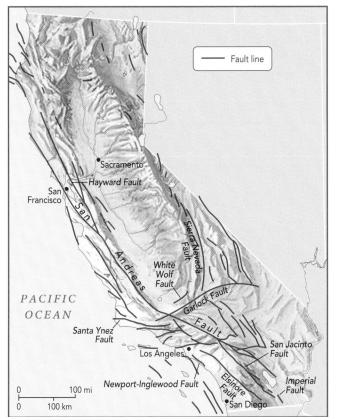

FAULT: *A break in the Earth's crust caused by movement.* Solid rock on one side of the fault no longer matches the solid rock on the other side. The movement may take place in any direction—up, down, or sideways. The movement may be a few inches or thousands of feet.

A fault that moves up or down is called a **dip-slip fault**. Niagara Falls cascades over an escarpment caused by this kind of movement.

A fault that moves sideways is called a **strike-slip fault**. The San Andreas fault is an example of this kind. Horizontal movement along this fault caused the devastating San Francisco earthquake in 1906 and will cause more earthquakes in the future. This happens because this fault marks the boundary between the Pacific Plate and the North American Plate (see page 20).

Where two parallel faults pull away from each other, they create a long, sunken valley between them called a **rift**. The Great Rift Valley in Africa is the world's most visible example (see page 91). Underwater, the huge Mid-Ocean Ridge is the longest rift on Earth (see pages 18–19).

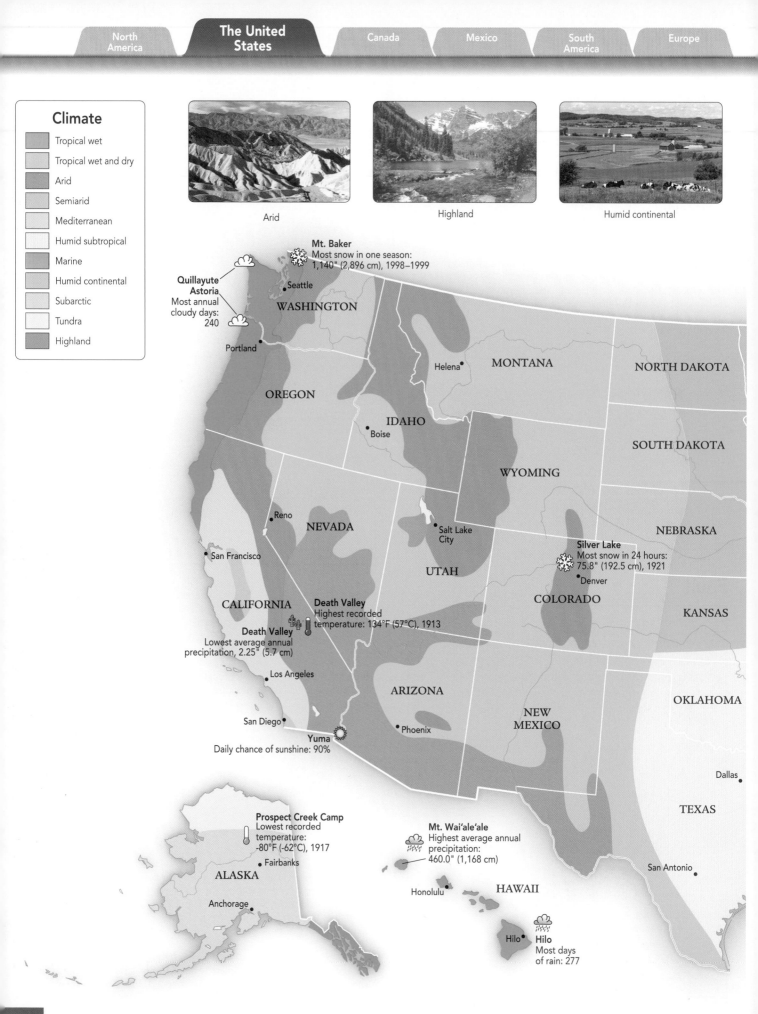

Climate

- Tropical wet
- Tropical wet and dry
- Arid
- Semiarid
- Mediterranean
- Humid subtropical
- Marine
- Humid continental
- Subarctic
- Tundra
- Highland

Arid

Highland

Humid continental

Mt. Baker
Most snow in one season:
1,140" (2,896 cm), 1998–1999

Quillayute
Astoria
Most annual
cloudy days:
240

Seattle

WASHINGTON

Portland

OREGON

MONTANA

Helena

NORTH DAKOTA

IDAHO

Boise

WYOMING

SOUTH DAKOTA

Reno

NEVADA

Salt Lake
City

San Francisco

UTAH

NEBRASKA

Silver Lake
Most snow in 24 hours:
75.8" (192.5 cm), 1921

Denver

COLORADO

KANSAS

CALIFORNIA

Death Valley
Highest recorded
temperature: 134°F (57°C), 1913

Death Valley
Lowest average annual
precipitation, 2.25" (5.7 cm)

Los Angeles

ARIZONA

San Diego

NEW
MEXICO

OKLAHOMA

Yuma
Daily chance of sunshine: 90%

Phoenix

Dallas

TEXAS

Prospect Creek Camp
Lowest recorded
temperature:
-80°F (-62°C), 1917

Fairbanks

ALASKA

Anchorage

Mt. Wai'ale'ale
Highest average annual
precipitation:
460.0" (1,168 cm)

Honolulu

HAWAII

San Antonio

Hilo

Hilo
Most days
of rain: 277

Humid subtropical

Marine

Mediterranean

Semiarid

Subarctic

Tropical wet

Tropical wet and dry

Tundra

MAINE

Mt. Washington
Highest wind gust:
231 mph (372 kph), 1934

Lake Superior

MINNESOTA

Portland

VT

NH

Minneapolis

WISCONSIN

MICHIGAN

Lake Michigan

Lake Huron

Lake Ontario

NEW YORK

Boston

Blue Hill
Highest average annual wind speed:
15.4 mph (24.8 kph)

MA

CT

RI

Buffalo

IOWA

Detroit

Lake Erie

PENNSYLVANIA

Johnstown
Deadliest flood: over 2,200 dead,
1889

New York City

Chicago

Great Midwest Flood
Costliest flood damage: $18 billion, 1993

ILLINOIS

INDIANA

OHIO

Philadelphia

NEW JERSEY

— **DELAWARE**

— **MARYLAND**

Indianapolis

Baltimore

Washington, D.C.

MISSOURI

**WEST
VIRGINIA**

St. Louis

VIRGINIA

Tri-State Tornado
Deadliest tornado: 689 dead, 1925

Lexington

KENTUCKY

Raleigh

Nashville

NORTH CAROLINA

TENNESSEE

ARKANSAS

**SOUTH
CAROLINA**

Atlanta

MISSISSIPPI

GEORGIA

ALABAMA

LOUISIANA

FLORIDA

Alvin
Most rain in 24 hours:
43.0" (109.2 cm), 1979

Houston

New
Orleans

Hurricane Katrina
Costliest hurricane damage:
over $80 billion, 2005

Galveston
Deadliest hurricane:
over 8,000 dead, 1900

Miami

Vegetation

- Tundra and alpine tundra
- Coniferous forest
- Midlatitude deciduous forest
- Subtropical broadleaf evergreen forest
- Mixed forest
- Midlatitude scrubland
- Midlatitude grassland
- Desert
- Tropical rain forest

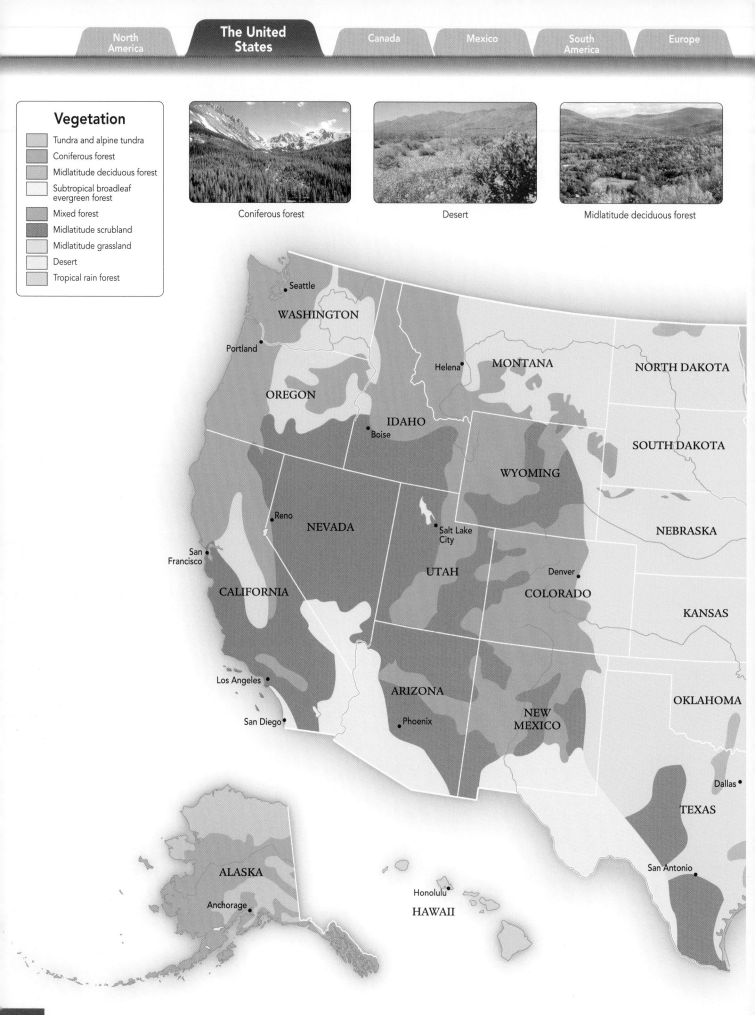

Coniferous forest

Desert

Midlatitude deciduous forest

Midlatitude grassland

Midlatitude scrubland

Mixed forest

Subtropical broadleaf evergreen forest

MINNESOTA

Minneapolis

WISCONSIN

Lake Superior

MICHIGAN

Lake Michigan

Lake Huron

IOWA

Chicago

Detroit

Lake Erie

Lake Ontario

Buffalo

NEW YORK

VERMONT

NEW HAMPSHIRE

MAINE

Portland

Boston   MASSACHUSETTS

RHODE ISLAND
CONNECTICUT

ILLINOIS   INDIANA

OHIO

PENNSYLVANIA

New York City

Philadelphia   NEW JERSEY

Indianapolis

Baltimore

Washington, D.C.   DELAWARE

MARYLAND

St. Louis

MISSOURI

WEST VIRGINIA

VIRGINIA

Lexington

KENTUCKY

Nashville

ARKANSAS

TENNESSEE

Raleigh

NORTH CAROLINA

SOUTH CAROLINA

Atlanta

MISSISSIPPI

ALABAMA   GEORGIA

LOUISIANA

Houston   New Orleans

FLORIDA

Miami

Tropical rain forest

Tundra and alpine tundra

63

Land Use

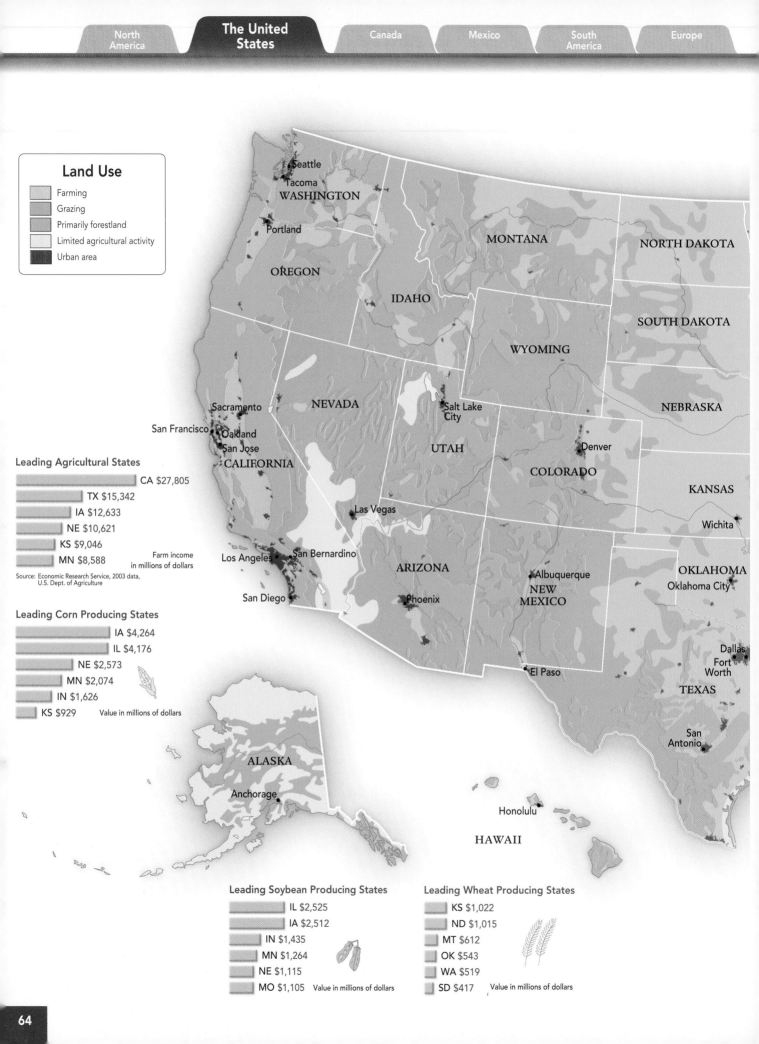

- Farming
- Grazing
- Primarily forestland
- Limited agricultural activity
- Urban area

Leading Agricultural States

CA	$27,805
TX	$15,342
IA	$12,633
NE	$10,621
KS	$9,046
MN	$8,588

Farm income
in millions of dollars

Source: Economic Research Service, 2003 data,
U.S. Dept. of Agriculture

Leading Corn Producing States

IA	$4,264
IL	$4,176
NE	$2,573
MN	$2,074
IN	$1,626
KS	$929

Value in millions of dollars

Leading Soybean Producing States

IL	$2,525
IA	$2,512
IN	$1,435
MN	$1,264
NE	$1,115
MO	$1,105

Value in millions of dollars

Leading Wheat Producing States

KS	$1,022
ND	$1,015
MT	$612
OK	$543
WA	$519
SD	$417

Value in millions of dollars

WASHINGTON — Seattle, Tacoma
Portland
OREGON
MONTANA
NORTH DAKOTA
IDAHO
SOUTH DAKOTA
WYOMING
NEVADA
Salt Lake City
NEBRASKA
Sacramento
San Francisco
Oakland
San Jose
CALIFORNIA
UTAH
Denver
COLORADO
KANSAS
Las Vegas
Wichita
Los Angeles
San Bernardino
ARIZONA
Albuquerque
NEW MEXICO
OKLAHOMA
Oklahoma City
San Diego
Phoenix
Dallas
Fort Worth
El Paso
TEXAS
San Antonio

ALASKA
Anchorage

Honolulu
HAWAII

Leading Beef Producing States

TX $6,135	
NE $3,605	
KS $2,827	
OK $1,951	
CO $1,849	
SD $1,451	Value in millions of dollars

Leading Hog Producing States

IA $3,264	
NC $2,065	
MN $1,505	
IL $938	
NE $717	
IN $685	Value in millions of dollars

Leading Poultry Producing States

GA $2,858	
AR $2,731	
AL $2,407	
NC $2,042	
MS $1,930	
TX $1,425	Value in millions of dollars

U.S. Percentage of World Production

	United States	World
Corn	42.3%	
Cotton	19.3%	
Rice	1.8%	
Soybean	39.9%	
Wheat	9.4%	

Source: Production, Supply and Distribution; 2004/2005 data, Foreign Agricultural Service, U.S. Dept. of Agriculture

Leading Vegetable Producing States

CA $5,191	
FL $1,157	
AZ $858	
GA $381	
TX $342	
NY $283	Value in millions of dollars

Leading Milk Producing States

CA $5,371	
WI $3,732	
NY $1,957	
PA $1,771	
ID $1,364	
MN $1,353	Value in millions of dollars

Source: National Agricultural Statistics Service, 2004 data, U.S. Dept. of Agriculture

65

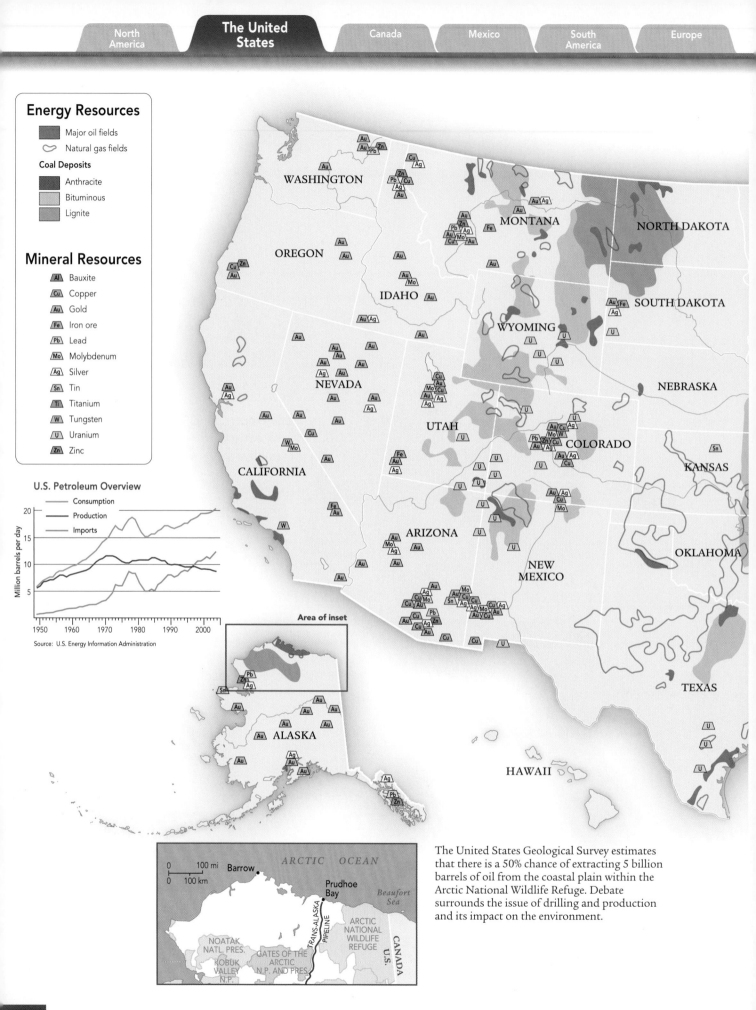

Energy Resources

- Major oil fields
- Natural gas fields

Coal Deposits
- Anthracite
- Bituminous
- Lignite

Mineral Resources

- Al Bauxite
- Cu Copper
- Au Gold
- Fe Iron ore
- Pb Lead
- Mo Molybdenum
- Ag Silver
- Sn Tin
- Ti Titanium
- W Tungsten
- U Uranium
- Zn Zinc

U.S. Petroleum Overview

Consumption
Production
Imports

Million barrels per day

20
15
10
5

1950 1960 1970 1980 1990 2000

Source: U.S. Energy Information Administration

The United States Geological Survey estimates that there is a 50% chance of extracting 5 billion barrels of oil from the coastal plain within the Arctic National Wildlife Refuge. Debate surrounds the issue of drilling and production and its impact on the environment.

Area of inset

ARCTIC OCEAN
Barrow
Prudhoe Bay
Beaufort Sea
TRANS-ALASKA PIPELINE
NOATAK NATL. PRES.
GATES OF THE ARCTIC N.P. AND PRES.
KOBUK VALLEY N.P.
ARCTIC NATIONAL WILDLIFE REFUGE
CANADA U.S.
0 100 mi
0 100 km

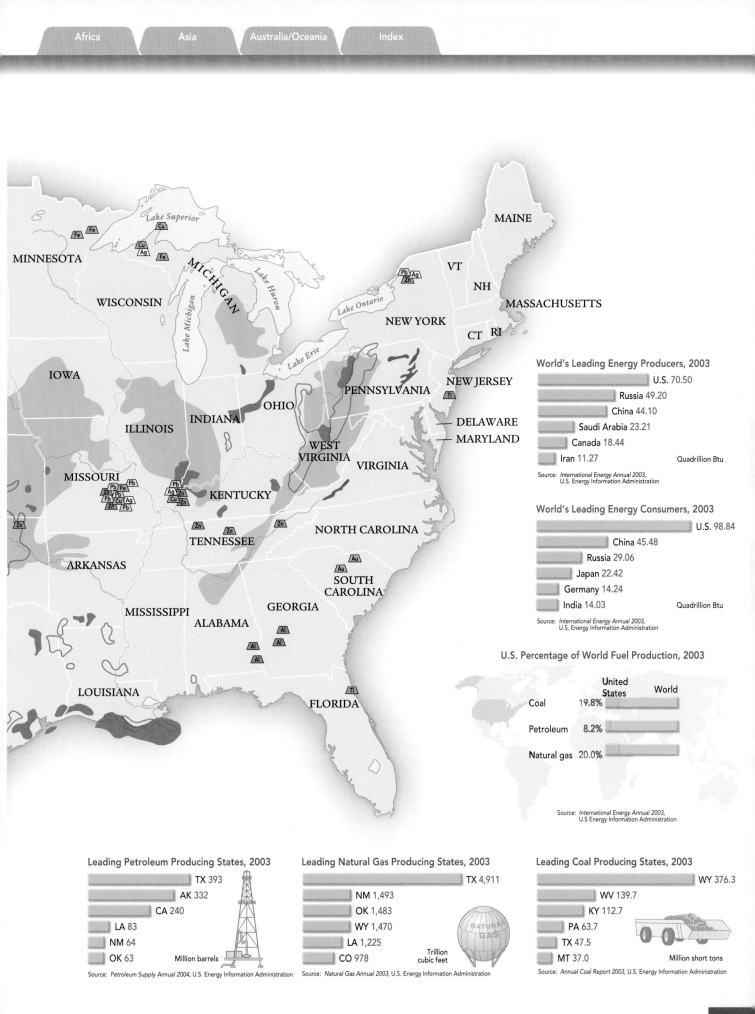

MINNESOTA

Lake Superior

MICHIGAN

WISCONSIN

Lake Michigan

Lake Huron

IOWA

Lake Ontario

MAINE

VT

NH

MASSACHUSETTS

NEW YORK

CT RI

Lake Erie

PENNSYLVANIA

NEW JERSEY

OHIO

INDIANA

DELAWARE

MARYLAND

ILLINOIS

WEST
VIRGINIA

VIRGINIA

MISSOURI

KENTUCKY

NORTH CAROLINA

TENNESSEE

ARKANSAS

SOUTH
CAROLINA

MISSISSIPPI

ALABAMA

GEORGIA

LOUISIANA

FLORIDA

World's Leading Energy Producers, 2003

- U.S. 70.50
- Russia 49.20
- China 44.10
- Saudi Arabia 23.21
- Canada 18.44
- Iran 11.27   Quadrillion Btu

Source: *International Energy Annual 2003*,
U.S. Energy Information Administration

World's Leading Energy Consumers, 2003

- U.S. 98.84
- China 45.48
- Russia 29.06
- Japan 22.42
- Germany 14.24
- India 14.03   Quadrillion Btu

Source: *International Energy Annual 2003*,
U.S. Energy Information Administration

U.S. Percentage of World Fuel Production, 2003

	United States	World
Coal	19.8%	
Petroleum	8.2%	
Natural gas	20.0%	

Source: *International Energy Annual 2003*,
U.S Energy Information Administration

Leading Petroleum Producing States, 2003

- TX 393
- AK 332
- CA 240
- LA 83
- NM 64
- OK 63   Million barrels

Source: *Petroleum Supply Annual 2004*, U.S. Energy Information Administration

Leading Natural Gas Producing States, 2003

- TX 4,911
- NM 1,493
- OK 1,483
- WY 1,470
- LA 1,225
- CO 978   Trillion cubic feet

Source: *Natural Gas Annual 2003*, U.S. Energy Information Administration

Leading Coal Producing States, 2003

- WY 376.3
- WV 139.7
- KY 112.7
- PA 63.7
- TX 47.5
- MT 37.0   Million short tons

Source: *Annual Coal Report 2003*, U.S. Energy Information Administration

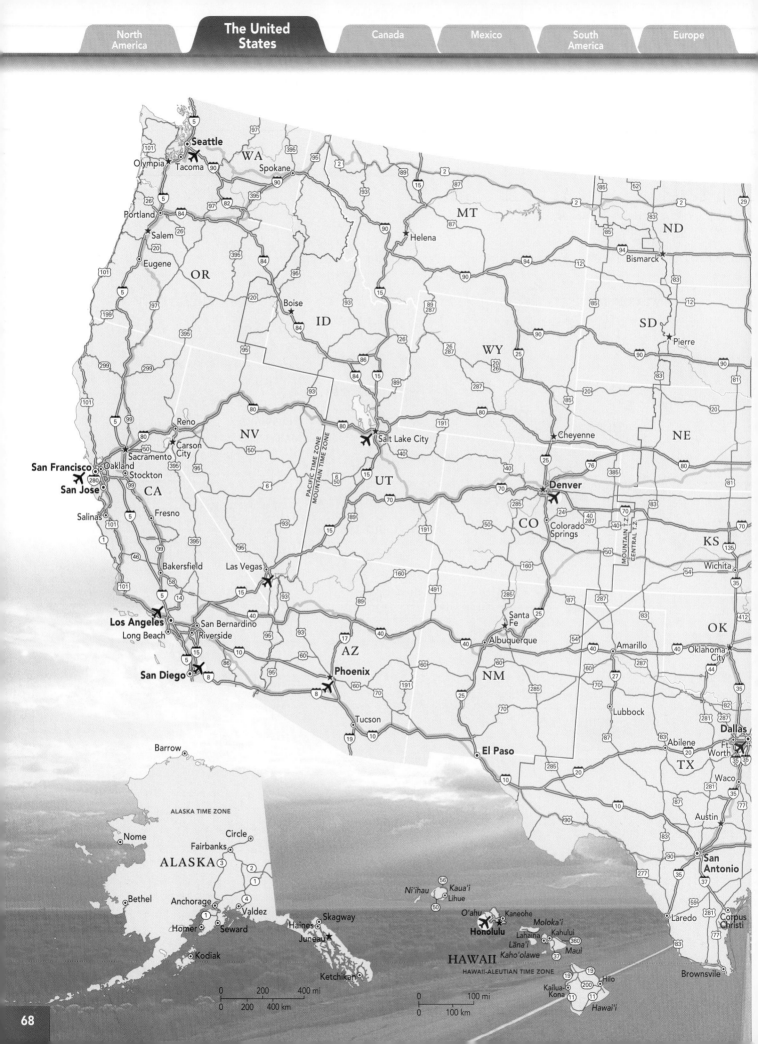

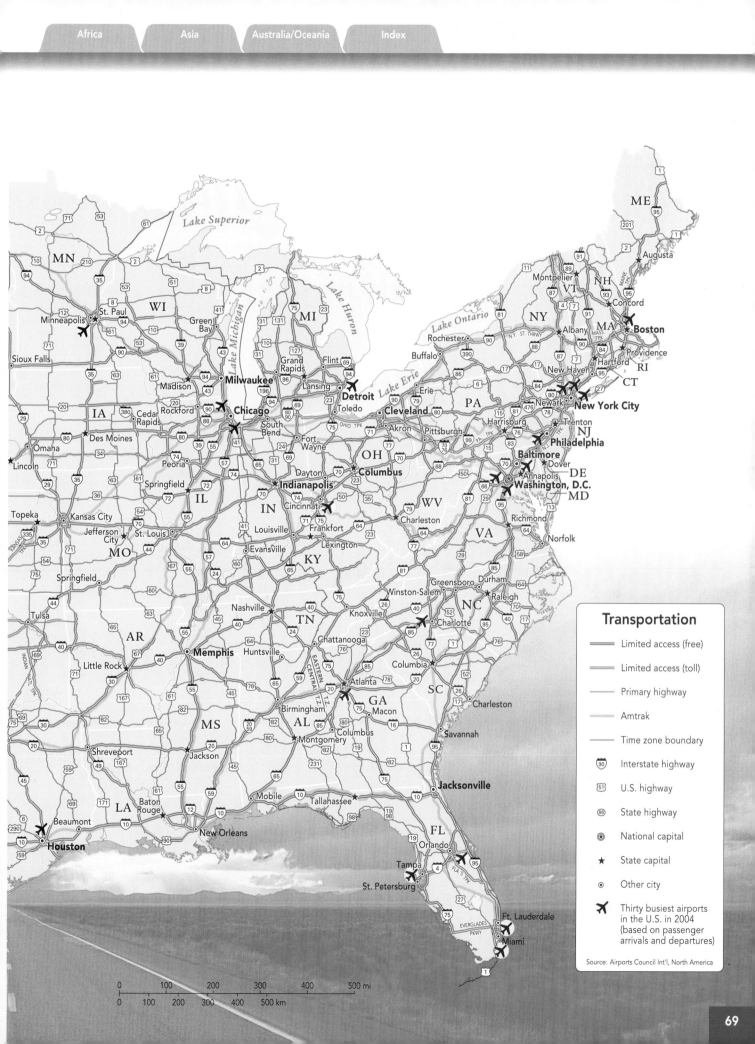

Transportation

═══ Limited access (free)

═══ Limited access (toll)

─── Primary highway

─── Amtrak

─── Time zone boundary

🛡 Interstate highway

🛡 U.S. highway

⬡ State highway

◉ National capital

★ State capital

⊙ Other city

✈ Thirty busiest airports in the U.S. in 2004 (based on passenger arrivals and departures)

Source: Airports Council Int'l, North America

Lake Superior

Lake Michigan

Lake Huron

Lake Ontario

Lake Erie

MN — Minneapolis, St. Paul, Sioux Falls

WI — Green Bay, Madison, Milwaukee

MI — Grand Rapids, Flint, Lansing, Detroit, Toledo

ME — Augusta

NH — Concord

VT — Montpelier

NY — Rochester, Buffalo, Albany, New York City

MA — Boston

RI — Providence

CT — New Haven, Hartford

PA — Erie, Pittsburgh, Harrisburg, Philadelphia

NJ — Newark, Trenton

DE — Dover

MD — Baltimore, Annapolis

Washington, D.C.

IA — Cedar Rapids, Des Moines

IL — Rockford, Peoria, Springfield, Chicago

IN — South Bend, Fort Wayne, Indianapolis

OH — Cleveland, Akron, Columbus, Dayton, Cincinnati

WV — Charleston

VA — Richmond, Norfolk

NE — Omaha, Lincoln

MO — Kansas City, Jefferson City, St. Louis, Springfield

KS — Topeka

KY — Louisville, Frankfort, Lexington, Evansville

TN — Nashville, Knoxville, Chattanooga, Memphis, Huntsville

NC — Greensboro, Durham, Winston-Salem, Raleigh, Charlotte

AR — Tulsa, Little Rock

MS — Jackson

AL — Birmingham, Montgomery, Columbus, Mobile

GA — Atlanta, Macon, Columbus, Savannah

SC — Columbia, Charleston

LA — Shreveport, Baton Rouge, New Orleans, Beaumont

TX — Houston

FL — Jacksonville, Tallahassee, Orlando, Tampa, St. Petersburg, Ft. Lauderdale, Miami

EVERGLADES PKWY

EASTERN CENTRAL T.Z.

0 100 200 300 400 500 mi

0 100 200 300 400 500 km

69

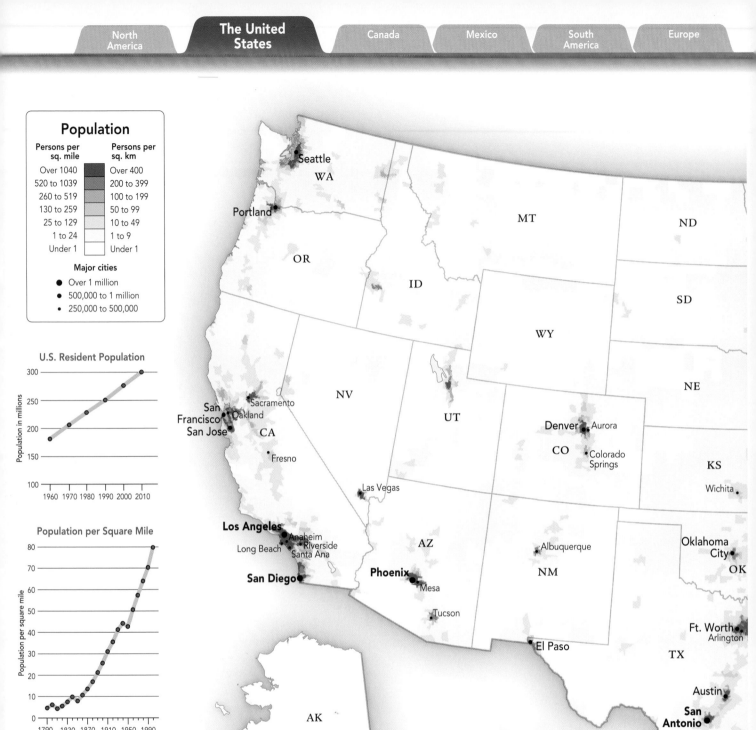

Population

Persons per sq. mile	Persons per sq. km
Over 1040	Over 400
520 to 1039	200 to 399
260 to 519	100 to 199
130 to 259	50 to 99
25 to 129	10 to 49
1 to 24	1 to 9
Under 1	Under 1

Major cities
- ● Over 1 million
- ● 500,000 to 1 million
- · 250,000 to 500,000

U.S. Resident Population

Population in millions — 100 to 300
1960 1970 1980 1990 2000 2010

Population per Square Mile

Population per square mile — 0 to 80
1790 1830 1870 1910 1950 1990

Source: U.S. Census Bureau

Distribution of Population by Region: 1900, 1950, 2000

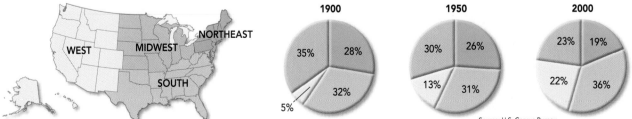

WEST | MIDWEST | NORTHEAST | SOUTH

1900
35% | 28% | 32% | 5%

1950
30% | 26% | 13% | 31%

2000
23% | 19% | 22% | 36%

Source: U.S. Census Bureau

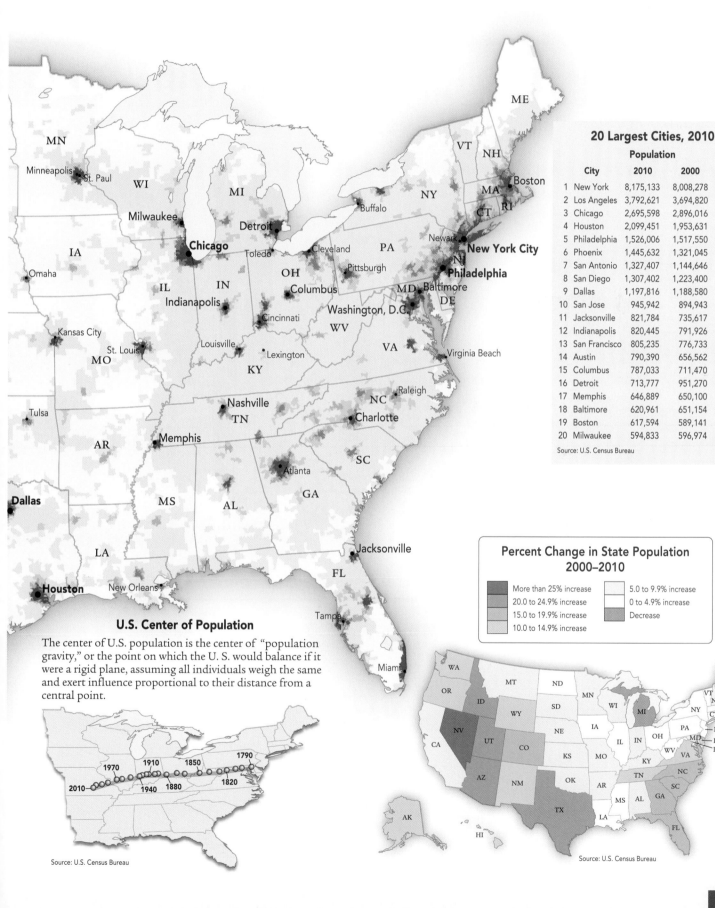

20 Largest Cities, 2010

Population

	City	2010	2000	Change
1	New York	8,175,133	8,008,278	2.08%
2	Los Angeles	3,792,621	3,694,820	2.65%
3	Chicago	2,695,598	2,896,016	-6.92%
4	Houston	2,099,451	1,953,631	7.46%
5	Philadelphia	1,526,006	1,517,550	0.56%
6	Phoenix	1,445,632	1,321,045	9.43%
7	San Antonio	1,327,407	1,144,646	15.97%
8	San Diego	1,307,402	1,223,400	6.87%
9	Dallas	1,197,816	1,188,580	0.78%
10	San Jose	945,942	894,943	5.70%
11	Jacksonville	821,784	735,617	11.71%
12	Indianapolis	820,445	791,926	3.60%
13	San Francisco	805,235	776,733	3.67%
14	Austin	790,390	656,562	20.38%
15	Columbus	787,033	711,470	10.62%
16	Detroit	713,777	951,270	-24.97%
17	Memphis	646,889	650,100	-0.49%
18	Baltimore	620,961	651,154	-4.64%
19	Boston	617,594	589,141	4.83%
20	Milwaukee	594,833	596,974	-0.36%

Source: U.S. Census Bureau

U.S. Center of Population

The center of U.S. population is the center of "population gravity," or the point on which the U. S. would balance if it were a rigid plane, assuming all individuals weigh the same and exert influence proportional to their distance from a central point.

Source: U.S. Census Bureau

Percent Change in State Population 2000–2010

More than 25% increase
20.0 to 24.9% increase
15.0 to 19.9% increase
10.0 to 14.9% increase
5.0 to 9.9% increase
0 to 4.9% increase
Decrease

Source: U.S. Census Bureau

71

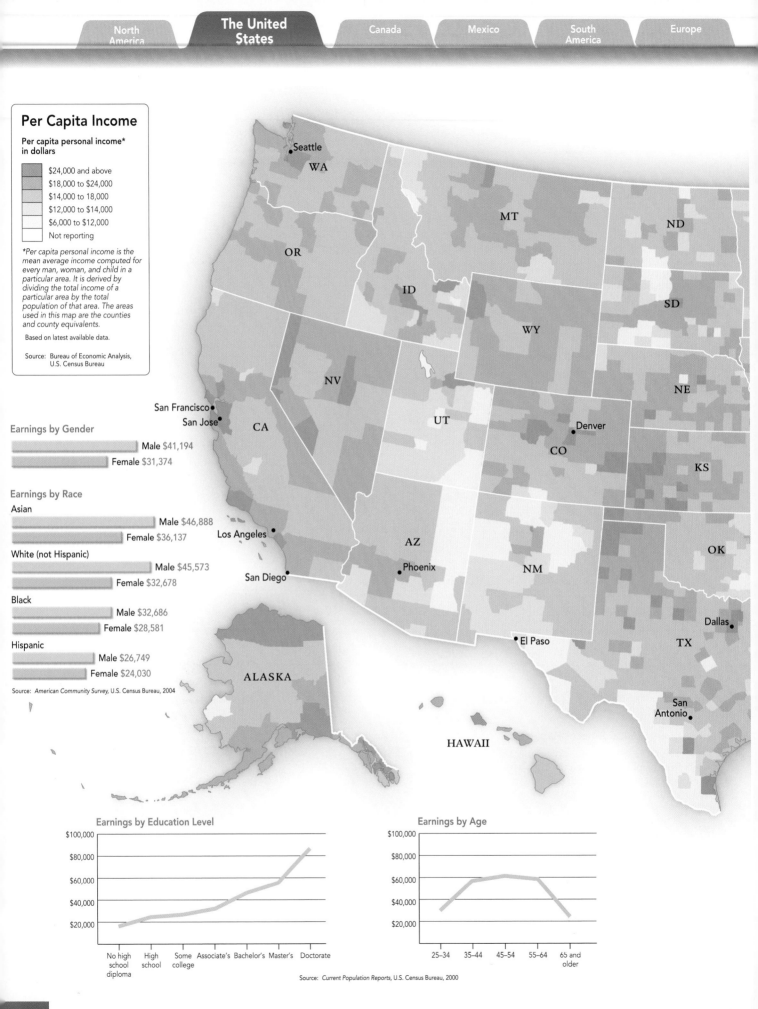

Per Capita Income

Per capita personal income*
in dollars

- $24,000 and above
- $18,000 to $24,000
- $14,000 to 18,000
- $12,000 to $14,000
- $6,000 to $12,000
- Not reporting

*Per capita personal income is the mean average income computed for every man, woman, and child in a particular area. It is derived by dividing the total income of a particular area by the total population of that area. The areas used in this map are the counties and county equivalents.

Based on latest available data.

Source: Bureau of Economic Analysis, U.S. Census Bureau

Earnings by Gender

Male $41,194
Female $31,374

Earnings by Race

Asian
Male $46,888
Female $36,137

White (not Hispanic)
Male $45,573
Female $32,678

Black
Male $32,686
Female $28,581

Hispanic
Male $26,749
Female $24,030

Source: American Community Survey, U.S. Census Bureau, 2004

Earnings by Education Level

$100,000
$80,000
$60,000
$40,000
$20,000

No high school diploma | High school | Some college | Associate's | Bachelor's | Master's | Doctorate

Earnings by Age

$100,000
$80,000
$60,000
$40,000
$20,000

25–34 | 35–44 | 45–54 | 55–64 | 65 and older

Source: Current Population Reports, U.S. Census Bureau, 2000

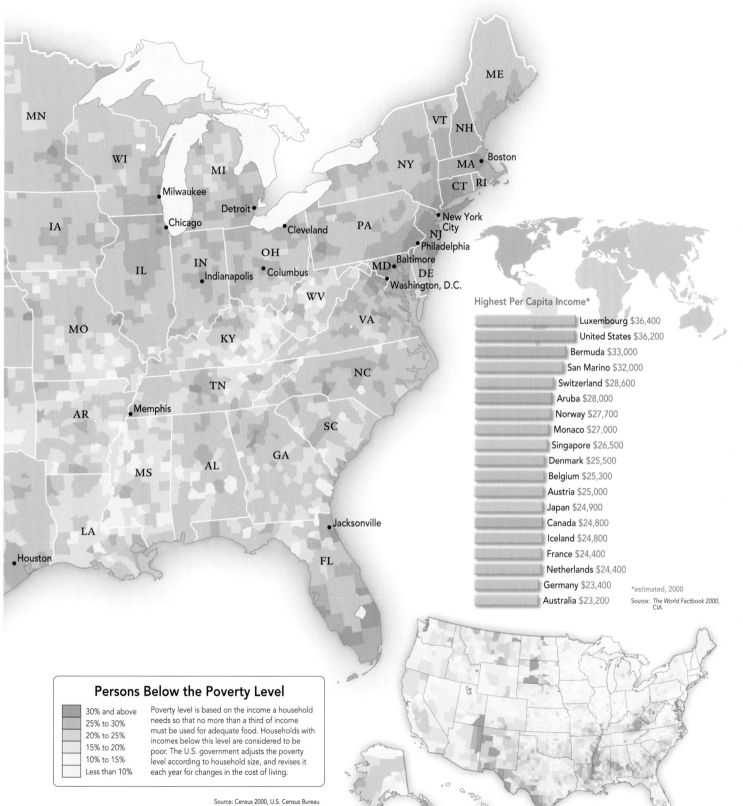

ME
VT
NH
NY
MA • Boston
CT RI
MN
WI
MI
• Milwaukee
• Detroit
• Chicago
• Cleveland
PA
• New York City
NJ
• Philadelphia
IA
IL
IN
OH
• Columbus
MD • Baltimore
DE
Washington, D.C.
• Indianapolis
WV
VA
MO
KY
NC
TN
SC
AR
• Memphis
GA
AL
MS
LA
Jacksonville
FL
• Houston

Highest Per Capita Income*

Luxembourg	$36,400
United States	$36,200
Bermuda	$33,000
San Marino	$32,000
Switzerland	$28,600
Aruba	$28,000
Norway	$27,700
Monaco	$27,000
Singapore	$26,500
Denmark	$25,500
Belgium	$25,300
Austria	$25,000
Japan	$24,900
Canada	$24,800
Iceland	$24,800
France	$24,400
Netherlands	$24,400
Germany	$23,400
Australia	$23,200

*estimated, 2000

Source: The World Factbook 2000, CIA

Persons Below the Poverty Level

- 30% and above
- 25% to 30%
- 20% to 25%
- 15% to 20%
- 10% to 15%
- Less than 10%

Poverty level is based on the income a household needs so that no more than a third of income must be used for adequate food. Households with incomes below this level are considered to be poor. The U.S. government adjusts the poverty level according to household size, and revises it each year for changes in the cost of living.

Source: Census 2000, U.S. Census Bureau

Canada

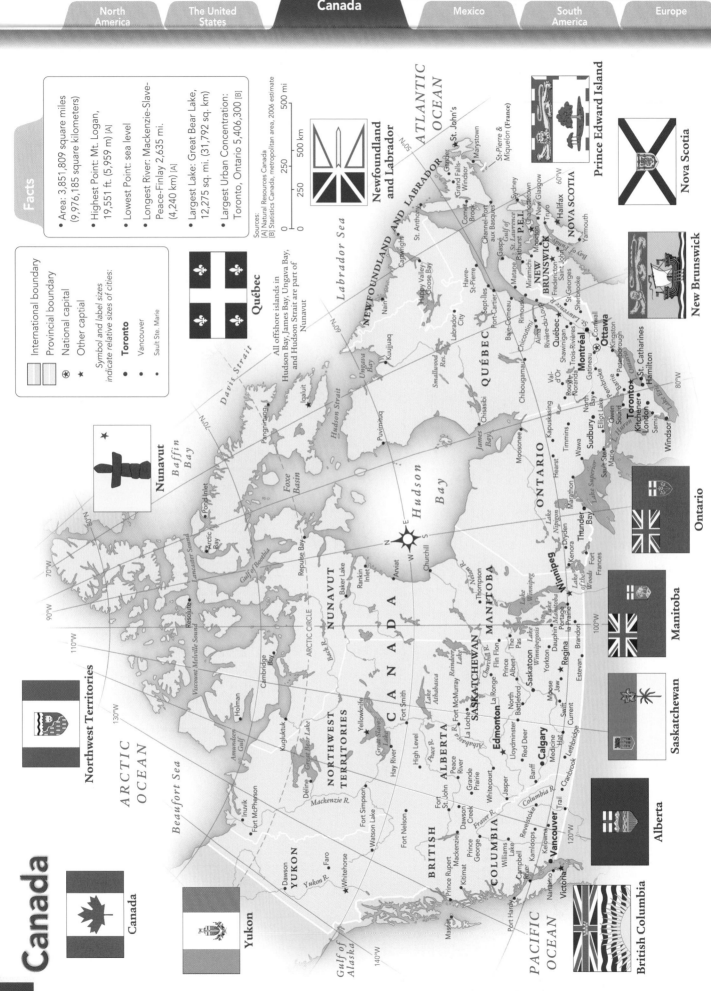

Facts

- Area: 3,851,809 square miles (9,976,185 square kilometers)
- Highest Point: Mt. Logan, 19,551 ft. (5,959 m) [A]
- Lowest Point: sea level
- Longest River: Mackenzie-Slave-Peace-Finlay 2,635 mi. (4,240 km) [A]
- Largest Lake: Great Bear Lake, 12,275 sq. mi. (31,792 sq. km)
- Largest Urban Concentration: Toronto, Ontario 5,406,300 [B]

Sources:
[A] Natural Resources Canada
[B] Statistics Canada, metropolitan area, 2006 estimate

All offshore islands in Hudson Bay, James Bay, Ungava Bay, and Hudson Strait are part of Nunavut

International boundary
Provincial boundary
⊛ National capital
★ Other capital

Symbol and label sizes indicate relative sizes of cities:
Toronto
Vancouver
Sault Ste. Marie

Newfoundland and Labrador
Nunavut
Québec
Prince Edward Island
Nova Scotia
New Brunswick
Ontario
Manitoba
Saskatchewan
Alberta
British Columbia
Yukon
Northwest Territories
Canada

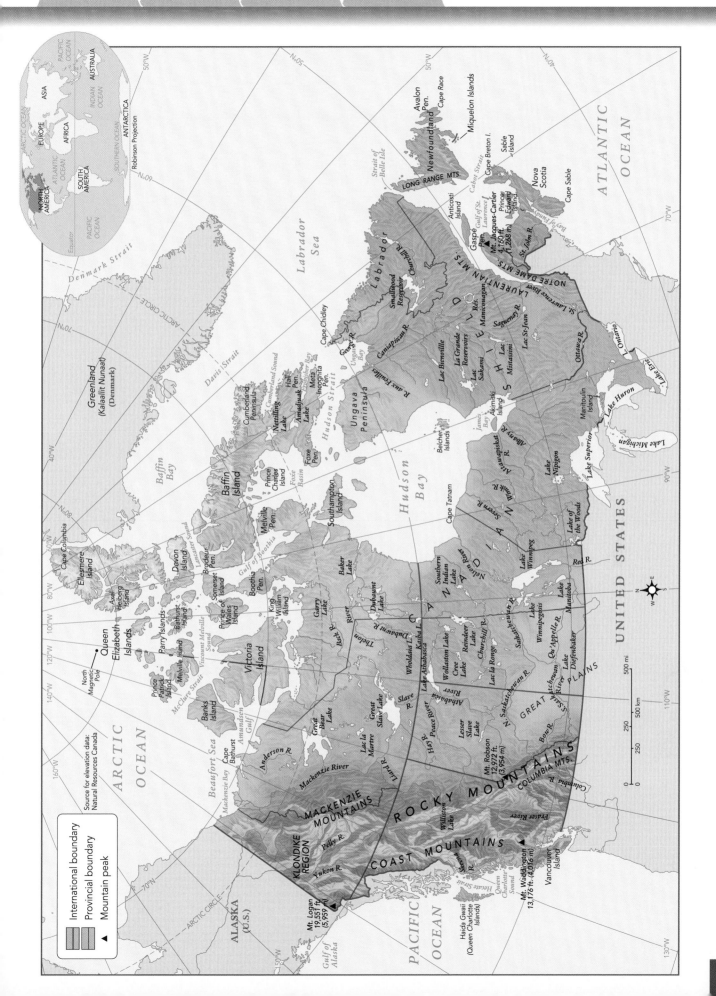

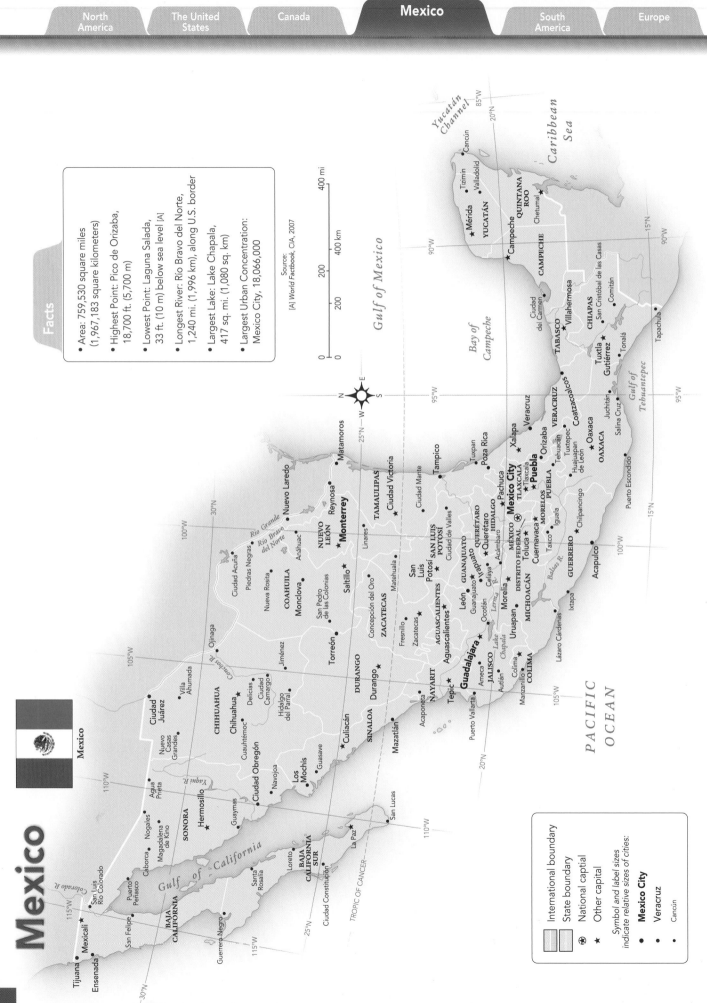

Mexico

Facts

- Area: 759,530 square miles (1,967,183 square kilometers)
- Highest Point: Pico de Orizaba, 18,700 ft. (5,700 m)
- Lowest Point: Laguna Salada, 33 ft. (10 m) below sea level [A]
- Longest River: Río Bravo del Norte, 1,240 mi. (1,996 km), along U.S. border
- Largest Lake: Lake Chapala, 417 sq. mi. (1,080 sq. km)
- Largest Urban Concentration: Mexico City, 18,066,000

Source:
[A] World Factbook, CIA, 2007

Mexico

International boundary
State boundary
National captial
Other capital

Symbol and label sizes
indicate relative sizes of cities:

Mexico City
Veracruz
Cancún

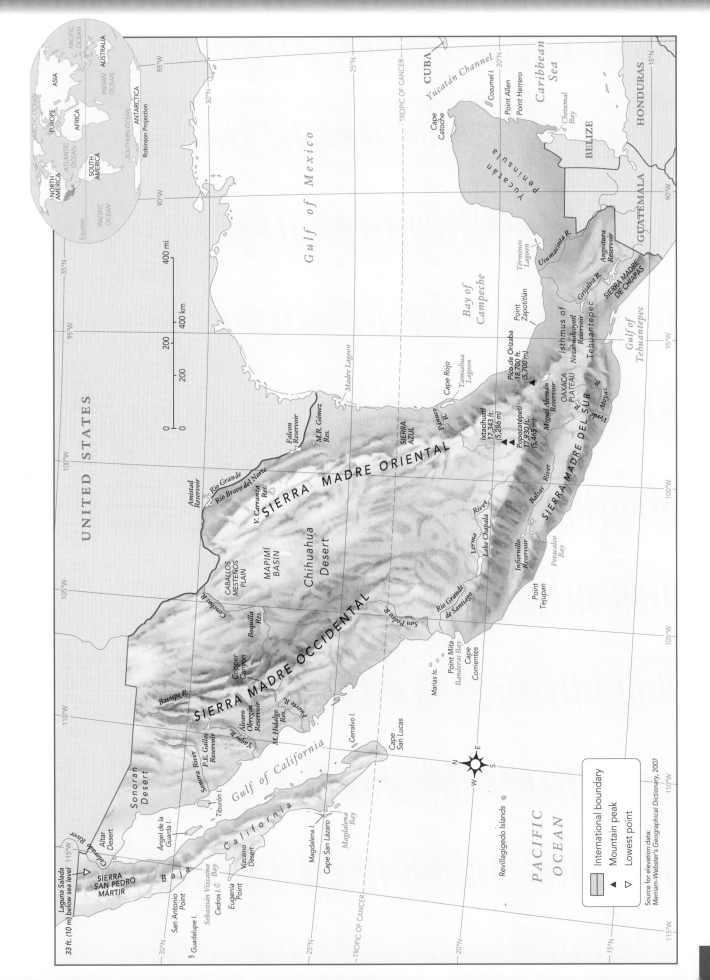

South America

Legend:
- International boundary
- ⊛ National capital
- ★ Other capital

Symbol and label sizes indicate relative sizes of cities:
- ● **Rio de Janeiro**
- • Santos
- · Jataí

Facts

- Area: 6,765,422 square miles (17,522,371 square kilometers) [A]

- Highest Point: Mt. Aconcagua, Argentina, 22,834 ft (6,960 m) [B]

- Lowest Point: Laguna del Carbón, Argentina, 344 ft (105 m) below sea level [B]

- Longest River: Amazon, 4,000 mi (6,437 km) [A]

- Largest Lake: Lake Titicaca, Peru/Bolivia, 3,200 sq. mi (8,288 sq. km) [A]

- Largest Country: Brazil, 3,286,488 sq. mi (8,511,965 sq. km) (slightly smaller than the United States) [B]

- Largest Urban Concentration: São Paulo, Brazil, 17,099,000 [A] [C]

Sources and notes:
[A] *World Almanac*, 2006
[B] *World Factbook*, CIA, 2007
[C] highest estimate is 20,400,000 - see www.citypopulation.de

NORTH
AMERICA

Caribbean Sea

80°W   70°W   60°W   50°W

NORTH
AMERICA   EUROPE   ASIA
ATLANTIC
OCEAN

Equator   AFRICA
PACIFIC
OCEAN   SOUTH
AMERICA   PACIFIC
OCEAN

INDIAN
OCEAN   AUSTRALIA

SOUTHERN OCEAN

ANTARCTICA

Robinson Projection

40°W

10°N

Gulf
of
Panama

Lake
Maracaibo

Cauca River

Magdalena River

LLANOS

Orinoco River

Angel Falls ≈
GUIANA   HIGHLANDS

ATLANTIC
OCEAN

Orinoco River

Rio Negro

EQUATOR

Galápagos
Islands

Gulf of
Guayaquil

Pariñas Pt.

AMAZON

Amazon (Solimões) River

Juruá River

Purus River

Amazon   River

Madeira River

Tapajós River

Xingu River   River

Teles Pires   River

Aragüaia River

Tocantins River

Parnaíba River

São Francisco River

Cape
São Roque

0°

BASIN

ANDES

Patumayo River

Marañón River

Ucayali River

▲ Mt. Huascarán
22,205 ft.
(6,768 m)

Beni River

Guaporé River

MATO GROSSO
PLATEAU

BRAZILIAN

HIGHLANDS

10°S

Paracas
Peninsula

Volcán Misti
19,101 ft.
(5,822 m) ▼

Lake
Titicaca

ALTIPLANO

Lake
Poopó

▲ Mt. Illimani
21,122 ft.
(6,438 m)

Mamoré River

Paraguay River

PACIFIC
OCEAN

Atacama Desert

ANDES

GRAN   CHACO

Pilcomayo   River

Grande River

SERRA DO MAR

20°S

TROPIC OF CAPRICORN

San Félix I.   San Ambrosio I.

Salado River

Paraná   River

Iguazú
Falls

River

TROPIC OF CAPRICORN

Juan
Fernández
Is.

Mt. Aconcagua
22,834 ft.
(6,960 m) ▲

Paraná

Uruguay River

ATLANTIC

OCEAN

30°S

Río de la Plata

Colorado River

PAMPAS

Negro River

Chiloé I.

Gulf of San Matías

40°S

Los Chonos
Archipelago

Patagonia

Gulf of
San Jorge

International boundary

▲ Mountain peak

▽ Lowest point

≈ Falls

Laguna del Carbón
344 ft (105 m) below sea level ▽

Sources for elevation data:
World Factbook, CIA, 2007
Smithsonian Global Volcanism Program

Santa Cruz
River

Strait of
Magellan

Falkland
Islands
(Islas Malvinas)

South
Georgia

Tierra del
Fuego

50°S

Cape Horn

A   B

100°W   90°W   80°W   70°W   60°W   50°W   40°W   30°W   20°W

N
W   E
S

Elevation Profile

Paracas Peninsula   Lake Titicaca   Andes Mountains

Mato Grosso Plateau

Brazilian Highlands

20,000 ft.

10,000 ft.

5,000 ft.

Sea   A
level

B

79

Major Metropolitan Areas

Argentina
Buenos Aires	11,298,000
Córdoba	1,209,000
Rosario	1,119,000

Bolivia
La Paz	1,484,000
Santa Cruz	1,136,000
Cochabamba	517,000

Brazil
São Paulo	17,834,000
Rio de Janeiro	10,612,000
Belo Horizonte	4,800,000
Porto Alegre	3,655,000
Recife	3,332,000
Salvador	3,018,000
Fortaleza	2,975,000
Brasília	2,942,000
Curitiba	2,726,000
Belém	1,816,000
Manaus	1,011,000

Chile
Santiago	4,647,000
Viña del Mar	299,000

Colombia
Bogotá	6,422,000
Cali	2,129,000
Medellín	1,885,000
Barranquilla	1,549,000

Ecuador
Guayaquil	2,118,000
Quito	1,616,000

French Guiana
Cayenne	50,000

Guyana
Georgetown	187,000

Paraguay
Asunción	513,000

Peru
Lima	6,988,000
Arequipa	830,000
Chiclayo	766,000

Suriname
Paramaribo	291,000

Uruguay
Montevideo	1,303,000

Venezuela
Caracas	3,061,000
Maracaibo	1,220,000
Barquisimeto	896,000
Valencia	742,000

International comparability of population data is limited by varying census methods. Where metropolitan population is unavailable, core city population is shown.

Population

Persons per sq. mile	Persons per sq. km
Over 520	Over 200
260 to 519	100 to 199
130 to 259	50 to 99
25 to 129	10 to 49
1 to 24	1 to 9
0	0

Major metropolitan areas
- ● Over 2 million
- ● 1 million to 2 million
- · Under 1 million

Estimated 2005 Population (in millions)

Brazil 186
Colombia 43
Argentina 40
Peru 28
Venezuela 25
Chile 16
Ecuador 13
Bolivia 9
Paraguay 6
All others 5

Source: U.S. Census Bureau

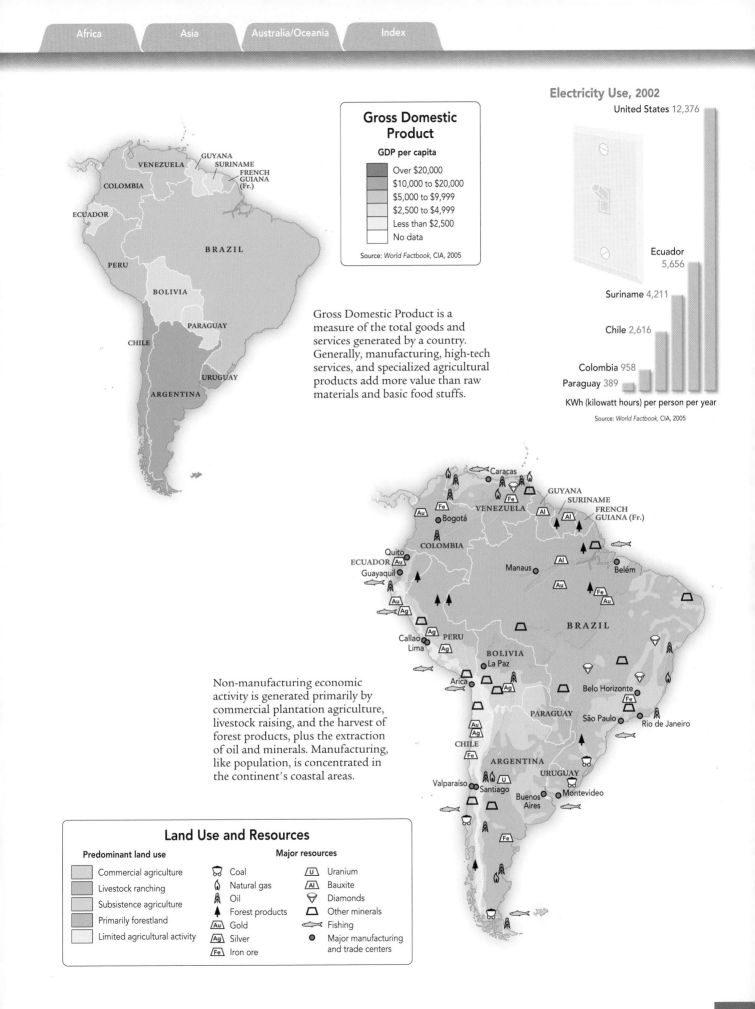

Gross Domestic Product

GDP per capita

- Over $20,000
- $10,000 to $20,000
- $5,000 to $9,999
- $2,500 to $4,999
- Less than $2,500
- No data

Source: *World Factbook*, CIA, 2005

Gross Domestic Product is a measure of the total goods and services generated by a country. Generally, manufacturing, high-tech services, and specialized agricultural products add more value than raw materials and basic food stuffs.

Electricity Use, 2002

United States 12,376
Ecuador 5,656
Suriname 4,211
Chile 2,616
Colombia 958
Paraguay 389

KWh (kilowatt hours) per person per year

Source: *World Factbook*, CIA, 2005

Non-manufacturing economic activity is generated primarily by commercial plantation agriculture, livestock raising, and the harvest of forest products, plus the extraction of oil and minerals. Manufacturing, like population, is concentrated in the continent's coastal areas.

Land Use and Resources

Predominant land use

- Commercial agriculture
- Livestock ranching
- Subsistence agriculture
- Primarily forestland
- Limited agricultural activity

Major resources

- Coal
- Natural gas
- Oil
- Forest products
- Au Gold
- Ag Silver
- Fe Iron ore
- U Uranium
- Al Bauxite
- Diamonds
- Other minerals
- Fishing
- Major manufacturing and trade centers

Most of the continent is under the influence of wet and tropical air. Warm currents in the Atlantic Ocean as well as wet lowland elevations lying within the confines of the tropical latitudes directly affect the climate of the majority of the land area. The Andes Mountains and cold currents that hug the Pacific coast keep the Western and Southern regions of the continent temperate but dry.

See photographs taken in different kinds of climates on pages 24–25.

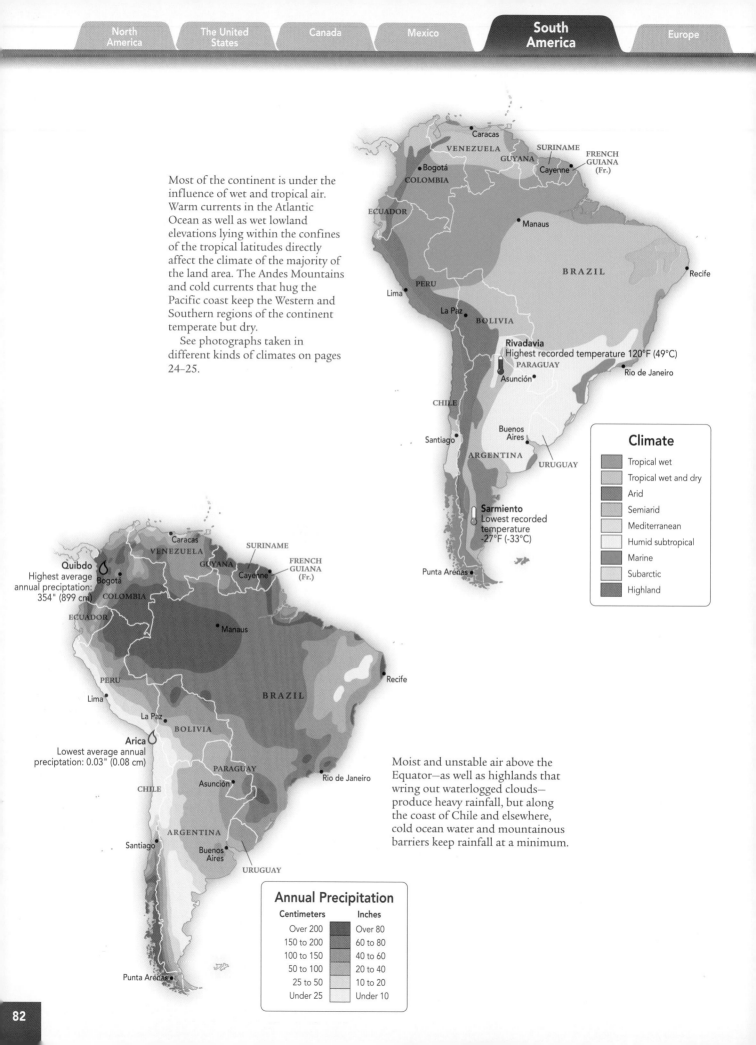

Caracas
VENEZUELA | GUYANA | SURINAME | FRENCH GUIANA (Fr.)
Bogotá | Cayenne
COLOMBIA
ECUADOR
Manaus
PERU
Lima
BRAZIL
Recife
La Paz
BOLIVIA
Rivadavia
Highest recorded temperature 120°F (49°C)
PARAGUAY
Asunción
Rio de Janeiro
CHILE
Buenos Aires
Santiago
ARGENTINA
URUGUAY
Sarmiento
Lowest recorded temperature -27°F (-33°C)
Punta Arenas

Climate

- Tropical wet
- Tropical wet and dry
- Arid
- Semiarid
- Mediterranean
- Humid subtropical
- Marine
- Subarctic
- Highland

Caracas
VENEZUELA | SURINAME
GUYANA | FRENCH GUIANA (Fr.)
Quibdo
Highest average annual precipitation: 354" (899 cm)
Bogotá | Cayenne
COLOMBIA
ECUADOR
Manaus
PERU
Lima
BRAZIL
Recife
La Paz
BOLIVIA
Arica
Lowest average annual precipitation: 0.03" (0.08 cm)
PARAGUAY
Asunción
Rio de Janeiro
CHILE
ARGENTINA
Santiago
Buenos Aires
URUGUAY

Moist and unstable air above the Equator—as well as highlands that wring out waterlogged clouds—produce heavy rainfall, but along the coast of Chile and elsewhere, cold ocean water and mountainous barriers keep rainfall at a minimum.

Punta Arenas

Annual Precipitation

Centimeters	Inches
Over 200	Over 80
150 to 200	60 to 80
100 to 150	40 to 60
50 to 100	20 to 40
25 to 50	10 to 20
Under 25	Under 10

Climate Graphs

Average daily temperature range (in °F)
- High
- Low

Average monthly precipitation (in inches)

ASUNCIÓN, Paraguay

BOGOTÁ, Colombia

BUENOS AIRES, Argentina

CARACAS, Venezuela

CAYENNE, French Guiana

LA PAZ, Bolivia

LIMA, Peru

MANAUS, Brazil

PUNTA ARENAS, Chile

RECIFE, Brazil

RIO DE JANEIRO, Brazil

SANTIAGO, Chile

South America is dominated by tropical vegetation, including Earth's most extensive rain forest. Farther south, a vast grassland, the Pampa, fades gradually into the dry and meager vegetation of Patagonia.
See photographs of the different kinds of vegetation on pages 26–27.

Vegetation

- Unclassified highlands or ice cap
- Midlatitude deciduous forest
- Mixed forest
- Midlatitude scrubland
- Midlatitude grassland
- Desert
- Tropical seasonal and scrub
- Tropical rain forest
- Tropical savanna

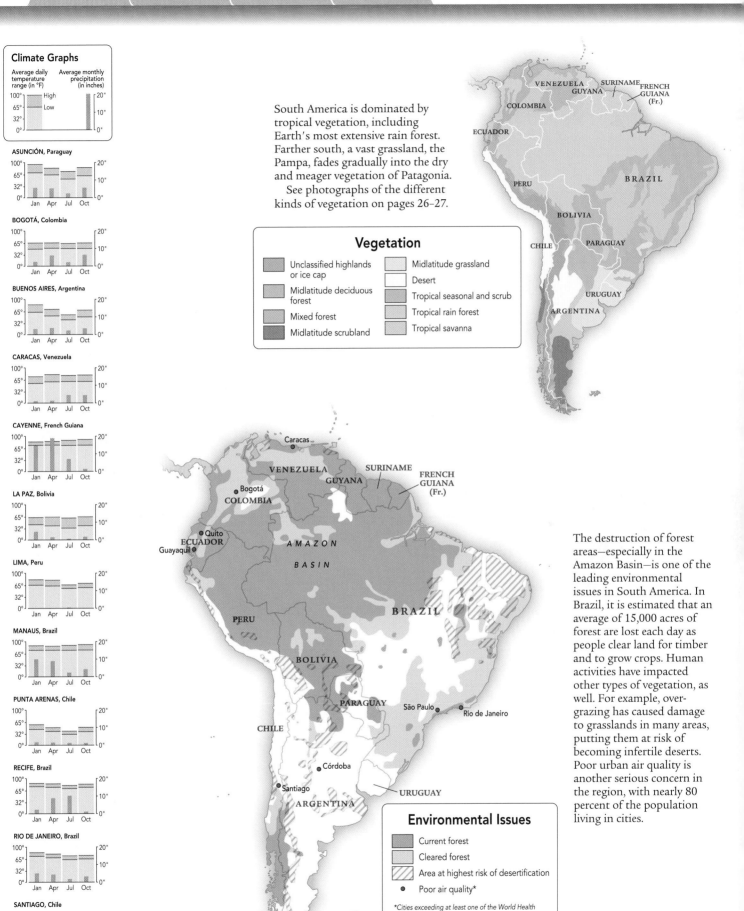

The destruction of forest areas—especially in the Amazon Basin—is one of the leading environmental issues in South America. In Brazil, it is estimated that an average of 15,000 acres of forest are lost each day as people clear land for timber and to grow crops. Human activities have impacted other types of vegetation, as well. For example, overgrazing has caused damage to grasslands in many areas, putting them at risk of becoming infertile deserts. Poor urban air quality is another serious concern in the region, with nearly 80 percent of the population living in cities.

Environmental Issues

- Current forest
- Cleared forest
- Area at highest risk of desertification
- Poor air quality*

Cities exceeding at least one of the World Health Organization's (WHO) annual mean guidelines for air quality

Sources: *Global Distribution of Original and Remaining Forests, UNEP-WCMC, 2002*
World Soil Resources Map Index, USDA/NRCS, 2002
World Development Indicators, World Bank, 1999

Europe

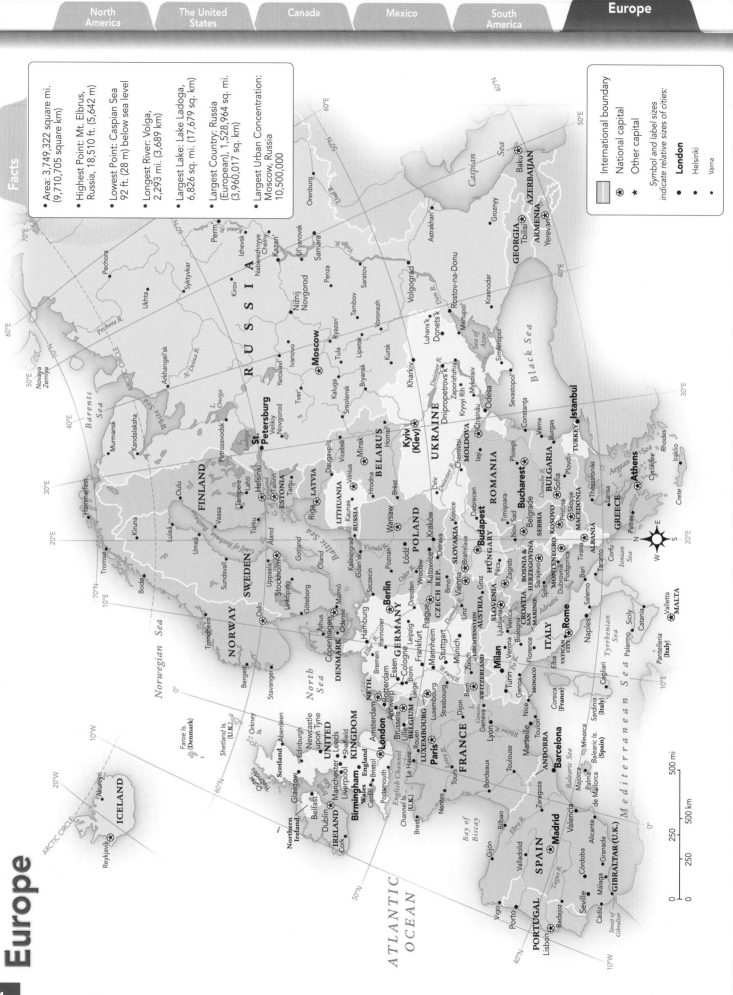

- Area: 3,749,322 square mi. (9,710,705 square km)
- Highest Point: Mt. Elbrus, Russia, 18,510 ft. (5,642 m)
- Lowest Point: Caspian Sea 92 ft. (28 m) below sea level
- Longest River: Volga, 2,293 mi. (3,689 km)
- Largest Lake: Lake Ladoga, 6,826 sq. mi. (17,679 sq. km)
- Largest Country: Russia (European) 1,528,964 sq. mi. (3,960,017 sq. km)
- Largest Urban Concentration: Moscow, Russia 10,500,000

International boundary
⊛ National capital
★ Other capital

Symbol and label sizes indicate relative sizes of cities:
● **London**
● Helsinki
· Varna

ASIA

ASIA

AFRICA

URAL MOUNTAINS

SCANDINAVIAN MTS

NORTHERN EUROPEAN PLAIN

CENTRAL RUSSIAN UPLAND

CARPATHIAN MTS.

ALPS

APENNINES

BALKAN MTS.

CAUCASUS MTS.

LESSER CAUCASUS

TRANSCAUCASIA

VOLGA UPLAND

DNIEPER UPLAND

DINARIC ALPS

PYRENEES

IBERIAN Peninsula

MASSIF CENTRAL

CANTABRIAN MTS.

SIERRA MORENA

TRANSYLVANIAN ALPS

Caspian Sea 92 ft. (28 m) below sea level

Mt. Elbrus 18,510 ft. (5,642 m)

Galdhøpiggen 8,100 ft. (2,469 m)

Mt. Blanc 15,771 ft. (4,807 m)

Mt. Etna 10,902 ft. (3,323 m)

Mulhacén 11,407 ft. (3,477 m)

Pico de Aneto 11,168 ft. (3,404 m)

Mt. Olympus 9,570 ft. (2,917 m)

Musala Peak 9,596 ft. (2,925 m)

Moldoveanu 8,343 ft. (2,543 m)

Wallachia

ATLANTIC OCEAN

Norwegian Sea

Barents Sea

White Sea

North Sea

Baltic Sea

Mediterranean Sea

Adriatic Sea

Black Sea

Caspian Sea

Caspian Depression

Sea of Azov

Bay of Biscay

Tyrrhenian Sea

Ligurian Sea

Ionian Sea

Aegean Sea

Sea of Marmara

Alboran Sea

Balearic Sea

Kattegat

Skagerrak

Irish Sea

Gulf of Bothnia

Gulf of Finland

Gulf of Riga

Gulf of Lions

Gulf of Taranto

Strait of Messina

Strait of Sicily

Strait of Gibraltar

English Channel

St. George's Channel

Strait of Dover

Volga-Don Canal

Kiel Canal

Ural River

Ural River

Kama River

Pechora R.

Northern Dvina R.

Sukhona R.

Vychegda R.

Volga River

Volgograd Reservoir

Kuybyshev Reservoir

Rybinsk Reservoir

Oka R.

Volga R.

Don R.

Donets R.

Dnieper River

Desna R.

Pripet River

W. Dvina R.

Dniester River

Prut R.

Danube River

Danube

Danube R.

Tisza

Sava R.

Drava R.

Po R.

Rhône R.

Rhine R.

Rhine Delta

Elbe River

Weser R.

Oder R.

Vistula R.

Bug R.

Seine River

Loire R.

Garonne R.

Ebro R.

Tagus River

Duero R.

Douro R.

Guadiana R.

Marne R.

Rhône R.

Klarälven

Göta R.

Glomma R.

Torneälven

Muonio R.

Kemi R.

Tornio R.

Osterdal

Vänern

Vättern

L. Constance

L. Geneva

Lake Balaton

Lake Onega

Lake Ladoga

Lake Saimaa

Lake Peipus

Tsimlyansk Reservoir

Kremenchuk Reservoir

Kakhovka Res.

Lake Sevan

Volga Delta

Danube Delta

Timan Ridge

Valdai Hills

SUDETEN MTS.

DONETS BASIN

LAPLAND

Kola Peninsula

Kanin Pen.

Crimea

Dalmatia

Peloponese Pen.

Brittany

Highlands

THE PENNINES

British Isles

Iceland

Vatnajökull

Faroe Is.

Shetland Is.

Orkney Islands

Outer Hebrides

Frisian Is.

Jutland

Åland Is.

Hiiumaa

Saaremaa

Gotland

Öland

Bornholm

Sicily

Sardinia

Corsica

Elba

Malta

Pantelleria

Balearic Is.

Majorca

Minorca

Ibiza

Crete

Rhodes

Kefallinía I.

Cyclades

Sea of Crete

North Cape

Cape Wrath

Land's End

Cape Clear

Cape Finisterre

Cape St. Vincent

Kolguyev I.

Kanin Pen.

Guernsey, Jersey

Po Valley

70°E

60°E

50°E

50°N

50°N

40°N

30°N

60°N

70°N

60°N

70°N

80°E

40°E

30°E

20°E

10°E

0°

10°W

20°W

30°W

ARCTIC CIRCLE

PRIME MERIDIAN

North Cape

International boundary
Canal
▲ Mountain peak
▽ Lowest point

N
W E
S

PACIFIC OCEAN
ASIA
AUSTRALIA
EUROPE
AFRICA
INDIAN OCEAN
ATLANTIC OCEAN
NORTH AMERICA
SOUTH AMERICA
ANTARCTICA
SOUTHERN OCEAN
PACIFIC OCEAN
ARCTIC OCEAN
Equator
Robinson Projection

250   500 mi
0
250   500 km
0

Note: elevation of Mt. Etna varies slightly between eruptions

A
B

Elevation Profile

Massif Central	Mt. Blanc	Alps	Carpathian Mountains	Black Sea	Sea of Azov	Caspian Depression	Caspian Sea		

15,000 ft.
10,000 ft.
5,000 ft.
Sea level

A
B

85

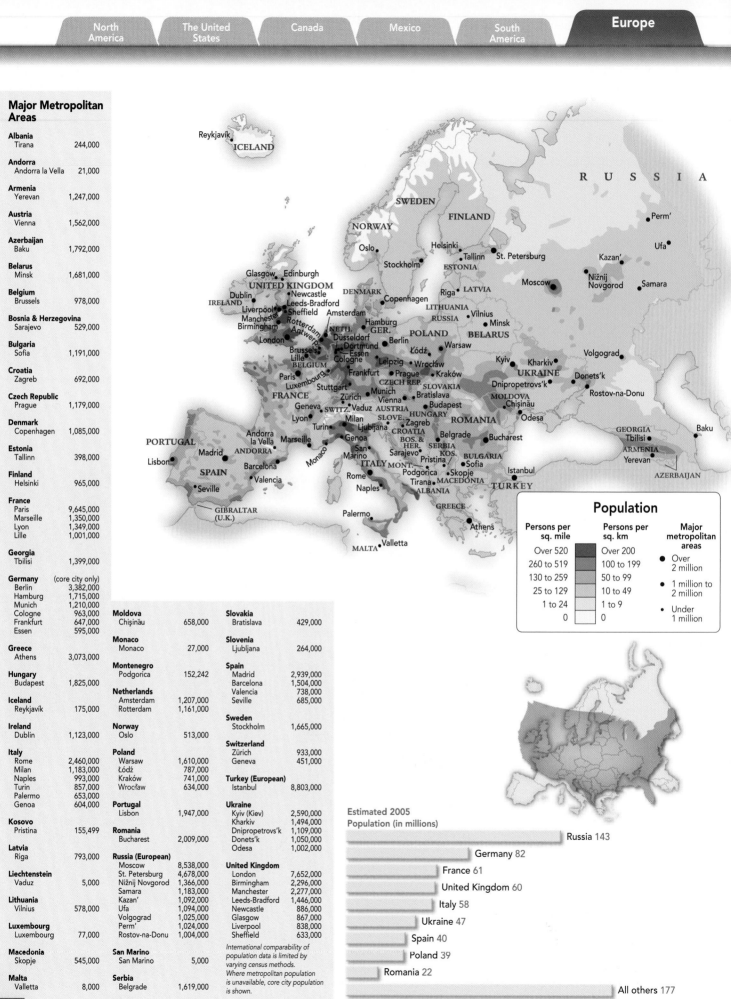

Major Metropolitan Areas

Albania
Tirana — 244,000

Andorra
Andorra la Vella — 21,000

Armenia
Yerevan — 1,247,000

Austria
Vienna — 1,562,000

Azerbaijan
Baku — 1,792,000

Belarus
Minsk — 1,681,000

Belgium
Brussels — 978,000

Bosnia & Herzegovina
Sarajevo — 529,000

Bulgaria
Sofia — 1,191,000

Croatia
Zagreb — 692,000

Czech Republic
Prague — 1,179,000

Denmark
Copenhagen — 1,085,000

Estonia
Tallinn — 398,000

Finland
Helsinki — 965,000

France
Paris — 9,645,000
Marseille — 1,350,000
Lyon — 1,349,000
Lille — 1,001,000

Georgia
Tbilisi — 1,399,000

Germany (core city only)
Berlin — 3,382,000
Hamburg — 1,715,000
Munich — 1,210,000
Cologne — 963,000
Frankfurt — 647,000
Essen — 595,000

Greece
Athens — 3,073,000

Hungary
Budapest — 1,825,000

Iceland
Reykjavík — 175,000

Ireland
Dublin — 1,123,000

Italy
Rome — 2,460,000
Milan — 1,183,000
Naples — 993,000
Turin — 857,000
Palermo — 653,000
Genoa — 604,000

Kosovo
Pristina — 155,499

Latvia
Riga — 793,000

Liechtenstein
Vaduz — 5,000

Lithuania
Vilnius — 578,000

Luxembourg
Luxembourg — 77,000

Macedonia
Skopje — 545,000

Malta
Valletta — 8,000

Moldova
Chişinău — 658,000

Monaco
Monaco — 27,000

Montenegro
Podgorica — 152,242

Netherlands
Amsterdam — 1,207,000
Rotterdam — 1,161,000

Norway
Oslo — 513,000

Poland
Warsaw — 1,610,000
Łódź — 787,000
Kraków — 741,000
Wrocław — 634,000

Portugal
Lisbon — 1,947,000

Romania
Bucharest — 2,009,000

Russia (European)
Moscow — 8,538,000
St. Petersburg — 4,678,000
Nižnij Novgorod — 1,366,000
Samara — 1,183,000
Kazan' — 1,092,000
Ufa — 1,094,000
Volgograd — 1,025,000
Perm' — 1,024,000
Rostov-na-Donu — 1,004,000

Slovakia
Bratislava — 429,000

Slovenia
Ljubljana — 264,000

Spain
Madrid — 2,939,000
Barcelona — 1,504,000
Valencia — 738,000
Seville — 685,000

Sweden
Stockholm — 1,665,000

Switzerland
Zürich — 933,000
Geneva — 451,000

Turkey (European)
Istanbul — 8,803,000

Ukraine
Kyiv (Kiev) — 2,590,000
Kharkiv — 1,494,000
Dnipropetrovs'k — 1,109,000
Donets'k — 1,050,000
Odesa — 1,002,000

United Kingdom
London — 7,652,000
Birmingham — 2,296,000
Manchester — 2,277,000
Leeds-Bradford — 1,446,000
Newcastle — 886,000
Glasgow — 867,000
Liverpool — 838,000
Sheffield — 633,000

San Marino
San Marino — 5,000

Serbia
Belgrade — 1,619,000

International comparability of population data is limited by varying census methods. Where metropolitan population is unavailable, core city population is shown.

Population

Persons per sq. mile	Persons per sq. km	Major metropolitan areas
Over 520	Over 200	● Over 2 million
260 to 519	100 to 199	
130 to 259	50 to 99	● 1 million to 2 million
25 to 129	10 to 49	
1 to 24	1 to 9	• Under 1 million
0	0	

Estimated 2005 Population (in millions)

Russia 143
Germany 82
France 61
United Kingdom 60
Italy 58
Ukraine 47
Spain 40
Poland 39
Romania 22
All others 177

Source: U.S. Census Bureau

Gross Domestic Product

GDP per capita

- Over $20,000
- $10,000 to $20,000
- $5,000 to $9,999
- $2,500 to $4,999
- Under $2,500
- No data

Source: *World Factbook*, CIA, 2005

Gross Domestic Product is a measure of the total goods and services generated by a country. Generally, manufacturing, high-tech services, and specialized agricultural products add more value than raw materials and basic food stuffs.

Electricity Use, 2002

- Iceland 25,922
- Finland 15,044
- United States 12,376
- France 6,837
- Russia 6,236*
- United Kingdom 5,582*
- Moldova 1,034

KWh (kilowatt hours) per person per year
*2003 data

Source: *World Factbook*, CIA, 2005

Land Use and Resources

Predominant land use

- Commercial agriculture
- Dairying
- Livestock ranching
- Nomadic herding
- Subsistence agriculture
- Primarily forestland
- Limited agricultural activity

Major resources

- Coal
- Natural gas
- Oil
- Au Gold
- Fe Iron ore
- Ag Silver
- U Uranium
- Al Bauxite
- Other minerals
- Fishing
- Major manufacturing and trade centers

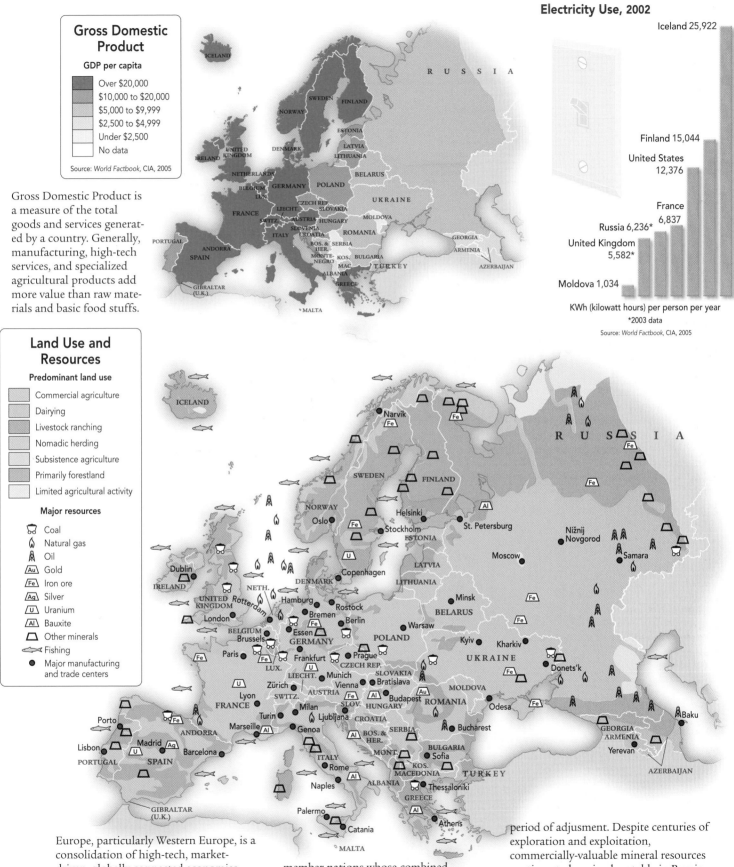

Europe, particularly Western Europe, is a consolidation of high-tech, market-driven, globally connected economies, where manufacturing and commercial agriculture predominate. Crucial to continental economic integration is the European Union, a partnership of 25 member nations whose combined economic clout rivals the U.S. Russia and former Soviet-satellite nations are, in large part, reaching harmony with the rest of Europe after an initial and unsettling period of adjustment. Despite centuries of exploration and exploitation, commercially-valuable mineral resources continue to be mined, notably in Russia, the Ukraine, and Scandinavia. The bountiful oil and gas fields of the North Sea are one of the most important and most recent discoveries.

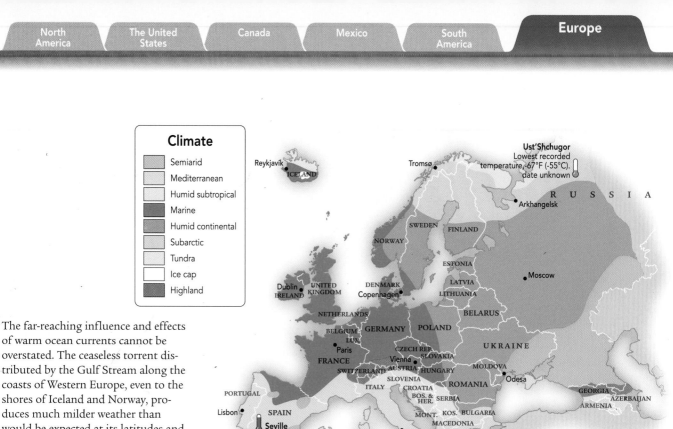

Climate

- Semiarid
- Mediterranean
- Humid subtropical
- Marine
- Humid continental
- Subarctic
- Tundra
- Ice cap
- Highland

Reykjavík · ICELAND

Tromsø ·

Ust'Shchugor
Lowest recorded
temperature, -67°F (-55°C),
date unknown

R U S S I A

· Arkhangelsk

NORWAY — SWEDEN — FINLAND

ESTONIA

· Moscow

Dublin · UNITED KINGDOM — DENMARK — Copenhagen — LATVIA — LITHUANIA

IRELAND

NETHERLANDS — BELARUS

BELGIUM — GERMANY — POLAND

LUX. — UKRAINE

Paris — CZECH REP. — SLOVAKIA

FRANCE — Vienna — AUSTRIA — HUNGARY — MOLDOVA

SWITZERLAND — SLOVENIA — ROMANIA — Odesa

PORTUGAL — ITALY — CROATIA — GEORGIA

BOS. & HER. — SERBIA — AZERBAIJAN

Lisbon · SPAIN — ARMENIA

MONT. — KOS. — BULGARIA

GIBRALTAR — Naples · — MACEDONIA

(U.K.) — ALBANIA

Seville
Highest recorded
temperature, 122°F (50°C), 1881

GREECE

· Athens

MALTA

The far-reaching influence and effects of warm ocean currents cannot be overstated. The ceaseless torrent distributed by the Gulf Stream along the coasts of Western Europe, even to the shores of Iceland and Norway, produces much milder weather than would be expected at its latitudes and provides a ready source of moisture. Along the Mediterranean margin of Europe the typical weather—mild, wet winters and hot, dry summers—has been defined as a climate category that is now used worldwide.

See photographs taken in different kinds of climates on pages 24–25.

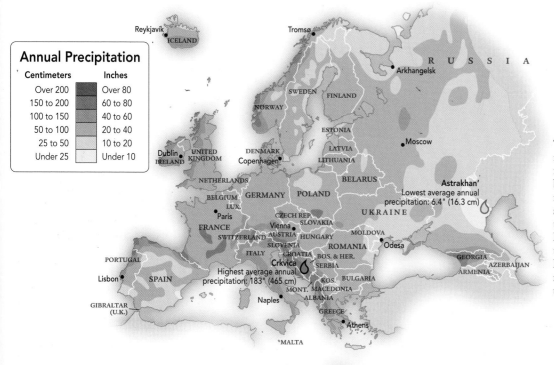

Annual Precipitation

Centimeters	Inches
Over 200	Over 80
150 to 200	60 to 80
100 to 150	40 to 60
50 to 100	20 to 40
25 to 50	10 to 20
Under 25	Under 10

Reykjavík · ICELAND

Tromsø ·

R U S S I A

· Arkhangelsk

NORWAY — SWEDEN — FINLAND

ESTONIA

· Moscow

Dublin · UNITED KINGDOM — DENMARK — LATVIA — LITHUANIA

IRELAND — Copenhagen

NETHERLANDS — BELARUS

BELGIUM — GERMANY — POLAND

LUX. — UKRAINE

Paris — CZECH REP.

FRANCE — Vienna — AUSTRIA — SLOVAKIA

SWITZERLAND — HUNGARY — MOLDOVA

SLOVENIA — ROMANIA — Odesa

PORTUGAL — ITALY — CROATIA — GEORGIA

BOS. & HER. — AZERBAIJAN

Lisbon · SPAIN — ARMENIA

Crkvica
Highest average annual
precipitation: 183" (465 cm)

Astrakhan'
Lowest average annual
precipitation: 6.4" (16.3 cm)

KOS. — BULGARIA

GIBRALTAR — MONT. — MACEDONIA

(U.K.) — Naples · — ALBANIA

GREECE

· Athens

MALTA

Though regionally formidable mountains rise to extract snow and rain, no continental-scale alpine barrier exists—thereby permitting moisture-laden, westerly winds springing from warm oceanic waters to distribute precipitation uniformly across Europe. However, by the time these currents of air reach the landlocked heart of Eastern Europe, northeast of the Black Sea, much of the moisture has already been spent.

Climate Graphs

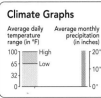

Average daily temperature range (in °F)   Average monthly precipitation (in inches)

High   Low

ARKHANGELSK, Russia

ATHENS, Greece

COPENHAGEN, Denmark

DUBLIN, Ireland

LISBON, Portugal

MOSCOW, Russia

NAPLES, Italy

ODESA, Ukraine

PARIS, France

REYKJAVÍK, Iceland

TROMSØ, Norway

VIENNA, Austria

Vegetation

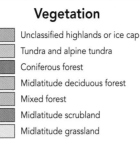

- Unclassified highlands or ice cap
- Tundra and alpine tundra
- Coniferous forest
- Midlatitude deciduous forest
- Mixed forest
- Midlatitude scrubland
- Midlatitude grassland

Forests, nourished by plentiful precipitation, dominate in Europe, but grassland and scrubland thrive where rainfall becomes sparse or is seasonal. Deciduous trees disappear as the winters grow harsh, replaced by vast and hardy stands of coniferous forest that are merely the western end of an immense belt stretching across Russia to the Pacific Ocean.

See photographs of the different kinds of vegetation on pages 26–27.

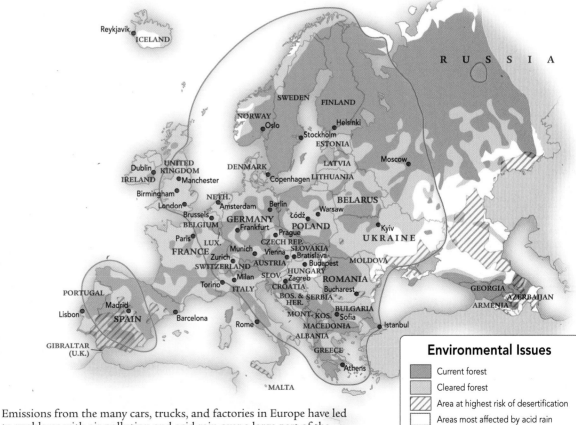

Environmental Issues

- Current forest
- Cleared forest
- Area at highest risk of desertification
- Areas most affected by acid rain
- • Poor air quality*

*Cities exceeding at least one of the World Health Organization's (WHO) annual mean guidelines for air quality

Sources: *Global Distribution of Original and Remaining Forests,* UNEP-WCMC, 2002
World Soil Resources Map Index, USDA/NRCS, 2002
World Development Indicators, World Bank, 1999

Emissions from the many cars, trucks, and factories in Europe have led to problems with air pollution and acid rain over a large part of the continent. Land and water pollution (from fertilizers, pesticides, and industrial waste) is also widespread. Since the 1960's, the amount of forest area in Western and Central Europe has actually increased, but many forests (nearly 60%) are damaged due to acidification, pollution, drought, or fires. Overfishing—especially in the North Sea—is a serious problem for marine ecosystems.

Africa

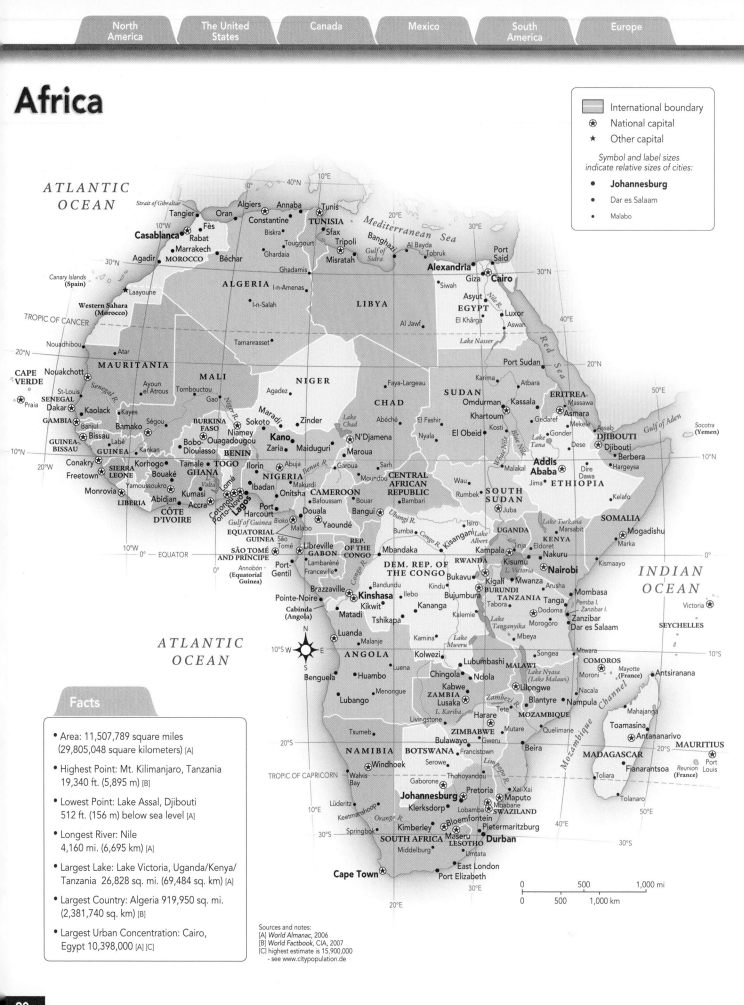

Legend:
- International boundary
- ⊛ National capital
- ★ Other capital

Symbol and label sizes indicate relative sizes of cities:
- ● **Johannesburg**
- • Dar es Salaam
- · Malabo

Facts

- Area: 11,507,789 square miles (29,805,048 square kilometers) [A]
- Highest Point: Mt. Kilimanjaro, Tanzania 19,340 ft. (5,895 m) [B]
- Lowest Point: Lake Assal, Djibouti 512 ft. (156 m) below sea level [A]
- Longest River: Nile 4,160 mi. (6,695 km) [A]
- Largest Lake: Lake Victoria, Uganda/Kenya/Tanzania 26,828 sq. mi. (69,484 sq. km) [A]
- Largest Country: Algeria 919,950 sq. mi. (2,381,740 sq. km) [B]
- Largest Urban Concentration: Cairo, Egypt 10,398,000 [A] [C]

Sources and notes:
[A] *World Almanac*, 2006
[B] *World Factbook*, CIA, 2007
[C] highest estimate is 15,900,000
    - see www.citypopulation.de

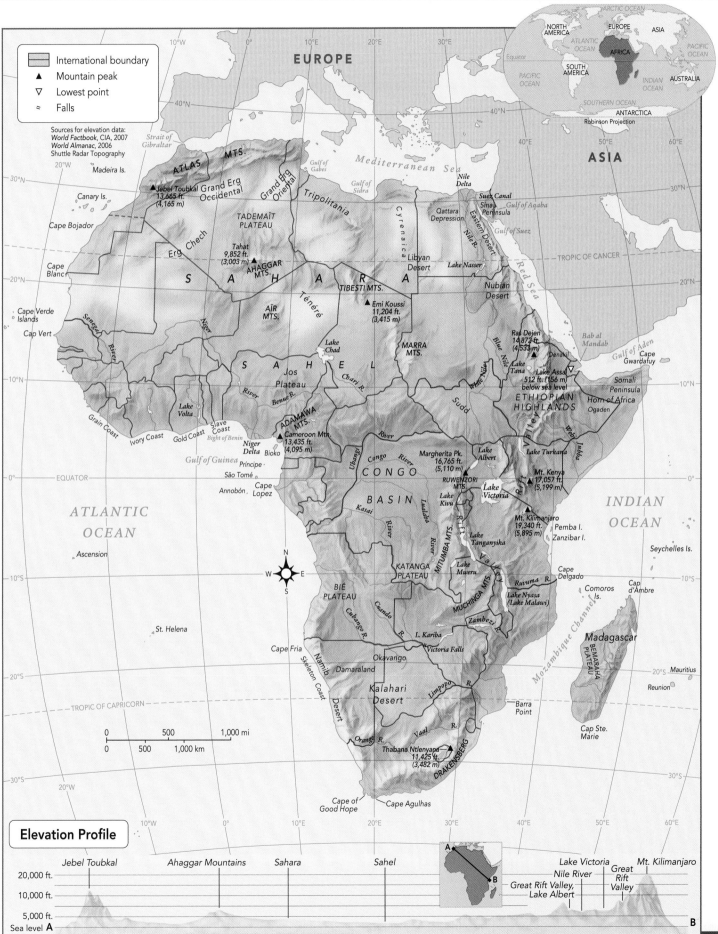

Legend

	International boundary
▲	Mountain peak
▽	Lowest point
≈	Falls

Sources for elevation data:
World Factbook, CIA, 2007
World Almanac, 2006
Shuttle Radar Topography

EUROPE

ASIA

ATLANTIC OCEAN

INDIAN OCEAN

Mediterranean Sea

ATLAS MTS.

▲ Jebel Toubkal
13,665 ft.
(4,165 m)

Grand Erg Occidental

Grand Erg Oriental

Tripolitania

TADEMAÏT PLATEAU

Erg Chech

Tahat
9,852 ft.
(3,003 m)

AHAGGAR MTS. ▲

S A H A R A

AÏR MTS.

Ténéré

TIBESTI MTS.

▲ Emi Koussi
11,204 ft.
(3,415 m)

Cyrenaica

Libyan Desert

Lake Nasser

Nubian Desert

Red Sea

Qattara Depression

Sinai Peninsula

Suez Canal

Nile Delta

Gulf of Gabes

Gulf of Sidra

Gulf of Aqaba

Gulf of Suez

Eastern Desert

Nile R.

MARRA MTS.

Ras Dejen
14,872 ft.
(4,533 m) ▲

Denakil ▽ Lake Assal
512 ft. (156 m)
below sea level

Bab al Mandab

Gulf of Aden

Cape Gwardafuy

Somali Peninsula

Horn of Africa

Ogaden

ETHIOPIAN HIGHLANDS

Lake Tana

Blue Nile

White Nile

Lake Turkana

Webi

Jubba

S A H E L

Jos Plateau

Lake Chad

Chari R.

Benue R.

River

Niger River

Senegal River

Lake Volta

Grain Coast

Ivory Coast

Gold Coast

Slave Coast

Bight of Benin

Niger Delta

ADAMAWA MTS.

▲ Cameroon Mtn.
13,435 ft.
(4,095 m)

Bioko

Gulf of Guinea

Príncipe

São Tomé

Annobón

Cape Lopez

EQUATOR

Ubangi River

Congo River

C O N G O   B A S I N

Kasai River

Lualaba River

KATANGA PLATEAU

BIÉ PLATEAU

Cubango R.

Cuando R.

Kalahari Desert

Damaraland

Okavango

Namib Desert

Skeleton Coast

Cape Fria

Orange R.

Vaal R.

Thabana Ntlenyana ▲
11,425 ft.
(3,482 m)

DRAKENSBERG

Limpopo R.

L. Kariba

Zambezi R.

Victoria Falls

Ruvuma R.

Lake Nyasa (Lake Malawi)

Lake Mweru

Lake Tanganyika

MUCHINGA MTS.

MITUMBA MTS.

Lake Kivu

Lake Victoria

RUWENZORI MTS.

Margherita Pk.
16,765 ft.
(5,110 m)

Lake Albert

Mt. Kenya
17,057 ft.
(5,199 m) ▲

Mt. Kilimanjaro
19,340 ft.
(5,895 m) ▲

Great Rift Valley

Sudd

Pemba I.

Zanzibar I.

Cape Delgado

Comoros Is.

Cap d'Ambre

Madagascar

BEMARAHA PLATEAU

Cap Ste. Marie

Mauritius

Reunion

Seychelles Is.

Mozambique Channel

Barra Point

Cape Agulhas

Cape of Good Hope

Ascension

St. Helena

Cape Verde Islands

Cap Vert

Cape Blanc

Cape Bojador

Canary Is.

Madeira Is.

Strait of Gibraltar

TROPIC OF CANCER

TROPIC OF CAPRICORN

0	500	1,000 mi

0	500	1,000 km

Elevation Profile

Jebel Toubkal	Ahaggar Mountains	Sahara	Sahel		Lake Victoria	Mt. Kilimanjaro
					Nile River	
					Great Rift Valley	
				Great Rift Valley, Lake Albert		

20,000 ft.

10,000 ft.

5,000 ft.

Sea level A

B

91

Major Metropolitan Areas

Algeria
Algiers 1,904,000 (metro)
Oran 745,000
Constantine 564,000

Angola
Luanda 1,822,000

Benin
Cotonou 537,000
Porto-Novo 179,000

Botswana
Gaborone 186,000

Burkina Faso
Ouagadougou 634,000

Burundi
Bujumbura 234,000

Cameroon
Douala 810,000
Yaoundé 649,000

Cape Verde
Praia 103,000

Central African Republic
Bangui 452,000

Chad
N'Djamena 547,000

Comoros
Moroni 30,000

Congo, Democratic Republic of the
Kinshasa 4,657,000
Lubumbashi 565,000

Congo, Republic of the
Brazzaville 596,000

Côte d'Ivoire
Abidjan 1,929,000
Yamoussoukro 107,000

Djibouti
Djibouti 62,000

Egypt
Cairo 6,801,000
Alexandria 3,339,000
Giza 2,222,000

Equatorial Guinea
Malabo 30,000

Eritrea
Asmara 358,000

Ethiopia
Addis Ababa 2,424,000

Gabon
Libreville 420,000

The Gambia
Banjul 271,000

Ghana
Accra 1,155,000

Guinea
Conakry 705,000

Guinea-Bissau
Bissau 109,000

Kenya
Nairobi 2,143,000
Mombasa 465,000

Lesotho
Maseru 138,000

Liberia
Monrovia 421,000

Libya
Tripoli 1,500,000

Madagascar
Antananarivo 1,103,000

Malawi
Blantyre 502,000
Lilongwe 440,000

Mali
Bamako 1,179,000

Mauritania
Nouakchott 612,000

Mauritius
Port Louis 128,000

Morocco
Casablanca 2,943,000
Rabat 1,220,000
Marrakesh 602,000

Mozambique
Maputo 989,000

Namibia
Windhoek 147,000

Niger
Niamey 397,000

Nigeria
Lagos 5,195,000
Kano 2,167,000
Ibadan 1,835,000

Rwanda
Kigali 234,000

São Tomé & Príncipe
São Tomé 6,000

Senegal
Dakar 1,977,000

Seychelles
Victoria 25,000

Sierra Leone
Freetown 470,000

Somalia
Mogadishu 230,000

South Africa
Durban 2,992,000
Cape Town 2,898,000
Johannesburg 2,885,000
Pretoria 2,086,000
Port Elizabeth 1,312,000

South Sudan
Juba 165,000

Sudan
Omdurman 1,271,000
Khartoum 947,000

Swaziland
Mbabane 38,000

Tanzania
Dar es Salaam 1,361,000

Togo
Lomé 450,000

Tunisia
Tunis 674,000

Uganda
Kampala 1,209,000

Western Sahara
el-Aaiún 90,000

Zambia
Lusaka 1,270,000

Zimbabwe
Harare 1,189,000

International comparability of population data is limited by varying census methods. Where metropolitan population is unavailable, core city population is shown

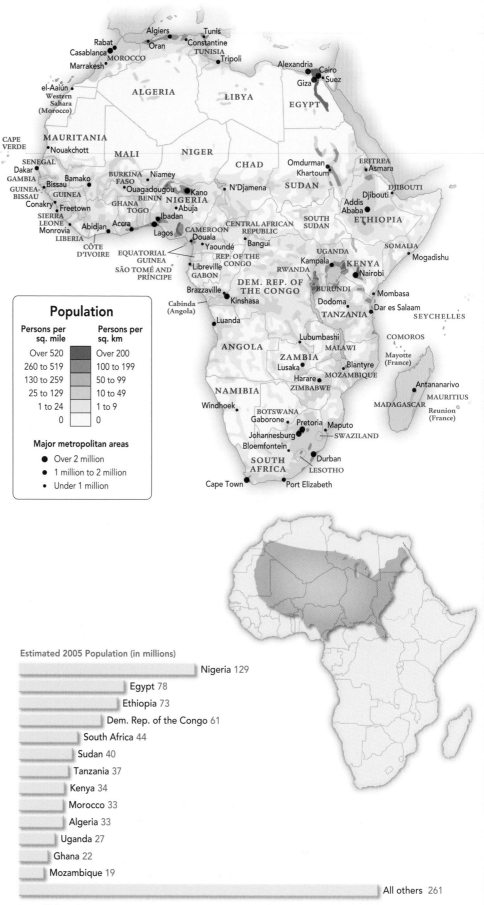

Population

Persons per sq. mile	Persons per sq. km
Over 520	Over 200
260 to 519	100 to 199
130 to 259	50 to 99
25 to 129	10 to 49
1 to 24	1 to 9
0	0

Major metropolitan areas
● Over 2 million
• 1 million to 2 million
· Under 1 million

Estimated 2005 Population (in millions)

Nigeria 129
Egypt 78
Ethiopia 73
Dem. Rep. of the Congo 61
South Africa 44
Sudan 40
Tanzania 37
Kenya 34
Morocco 33
Algeria 33
Uganda 27
Ghana 22
Mozambique 19
All others 261

Source: U.S. Census Bureau

Gross Domestic Product is a measure of the total goods and services generated by a country. Generally, manufacturing, high-tech services, and specialized agricultural products add more value than raw materials and basic food stuffs.

South Africa is the only African nation considered to have a developed economy, even though their GDP is less then half that of the United States.

Electricity Use, 2002

United States 12,376

South Africa 4,271

Libya 3,370

Botswana 1,152
Zambia 475
Nigeria 143

KWh (kilowatt hours) per person per year

Source: *World Factbook*, CIA, 2005

Gross Domestic Product

GDP per capita

- Over $20,000
- $10,000 to $20,000
- $5,000 to $9,999
- $2,500 to $4,999
- Under $2,500
- No data

Source: *World Factbook*, CIA, 2005

Agriculture supplies the livelihood for the vast majority of Africans. Agricultural exports include coffee, cocoa beans, peanuts, palm oil, and spices. These important export crops are mainly cultivated on plantations and large farms. Areas of subsistence farming supply the needs of local communities.

Unfortunately, poor soils and unfavorable climate conditions, as well as political unrest and unstable economies, all have an adverse impact on agricultural activity and therefore the standard of living.

Minerals account for more then one half of Africa's exports. Oil, diamonds, gold, cobalt, and several other minerals are leading exports. However, important mineral deposits are limited to a handful of countries.

Manufacturing has been slow to develop on the continent. Lack of money and skilled labor are the main deterrents.

Land Use and Resources

Predominant land use
- Commercial agriculture
- Livestock ranching
- Subsistence agriculture
- Nomadic herding
- Primarily forestland
- Limited agricultural activity

Major resources
- Coal
- Natural gas
- Oil
- Au Gold
- Fe Iron ore
- Pt Platinum
- U Uranium
- Al Bauxite
- Diamonds
- Other minerals
- Fishing
- Major manufacturing and trade centers

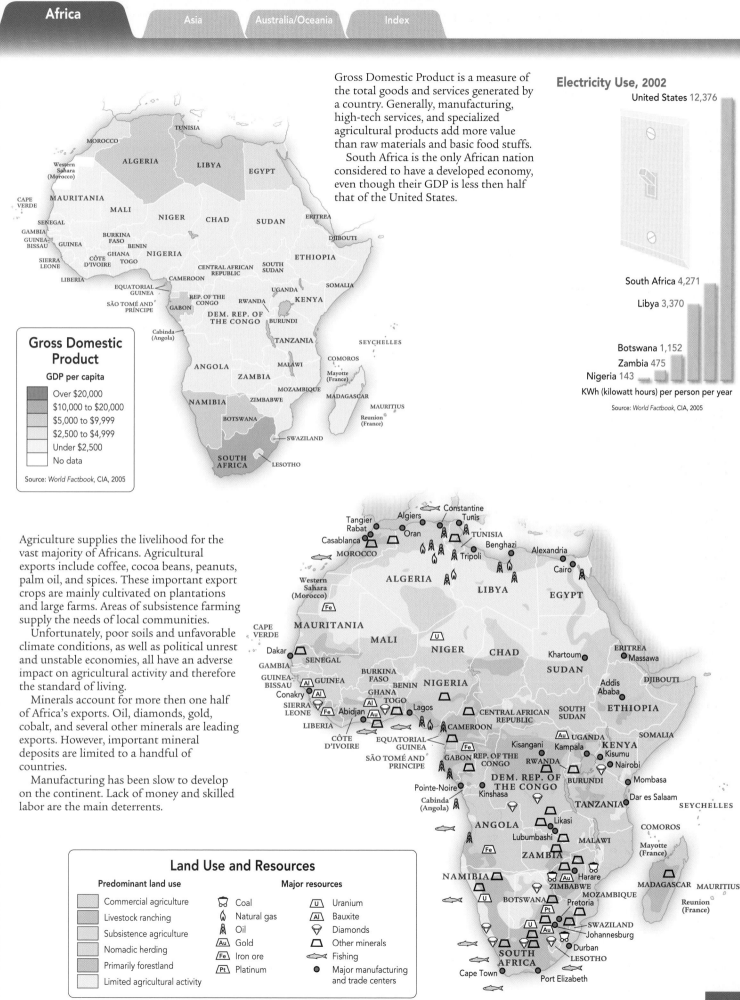

The climate of Africa is clearly a study in geographic contrasts. Perpetually wet and tropical areas surrounding the Equator quickly acquire seasonal variety as you move north and south. Roaming even farther leads to the vast, hot and arid zones of northern and southern Africa. The influence of neighboring water bodies is limited to small regions of northern Africa, namely Morocco, Algeria, and Libya, where the mild currents of the Mediterranean Sea temper the climate, and eastern South Africa, where the mixture of warm currents flowing close to shore and the seasonal onshore winds striking the Drakensberg uplands provide for a moist and temperate marine coast climate.

See photographs taken in different kinds of climates on pages 24–25.

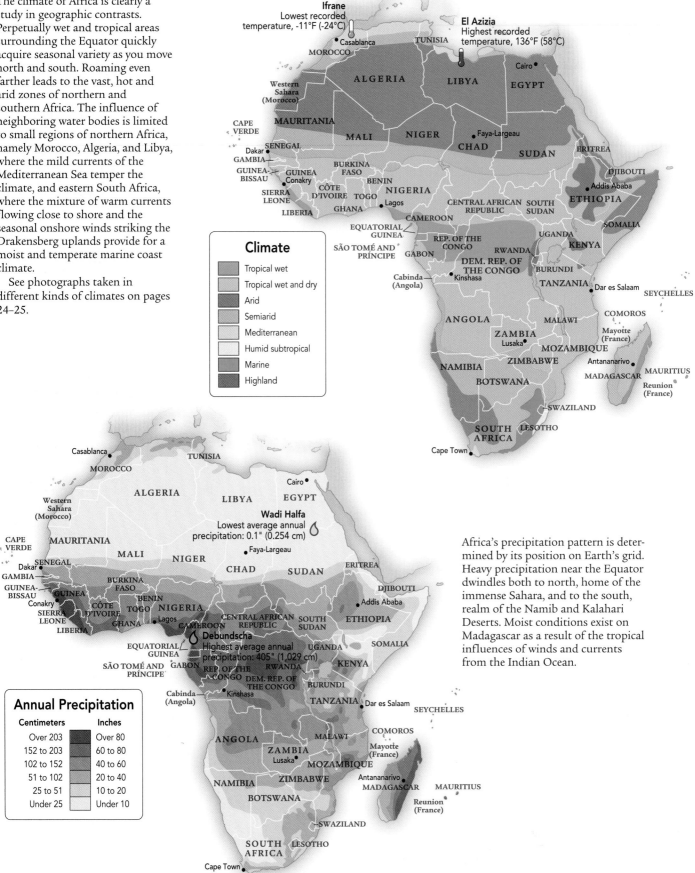

Climate

- Tropical wet
- Tropical wet and dry
- Arid
- Semiarid
- Mediterranean
- Humid subtropical
- Marine
- Highland

Ifrane
Lowest recorded temperature, -11°F (-24°C)

El Azizia
Highest recorded temperature, 136°F (58°C)

Wadi Halfa
Lowest average annual precipitation: 0.1" (0.254 cm)

Debundscha
Highest average annual precipitation: 405" (1,029 cm)

Africa's precipitation pattern is determined by its position on Earth's grid. Heavy precipitation near the Equator dwindles both to north, home of the immense Sahara, and to the south, realm of the Namib and Kalahari Deserts. Moist conditions exist on Madagascar as a result of the tropical influences of winds and currents from the Indian Ocean.

Annual Precipitation

Centimeters	Inches
Over 203	Over 80
152 to 203	60 to 80
102 to 152	40 to 60
51 to 102	20 to 40
25 to 51	10 to 20
Under 25	Under 10

Climate Graphs

Average daily temperature range (in °F)

Average monthly precipitation (in inches)

100° — High
65° — Low
32°
0°

20"
10"
0"

ADDIS ABABA, Ethiopia

ANTANANARIVO, Madagascar

CAIRO, Egypt

CAPE TOWN, South Africa

CASABLANCA, Morocco

CONAKRY, Guinea — 51.1

DAKAR, Senegal

DAR ES SALAAM, Tanzania

FAYA-LARGEAU, Chad

KINSHASA, Dem. Rep. of the Congo

LAGOS, Nigeria

LUSAKA, Zambia

The dense, tropical rain forest surrounding the Equator is offset by the contrastingly sparse vegetation on the rest of the continent. Vast areas consist of grassland and scrub vegetation with trees only occasionally dotting the landscape. Evergreen and mixed forests of more temperate climates are limited to the Mediterranean areas of Morocco and Algeria, the Ethiopian Highlands, and Kenya.

See photographs of the different kinds of vegetation on pages 26–27.

Vegetation

- Coniferous forest
- Mixed forest
- Midlatitude scrubland
- Midlatitude grassland
- Desert
- Tropical seasonal and scrub
- Tropical rain forest
- Tropical savanna

Environmental Issues

- Current forest
- Cleared forest
- Area at highest risk of desertification
- Poor air quality*

*Cities exceeding at least one of the World Health Organization's (WHO) annual mean guidelines for air quality

Sources: *Global Distribution of Original and Remaining Forests,* UNEP-WCMC, 2002
World Soil Resources Map Index, USDA/NRCS, 2002
World Development Indicators, World Bank, 1999

Desertification (land turning into desert) is one of the leading environmental issues in Africa. Two leading causes of desertification are the removal of vegetation (often for cooking fuel) and overgrazing, especially in semiarid and drought-prone areas. Other environmental problems include deforestation, soil loss, declining biodiversity, and decreasing air and water quality. Water scarcity is also a concern in many African countries, such as Egypt, Libya, Algeria, Tunisia, and Morocco.

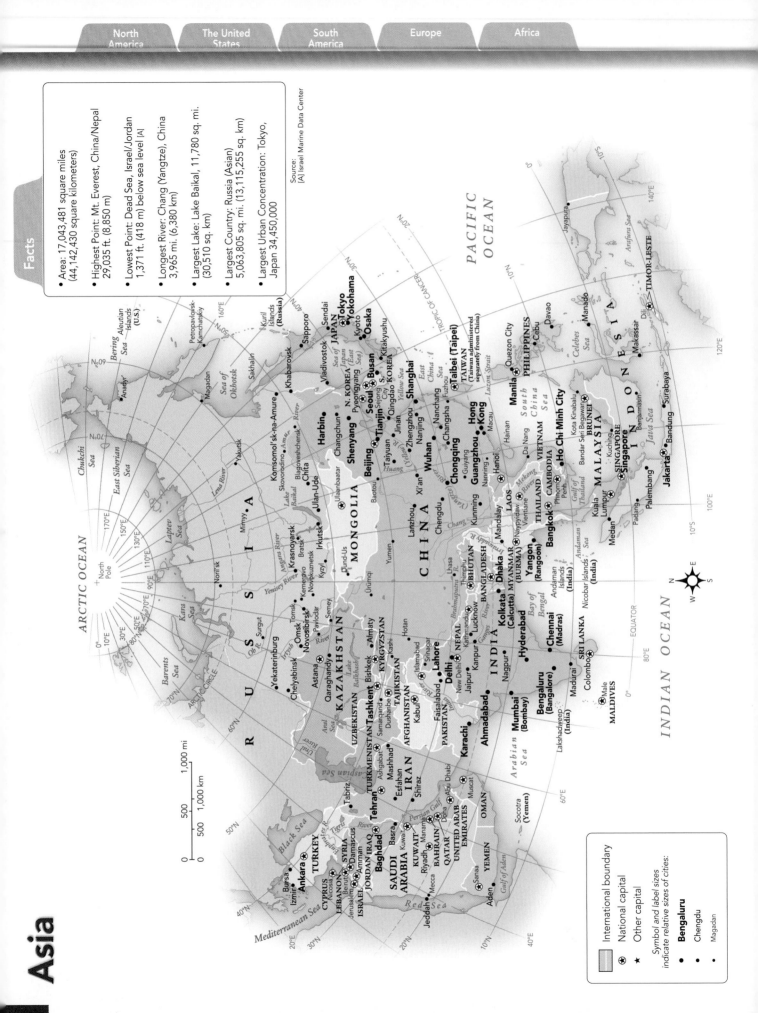

Asia

Facts

- Area: 17,043,481 square miles (44,142,430 square kilometers)
- Highest Point: Mt. Everest, China/Nepal 29,035 ft. (8,850 m)
- Lowest Point: Dead Sea, Israel/Jordan 1,371 ft. (418 m) below sea level [A]
- Longest River: Chang (Yangtze), China 3,965 mi. (6,380 km)
- Largest Lake: Lake Baikal, 11,780 sq. mi. (30,510 sq. km)
- Largest Country: Russia (Asian) 5,063,805 sq. mi. (13,115,255 sq. km)
- Largest Urban Concentration: Tokyo, Japan 34,450,000

Source:
[A] Israel Marine Data Center

International boundary
National capital
Other capital

Symbol and label sizes indicate relative sizes of cities:

Bengaluru
Chengdu
Magadan

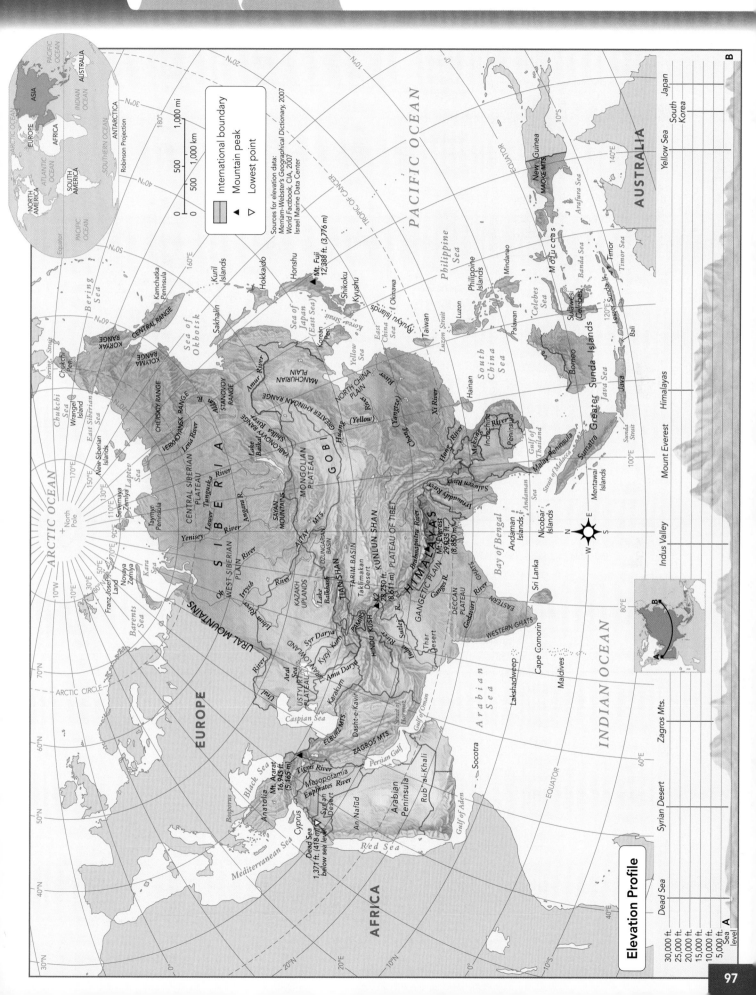

PACIFIC OCEAN

ARCTIC OCEAN

INDIAN OCEAN

EUROPE

AFRICA

AUSTRALIA

International boundary
▲ **Mountain peak**
▽ **Lowest point**

Sources for elevation data:
Merriam-Webster's Geographical Dictionary, 2007
World Factbook, CIA, 2007
Israel Marine Data Center

1,000 mi
1,000 km

Robinson Projection

North Pole

ARCTIC CIRCLE

SIBERIA

URAL MOUNTAINS

CENTRAL SIBERIAN PLATEAU

WEST SIBERIAN PLAIN

KAZAKH UPLANDS

Yenisey River

Ob River

Irtysh River

Lena River

Aldan River

STANOVOY RANGE

CHERSKIY RANGE

VERKHOYANSK RANGE

KOLYMA RANGE

KORYAK RANGE

CENTRAL RANGE

Kamchatka Peninsula

Bering Strait

Bering Sea

Sea of Okhotsk

Chukchi Sea

East Siberian Sea

Laptev Sea

Kara Sea

Barents Sea

New Siberian Islands

Wrangel Island

Novaya Zemlya

Franz Josef Land

Severnaya Zemlya

Taymyr Peninsula

MONGOLIAN PLATEAU

GOBI

ALTAY MTS.

SAYAN MOUNTAINS

YABLONOVYY RANGE

Lake Baikal

Shilka River

Amur River

GREATER KHINGAN RANGE

MANCHURIAN PLAIN

NORTH CHINA PLAIN

Huang (Yellow) River

Chang (Yangtze) River

Xi River

Hong River

Mekong River

TIAN SHAN

DZUNGARIAN BASIN

TARIM BASIN

Taklimakan Desert

KUNLUN SHAN

PLATEAU OF TIBET

HIMALAYAS

Mt. Everest 29,035 ft (8,850 m)

K2 28,250 ft (8,611 m)

PAMIRS

HINDU KUSH

TURAN LOWLAND

USTYURT PLATEAU

Aral Sea

Caspian Sea

Lake Balkhash

Syr Darya

Amu Darya

Kyzyl Kum

Karakum

Ishim River

Ural River

Tobol River

Indus River

Sutlej River

Thar Desert

GANGETIC PLAIN

Ganges R.

Brahmaputra River

DECCAN PLATEAU

EASTERN GHATS

WESTERN GHATS

Godavari River

Cape Comorin

Sri Lanka

Maldives

Lakshadweep

Socotra

Gulf of Aden

Red Sea

Arabian Peninsula

Rub' al-Khali

An Nafūd

Syrian Desert

Mesopotamia

Tigris River

Euphrates River

Persian Gulf

Gulf of Oman

Strait of Hormuz

ZAGROS MTS.

ELBURZ MTS.

Dasht-e-Kavir

Mt. Ararat 16,945 ft (5,165 m) ▲

Anatolia

Cyprus

Black Sea

Bosporus

Mediterranean Sea

Dead Sea 1,371 ft. (418 m) below sea level ▽

Arabian Sea

Bay of Bengal

Andaman Islands

Nicobar Islands

Andaman Sea

Indochina Peninsula

Gulf of Thailand

Malay Peninsula

Strait of Malacca

Sumatra

Borneo

Java

Bali

Greater Sunda Islands

Lesser Sunda Islands

Sunda Strait

Java Sea

Celebes Sea

Sulawesi (Celebes)

Banda Sea

Molucca s

Arafura Sea

Timor Sea

New Guinea

MAOKE MTS.

Timor

Mentawai Islands

South China Sea

Hainan

Philippine Islands

Luzon

Mindanao

Palawan

Luzon Strait

Philippine Sea

Taiwan

Okinawa

Ryukyu Islands

East China Sea

Yellow Sea

Korean Pen.

Korea Strait

Sea of Japan (East Sea)

Hokkaido

Honshu

Shikoku

Kyushu

Mt. Fuji 12,388 ft. (3,776 m) ▲

Kuril Islands

Sakhalin

Bering Strait

TROPIC OF CANCER

EQUATOR

North America

South America

Europe

Africa

Asia

Australia

Antarctica

PACIFIC OCEAN

INDIAN OCEAN

ATLANTIC OCEAN

ARCTIC OCEAN

SOUTHERN OCEAN

Elevation Profile

A							B
Dead Sea	Syrian Desert	Zagros Mts.	Indus Valley	Mount Everest	Himalayas	South Korea	Japan

30,000 ft.
25,000 ft.
20,000 ft.
15,000 ft.
10,000 ft.
5,000 ft.
Sea level

97

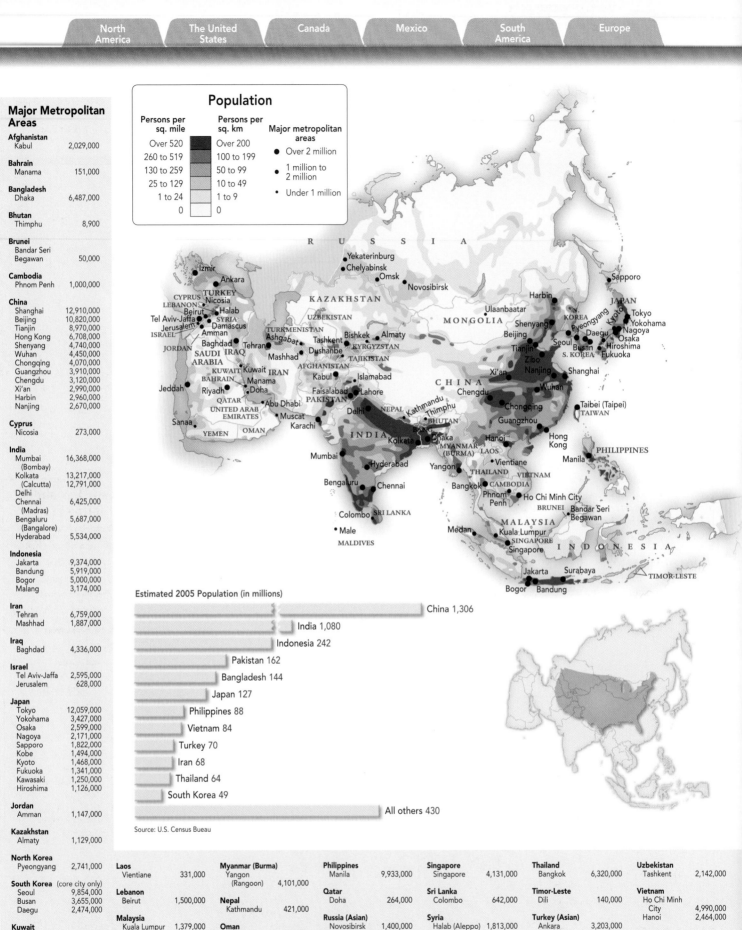

Major Metropolitan Areas

Afghanistan
Kabul — 2,029,000

Bahrain
Manama — 151,000

Bangladesh
Dhaka — 6,487,000

Bhutan
Thimphu — 8,900

Brunei
Bandar Seri Begawan — 50,000

Cambodia
Phnom Penh — 1,000,000

China
Shanghai — 12,910,000
Beijing — 10,820,000
Tianjin — 8,970,000
Hong Kong — 6,708,000
Shenyang — 4,740,000
Wuhan — 4,450,000
Chongqing — 4,070,000
Guangzhou — 3,910,000
Chengdu — 3,120,000
Xi'an — 2,990,000
Harbin — 2,960,000
Nanjing — 2,670,000

Cyprus
Nicosia — 273,000

India
Mumbai (Bombay) — 16,368,000
Kolkata (Calcutta) — 13,217,000
Delhi — 12,791,000
Chennai (Madras) — 6,425,000
Bengaluru (Bangalore) — 5,687,000
Hyderabad — 5,534,000

Indonesia
Jakarta — 9,374,000
Bandung — 5,919,000
Bogor — 5,000,000
Malang — 3,174,000

Iran
Tehran — 6,759,000
Mashhad — 1,887,000

Iraq
Baghdad — 4,336,000

Israel
Tel Aviv-Jaffa — 2,595,000
Jerusalem — 628,000

Japan
Tokyo — 12,059,000
Yokohama — 3,427,000
Osaka — 2,599,000
Nagoya — 2,171,000
Sapporo — 1,822,000
Kobe — 1,494,000
Kyoto — 1,468,000
Fukuoka — 1,341,000
Kawasaki — 1,250,000
Hiroshima — 1,126,000

Jordan
Amman — 1,147,000

Kazakhstan
Almaty — 1,129,000

North Korea
Pyeongyang — 2,741,000

South Korea (core city only)
Seoul — 9,854,000
Busan — 3,655,000
Daegu — 2,474,000

Kuwait
Kuwait — 193,000

Kyrgyzstan
Bishkek — 753,000

Laos
Vientiane — 331,000

Lebanon
Beirut — 1,500,000

Malaysia
Kuala Lumpur — 1,379,000

Maldives
Male — 74,000

Mongolia
Ulaanbaatar — 760,000

Myanmar (Burma)
Yangon (Rangoon) — 4,101,000

Nepal
Kathmandu — 421,000

Oman
Muscat — 477,000

Pakistan
Karachi — 9,339,000
Lahore — 5,143,000
Faisalabad — 2,009,000
Islamabad — 529,000

Philippines
Manila — 9,933,000

Qatar
Doha — 264,000

Russia (Asian)
Novosibirsk — 1,400,000
Yekaterinburg — 1,314,000
Omsk — 1,177,000
Chelyabinsk — 1,111,000

Saudi Arabia
Riyadh — 2,776,000
Jeddah — 2,046,000

Singapore
Singapore — 4,131,000

Sri Lanka
Colombo — 642,000

Syria
Halab (Aleppo) — 1,813,000
Damascus — 1,394,000

Taiwan
Taibei (Taipei) — 2,720,000

Tajikistan
Dushanbe — 529,000

Thailand
Bangkok — 6,320,000

Timor-Leste
Dili — 140,000

Turkey (Asian)
Ankara — 3,203,000
Izmir — 2,232,000

Turkmenistan
Ashgabat — 407,000

United Arab Emirates
Abu Dhabi — 904,000

Uzbekistan
Tashkent — 2,142,000

Vietnam
Ho Chi Minh City — 4,990,000
Hanoi — 2,464,000

Yemen
Sanaa — 927,000

International comparability of population data is limited by varying census methods. Where metropolitan population is unavailable, core city population is shown.

Population

Persons per sq. mile
Over 520
260 to 519
130 to 259
25 to 129
1 to 24
0

Persons per sq. km
Over 200
100 to 199
50 to 99
10 to 49
1 to 9
0

Major metropolitan areas
● Over 2 million
• 1 million to 2 million
· Under 1 million

Estimated 2005 Population (in millions)

China 1,306
India 1,080
Indonesia 242
Pakistan 162
Bangladesh 144
Japan 127
Philippines 88
Vietnam 84
Turkey 70
Iran 68
Thailand 64
South Korea 49
All others 430

Source: U.S. Census Bueau

Gross Domestic Product is a measure of the total goods and services generated by a country. Generally, manufacturing, high-tech services, and specialized agricultural products add more value than raw materials and basic food stuffs. The high-tech and oil producing countries on the fringes of Asia are the exceptions in this generally poor continent.

Gross Domestic Product

GDP per capita

Over $20,000
$10,000 to $20,000
$5,000 to $9,999
$2,500 to $4,999
Less than $2,500
No data

Source: *World Factbook*, CIA, 2005

Electricity Use, 2002

United Arab Emirates 14,244
United States 12,376
Japan 7,621
Israel 6,102
Vietnam 2,351
China 1,248*
India 472
Myanmar (Burma) 74*

KWh (kilowatt hours) per person per year
*2003 data
Source: *World Factbook*, CIA, 2005

Agriculture is the predominant land use in Asia, though only one-sixth of the land is arable. Wet grains, such as rice, are the principal crops of China and Southeast Asian countries. Dry grains, such as wheat, are grown in limited areas of Russia and China. A lack of modern farming methods, except in Japan, Russia, and Israel, has historically limited food production. However, production is increasing in some countries as governments supply the needed technology. The rugged land and climate in Northern, Central and Southwest Asia limits land use to nomadic herding. Here, animals supply food, shelter, clothing, and transportation.

Land Use and Resources

Predominant land use

Commercial agriculture
Nomadic herding
Subsistence agriculture
Primarily forestland
Limited agricultural activity

Major resources

Coal
Natural gas
Oil
Forest products
Au Gold
Ag Silver
Fe Iron ore
U   Uranium
Al Bauxite
Diamonds
Other minerals
Fishing
Major manufacturing and trade centers

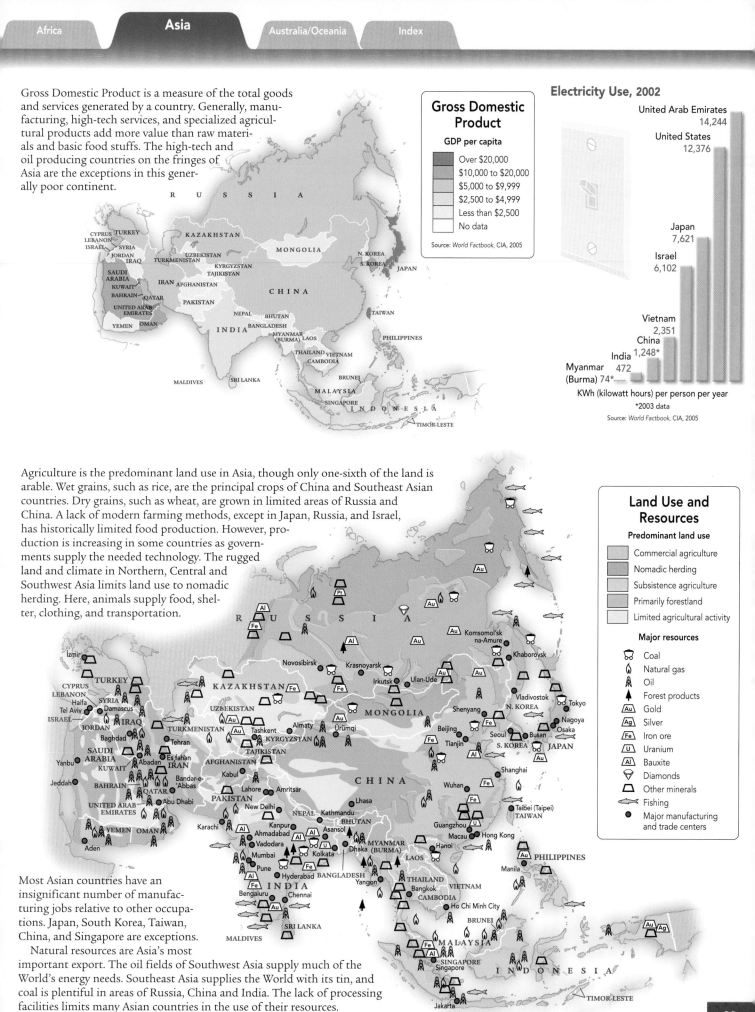

Most Asian countries have an insignificant number of manufacturing jobs relative to other occupations. Japan, South Korea, Taiwan, China, and Singapore are exceptions.

Natural resources are Asia's most important export. The oil fields of Southwest Asia supply much of the World's energy needs. Southeast Asia supplies the World with its tin, and coal is plentiful in areas of Russia, China and India. The lack of processing facilities limits many Asian countries in the use of their resources.

Asia has many climates. This can be expected on a landmass that covers an area from below the Equator to the Arctic Ocean and from the Mediterranean Sea to the Pacific Ocean. Weather conditions fluctuate from the sub-freezing temperatures and snow of the tundra climate in Northern Russia, through the more temperate humid continental climate, past the arid conditions of Southwest and Central Asia, and finally to the warm and wet zones of South and Southeast Asia.

See photographs taken in different kinds of climates on pages 24–25.

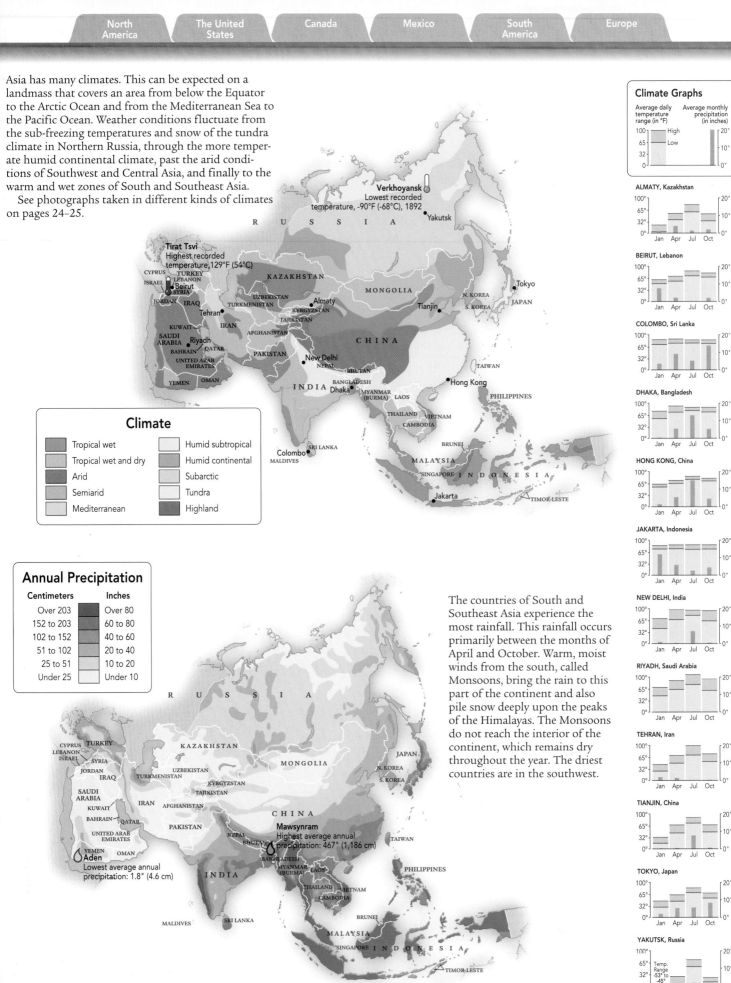

Climate

- Tropical wet
- Tropical wet and dry
- Arid
- Semiarid
- Mediterranean
- Humid subtropical
- Humid continental
- Subarctic
- Tundra
- Highland

Annual Precipitation

Centimeters	Inches
Over 203	Over 80
152 to 203	60 to 80
102 to 152	40 to 60
51 to 102	20 to 40
25 to 51	10 to 20
Under 25	Under 10

Verkhoyansk
Lowest recorded temperature, -90°F (-68°C), 1892

Tirat Tsvi
Highest recorded temperature, 129°F (54°C)

Mawsynram
Highest average annual precipitation: 467" (1,186 cm)

Aden
Lowest average annual precipitation: 1.8" (4.6 cm)

The countries of South and Southeast Asia experience the most rainfall. This rainfall occurs primarily between the months of April and October. Warm, moist winds from the south, called Monsoons, bring the rain to this part of the continent and also pile snow deeply upon the peaks of the Himalayas. The Monsoons do not reach the interior of the continent, which remains dry throughout the year. The driest countries are in the southwest.

Climate Graphs

Average daily temperature range (in °F)
Average monthly precipitation (in inches)

ALMATY, Kazakhstan
BEIRUT, Lebanon
COLOMBO, Sri Lanka
DHAKA, Bangladesh
HONG KONG, China
JAKARTA, Indonesia
NEW DELHI, India
RIYADH, Saudi Arabia
TEHRAN, Iran
TIANJIN, China
TOKYO, Japan
YAKUTSK, Russia

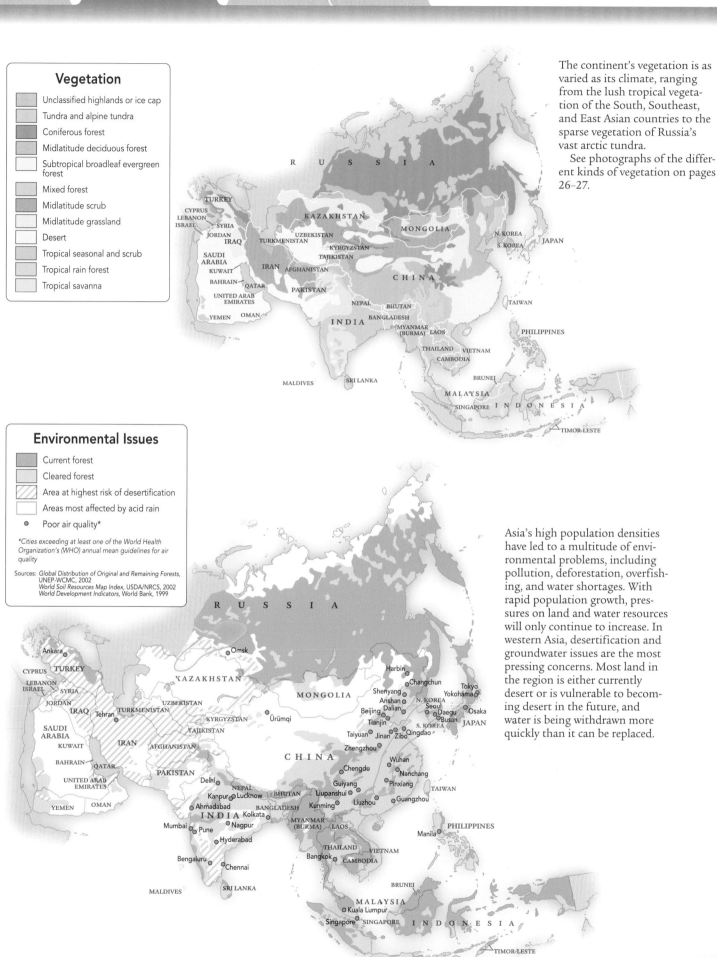

Vegetation

- Unclassified highlands or ice cap
- Tundra and alpine tundra
- Coniferous forest
- Midlatitude deciduous forest
- Subtropical broadleaf evergreen forest
- Mixed forest
- Midlatitude scrub
- Midlatitude grassland
- Desert
- Tropical seasonal and scrub
- Tropical rain forest
- Tropical savanna

The continent's vegetation is as varied as its climate, ranging from the lush tropical vegetation of the South, Southeast, and East Asian countries to the sparse vegetation of Russia's vast arctic tundra.

See photographs of the different kinds of vegetation on pages 26–27.

Environmental Issues

- Current forest
- Cleared forest
- Area at highest risk of desertification
- Areas most affected by acid rain
- • Poor air quality*

*Cities exceeding at least one of the World Health Organization's (WHO) annual mean guidelines for air quality

Sources: *Global Distribution of Original and Remaining Forests,* UNEP-WCMC, 2002
World Soil Resources Map Index, USDA/NRCS, 2002
World Development Indicators, World Bank, 1999

Asia's high population densities have led to a multitude of environmental problems, including pollution, deforestation, overfishing, and water shortages. With rapid population growth, pressures on land and water resources will only continue to increase. In western Asia, desertification and groundwater issues are the most pressing concerns. Most land in the region is either currently desert or is vulnerable to becoming desert in the future, and water is being withdrawn more quickly than it can be replaced.

Australia/Oceania

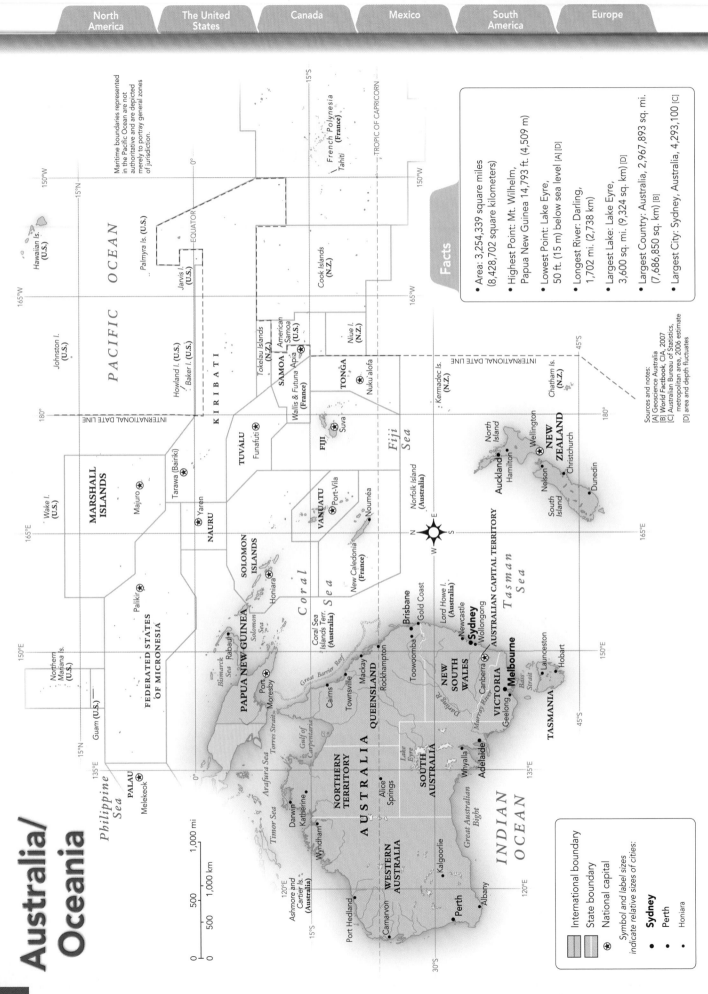

Facts

- Area: 3,254,339 square miles (8,428,702 square kilometers)
- Highest Point: Mt. Wilhelm, Papua New Guinea 14,793 ft. (4,509 m)
- Lowest Point: Lake Eyre, 50 ft. (15 m) below sea level [A][D]
- Longest River: Darling, 1,702 mi. (2,738 km)
- Largest Lake: Lake Eyre, 3,600 sq. mi. (9,324 sq. km) [D]
- Largest Country: Australia, 2,967,893 sq. mi. (7,686,850 sq. km) [B]
- Largest City: Sydney, Australia, 4,293,100 [C]

Sources and notes:
[A] Geoscience Australia
[B] World Factbook, CIA, 2007
[C] Australian Bureau of Statistics, metropolitan area, 2006 estimate
[D] area and depth fluctuates

Maritime boundaries represented in the Pacific Ocean are not authoritative and are depicted merely to portray general zones of jurisdiction.

International boundary
State boundary
National capital

Symbol and label sizes indicate relative sizes of cities:

Sydney
• Perth
· Honiara

1,000 mi
1,000 km
0   500
0   500

Labels on map:

PACIFIC OCEAN
INDIAN OCEAN
Philippine Sea
Coral Sea
Fiji Sea
Tasman Sea
Timor Sea
Arafura Sea
Bismarck Sea
Solomon Sea
Gulf of Carpentaria
Great Australian Bight

TROPIC OF CAPRICORN
EQUATOR
INTERNATIONAL DATE LINE

PALAU — Melekeok
FEDERATED STATES OF MICRONESIA — Palikir
Guam (U.S.)
Northern Mariana Is. (U.S.)
Wake I. (U.S.)
MARSHALL ISLANDS — Majuro
NAURU — Yaren
Tarawa (Bairiki) — KIRIBATI
TUVALU — Funafuti
Howland I. (U.S.)
Baker I. (U.S.)
Johnston I. (U.S.)
Hawaiian Is. (U.S.)
Palmyra Is. (U.S.)
Jarvis I. (U.S.)
Tokelau Islands (N.Z.)
SAMOA — Apia
American Samoa (U.S.)
Wallis & Futuna Is. (France)
TONGA — Nuku'alofa
Niue I. (N.Z.)
Cook Islands (N.Z.)
French Polynesia (France) — Tahiti
FIJI — Suva
VANUATU — Port-Vila
New Caledonia (France) — Nouméa
SOLOMON ISLANDS — Honiara
PAPUA NEW GUINEA — Port Moresby, Rabaul
Coral Sea Islands Terr. (Australia)
Norfolk Island (Australia)
Kermadec Is. (N.Z.)
Chatham Is. (N.Z.)
Lord Howe I. (Australia)

NEW ZEALAND — Wellington
North Island
South Island
Auckland, Hamilton, Nelson, Christchurch, Dunedin

AUSTRALIA
WESTERN AUSTRALIA
NORTHERN TERRITORY
SOUTH AUSTRALIA
QUEENSLAND
NEW SOUTH WALES
VICTORIA
TASMANIA
AUSTRALIAN CAPITAL TERRITORY
Ashmore and Cartier Is. (Australia)

Port Hedland, Carnarvon, Wyndham, Darwin, Katherine, Kalgoorlie, Albany, Perth, Whyalla, Adelaide, Alice Springs, Geelong, Melbourne, Canberra, Launceston, Hobart, Wollongong, Sydney, Newcastle, Gold Coast, Brisbane, Toowoomba, Rockhampton, Mackay, Townsville, Cairns

Lake Eyre
Great Barrier Reef
Darling R.
Murray R.
Torres Strait
Bass Strait

102

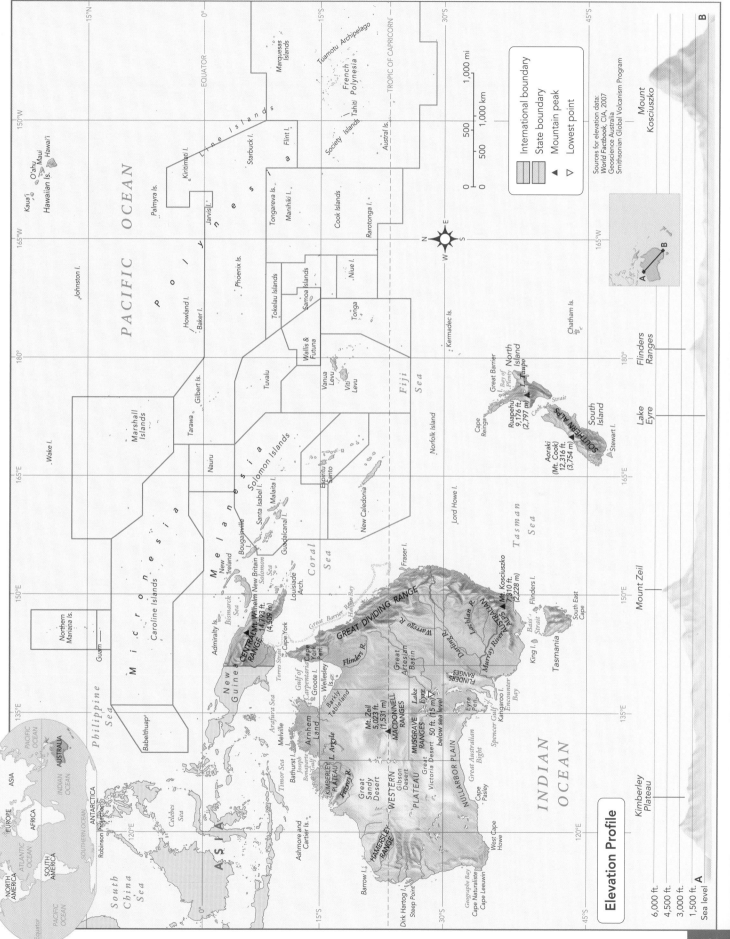

Major Metropolitan Areas

Australia
Sydney	3,997,000
Melbourne	3,367,000
Brisbane	1,628,000
Perth	1,340,000
Adelaide	1,073,000
Newcastle	471,000
Gold Coast (Southport)	397,000
Canberra	312,000

Fiji
| Suva | 167,000 |
| Lautoka | 29,000 |

Kiribati
| Tarawa (Bairiki) | 25,000 |

Marshall Islands
| Majuro | 18,000 |

Micronesia
| Weno | 15,000 |
| Colonia | 3,000 |

Nauru
| Yaren | 4,000 |

New Zealand
Auckland	1,075,000
Wellington	340,000
Christchurch	334,000

Palau
| Melekeok | 400 |

Papua New Guinea
Port Moresby	332,000
Lae	81,000
Madang	27,000
Wewak	23,000

Samoa
| Apia | 34,000 |

Solomon Islands
| Honiara | 61,000 |

Tonga
| Nuku'alofa | 30,000 |

Tuvalu
| Funafuti | 4,000 |

Vanuatu
| Port-Vila | 30,000 |

International comparability of population data is limited by varying census methods. Where metropolitan population is unavailable, core city population is shown.

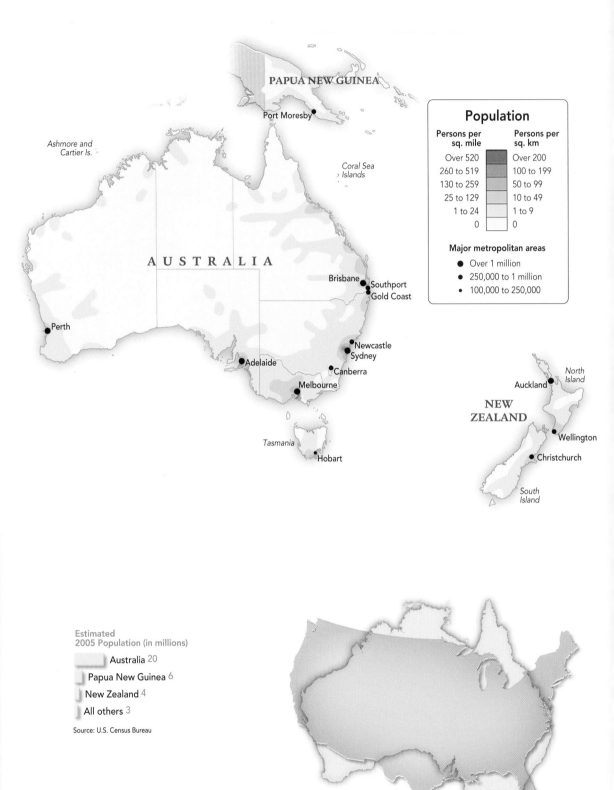

Population

Persons per sq. mile	Persons per sq. km
Over 520	Over 200
260 to 519	100 to 199
130 to 259	50 to 99
25 to 129	10 to 49
1 to 24	1 to 9
0	0

Major metropolitan areas
● Over 1 million
• 250,000 to 1 million
· 100,000 to 250,000

Estimated 2005 Population (in millions)
Australia 20
Papua New Guinea 6
New Zealand 4
All others 3

Source: U.S. Census Bureau

Gross Domestic Product is a measure of the total goods and services generated by a country. Generally, manufacturing, high-tech services, and specialized agricultural products add more value than raw materials and basic food stuffs.

Australia derives its wealth and high standard of living from service industries and mineral extraction and processing. New Zealand's economy is oriented towards the export of animal products. Papua New Guinea's subsistence economy generates little excess wealth.

Electricity Use, 2002

United States 12,376
Australia 9,736
New Zealand 8,849
Fiji 781
Papua New Guinea 282

KWh (kilowatt hours) per person per year

Source: World Factbook, CIA, 2005

Gross Domestic Product

GDP per capita

- Over $20,000
- $10,000 to $20,000
- $5,000 to $9,999
- $2,500 to $4,999
- Less than $2,500
- No data

Source: World Factbook, CIA, 2005

GDP of Island Nations

Fiji, Kiribati, Marshall Islands, Micronesia, Nauru, Palau, Samoa, Solomon Islands, Tonga, Tuvalu, Vanuatu

GDP of Island Territories

American Samoa (U.S.), Cook Is. (N.Z.), French Polynesia (Fr.), Guam (U.S.), New Caledonia (Fr.), Niue (N.Z.), Northern Mariana Is. (U.S.), Tokelau (N.Z.), Wallis & Futuna (Fr.)

Land Use and Resources

Predominant land use
- Commercial agriculture
- Dairying
- Livestock ranching
- Primarily forestland
- Limited agricultural activity

Major resources
Coal, Natural gas, Oil, Forest products, Gold, Silver, Iron ore, Uranium, Bauxite, Diamonds, Other minerals, Fishing, Major manufacturing and trade centers

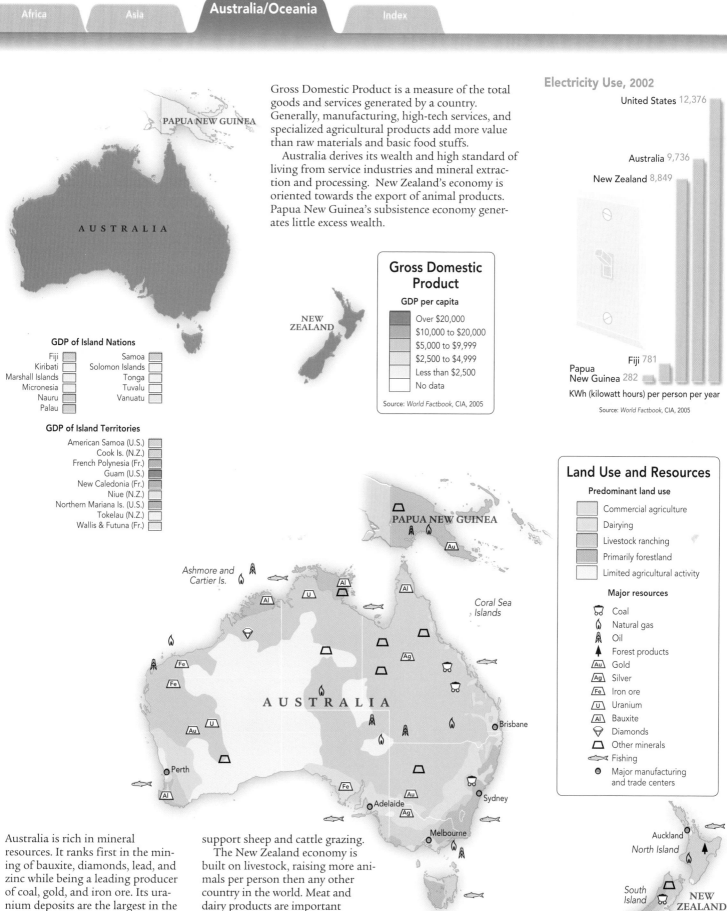

Australia is rich in mineral resources. It ranks first in the mining of bauxite, diamonds, lead, and zinc while being a leading producer of coal, gold, and iron ore. Its uranium deposits are the largest in the world, though largely undeveloped. Modern methods of farming and irrigation allow a very limited area of commercial agriculture to be highly productive. Despite arid conditions, vast areas of the interior support sheep and cattle grazing.

The New Zealand economy is built on livestock, raising more animals per person then any other country in the world. Meat and dairy products are important exports.

The economies of Papua New Guinea and the other island nations in the region rely primarily on subsistence agriculture and tourism.

105

Australia's climate is predominately warm and dry. The northern half of the country lies within the tropics and has very warm conditions year round. The southern half of the country lies below the tropics and experiences a warm summer and a cool winter.

New Zealand's climate is like that of the U.S. Pacific Northwest—mild and moist. Papua New Guinea and other island nations surrounding the equator have climates that are mainly very warm and moist year round.

See photographs taken in different kinds of climates on pages 24–25.

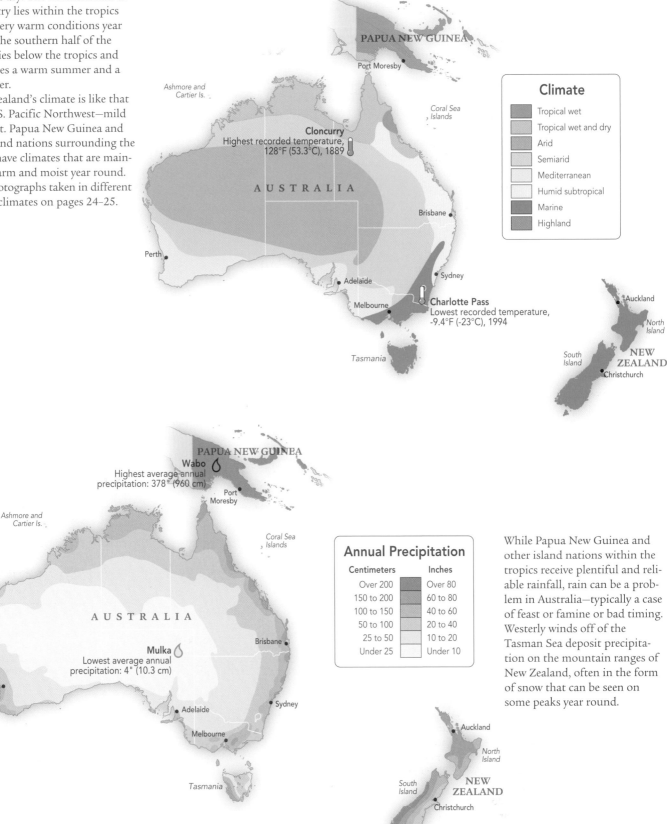

Climate

- Tropical wet
- Tropical wet and dry
- Arid
- Semiarid
- Mediterranean
- Humid subtropical
- Marine
- Highland

PAPUA NEW GUINEA
Port Moresby
Coral Sea Islands
Ashmore and Cartier Is.

Cloncurry
Highest recorded temperature, 128°F (53.3°C), 1889

AUSTRALIA

Brisbane

Perth

Adelaide
Sydney

Melbourne
Charlotte Pass
Lowest recorded temperature, -9.4°F (-23°C), 1994

Tasmania

Auckland
North Island
South Island
NEW ZEALAND
Christchurch

PAPUA NEW GUINEA
Wabo
Highest average annual precipitation: 378" (960 cm)
Port Moresby
Coral Sea Islands
Ashmore and Cartier Is.

AUSTRALIA

Mulka
Lowest average annual precipitation: 4" (10.3 cm)

Brisbane
Perth
Adelaide
Sydney
Melbourne
Tasmania

Annual Precipitation

Centimeters	Inches
Over 200	Over 80
150 to 200	60 to 80
100 to 150	40 to 60
50 to 100	20 to 40
25 to 50	10 to 20
Under 25	Under 10

While Papua New Guinea and other island nations within the tropics receive plentiful and reliable rainfall, rain can be a problem in Australia—typically a case of feast or famine or bad timing. Westerly winds off of the Tasman Sea deposit precipitation on the mountain ranges of New Zealand, often in the form of snow that can be seen on some peaks year round.

Auckland
North Island
South Island
NEW ZEALAND
Christchurch

Climate Graphs

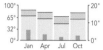

Average daily temperature range (in °F)

Average monthly precipitation (in inches)

BRISBANE, Australia

PERTH, Australia

AUCKLAND, New Zealand

PORT MORESBY, Papua New Guinea

ADELAIDE, Australia

MELBOURNE, Australia

SYDNEY, Australia

CHRISTCHURCH, New Zealand

Abundant Australian forest-lands are limited to relatively narrow coastal regions where moisture, even if seasonal, is adequate. Most of the rest of the continent is covered by species of trees, bush, and grasses adapted to arid conditions. Eucalyptus are the most common trees in Australia.

Papua New Guinea has dense tropical rain forests, and New Zealand has mixed forests and grasslands arising from its temperate climate.

See photographs of different kinds of vegetation on pages 26–27.

Vegetation

- Subtropical broadleaf evergreen forest
- Mixed forest
- Midlatitude scrubland
- Midlatitude grassland
- Desert
- Tropical seasonal and scrub
- Tropical rain forest
- Tropical savanna

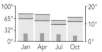

Environmental Issues

- Current forest
- Cleared forest
- Area at highest risk of desertification
- ● Poor air quality*

*Cities exceeding at least one of the World Health Organization's (WHO) annual mean guidelines for air quality

Sources: *Global Distribution of Original and Remaining Forests*, UNEP-WCMC, 2002
World Soil Resources Map Index, USDA/NRCS, 2002
World Development Indicators, World Bank, 1999

Biodiversity loss (a decrease in the variety of life forms and ecosystems) is a leading environmental problem in both Australia and New Zealand. Over the past two hundred years, vast areas have been cleared for settlements and farmland. This land clearing, along with the introduction of non-native plant and animal species, has permanently altered the ecological balance. In New Zealand, it is estimated that eighty-five percent of the original lowland forests and wetlands have been lost due to human influences. Desertification, often brought on by overgrazing, is another serious environmental threat in many parts of Australia.

107

Name	Page	Latitude	Longitude
state, Austl.	102	29°00'S	149°00'E
New York, NY	51	40°43'N	74°00'W
New York, state, U.S.	51	44°00'N	75°00'W
New Zealand, country	102	42°00'S	175°00'E
Nezahualcóyotl Res., lake	77	17°00'N	94°00'W
Niagara Falls, falls	45	44°00'N	83°00'W
Niamey, Niger	90	13°31'N	2°07'E
Nicaragua, country	44	12°00'N	84°00'W
Nicaragua, L., lake	45	12°00'N	85°00'W
Nice, France	84	43°43'N	7°16'E
Nicobar Is., islands	97	8°00'N	93°00'E
Nicosia, Cyprus	96	35°07'N	33°21'E
Niger, country	90	19°00'N	10°00'E
Niger, river	91	17°00'N	0°00'
Niger Delta, delta	91	5°00'N	6°00'E
Nigeria, country	90	9°00'N	9°00'E
Niihau, island	54	22°00'N	160°00'W
Nile, river	91	25°00'N	32°00'E
Nile Delta, delta	91	31°00'N	31°00'E
Niobrara, river	54	43°00'N	102°00'W
Nipigon, L., lake	75	50°00'N	89°00'W
Niterói, Brazil	78	22°52'S	43°08'W
Niue I., dependency, N.Z.	102	19°00'S	170°00'W
Niue I., island	103	19°00'S	170°00'W
Niznij Novgorod, Russia	84	56°19'N	43°56'E
Nogales, Mexico	76	31°19'N	110°56'W
Nome, AK	50	64°30'N	165°24'W
Norfolk, VA	51	36°51'N	76°17'W
Norfolk I., dependency, Austl.	102	29°00'S	168°00'E
Norfolk I., island	103	29°00'S	168°00'E
Noril'sk, Russia	96	69°24'N	88°10'E
North America, continent	14	50°00'N	100°00'W
North Battleford, Canada	74	52°47'N	108°18'W
North Bay, Canada	74	46°19'N	79°28'W
North C., cape	85	71°00'N	25°00'E
North Carolina, state, U.S.	51	35°00'N	79°00'W
North China Plain, plateau	97	37°00'N	118°00'E
North Dakota, state, U.S.	50	48°00'N	101°00'W
Northern Dvina, river	85	64°00'N	42°00'E
Northern European Plain, plain	85	55°00'N	22°00'E
Northern Ireland, division, U.K.	84	55°00'N	8°00'W
Northern Mariana Is., dependency, U.S.	102	16°00'N	146°00'E
Northern Mariana Is., islands	103	16°00'N	146°00'E
Northern Terr., state, Austl.	102	18°00'S	133°00'E
North I., island	103	39°00'S	176°00'E
North Korea, country	96	41°00'N	128°00'E
North Platte, river	54	43°00'N	105°00'W
North Pole, pole	14	90°00'N	0°00'
North Saskatchewan, river	75	54°00'N	111°00'W
North Sea, sea	85	56°00'N	3°00'E
Northwest Territories, territory, Can.	74	65°00'N	119°00'W
Norway, country	84	62°00'N	9°00'E
Norwegian Sea, sea	85	67°00'N	6°00'E
Notre Dame Mts., mountains	75	47°00'N	70°00'W
Nouadhibou, Mauritania	90	20°55'N	17°02'W
Nouakchott, Mauritania	90	18°05'N	15°58'W
Nouméa, New Caledonia	102	22°10'S	166°46'E
Nova Scotia, peninsula	75	45°00'N	65°00'W
Nova Scotia, province, Can.	74	47°00'N	65°00'W
Novaya Zemlya, islands	97	74°00'N	57°00'E
Novi Sad, Serbia	84	45°15'N	19°51'E
Novokuznetsk, Russia	96	53°46'N	87°11'E
Novosibirsk, Russia	96	55°02'N	82°56'E
Nubian Desert, desert	91	20°00'N	35°00'E
Nueces, river	55	28°00'N	98°00'W
Nueva Rosita, Mexico	76	27°56'N	101°12'W
Nuevo Casas Grandes, Mexico	76	30°25'N	107°55'W
Nuevo Laredo, Mexico	76	27°29'N	99°30'W
Nuevo León, state, Mex.	76	26°00'N	100°00'W
Nuku'alofa, Tonga	102	21°11'S	175°11'W
Nullarbor Plain, plain	103	31°00'S	127°00'E
Nunavut, territory, Can.	74	65°00'N	90°00'W
Nuuk (Godthåb), Greenland	44	64°10'N	51°41'W
Nyala, Sudan	90	12°02'N	24°53'E
Nyasa, L. (L. Malawi), lake	91	12°00'S	35°00'E

O

Name	Page	Latitude	Longitude
Oahe, L., lake	54	45°00'N	100°00'W
Oahu, island	54	22°00'N	158°00'W
Oakland, CA	50	37°48'N	122°16'W
Oaxaca, Mexico	76	17°04'N	96°43'W
Oaxaca, state, Mex.	76	17°00'N	97°00'W
Oaxaca Plat., plateau	77	17°00'N	89°00'W
Ob, river	97	62°00'N	69°00'E
Ocmulgee, river	55	33°00'N	83°00'W
Oconee, river	55	33°00'N	82°00'W
Ocotlán, Mexico	76	20°21'N	102°47'W
Odense, Denmark	84	55°24'N	10°23'E
Oder, river	85	52°00'N	17°00'E
Odesa, Ukraine	84	46°28'N	30°46'E
Odessa, TX	50	31°51'N	102°22'W
Ogaden, region	91	8°00'N	46°00'E
Ogden, UT	50	41°13'N	111°58'W
Ohio, river	55	39°00'N	86°00'W
Ohio, state, U.S.	51	41°00'N	84°00'W
Ojinaga, Mexico	76	29°34'N	104°25'W
Oka, river	85	55°00'N	37°00'E
Okavango, region	91	19°00'S	19°00'E
Okeechobee, L., lake	55	27°00'N	81°00'W
Okhotsk, Sea of, sea	97	55°00'N	149°00'E
Okinawa, island	97	26.3°00'N	128°00'E
Oklahoma, state, U.S.	50	37°00'N	99°00'W
Oklahoma City, OK	50	35°28'N	97°31'W
Öland, island	85	57°00'N	19°00'E
Olympia, WA	50	47°02'N	122°54'W
Olympus, Mt., peak	85	40°00'N	22°00'E
Omaha, NE	51	41°16'N	95°56'W
Oman, country	96	19°00'N	55°00'E
Oman, G. of, gulf	97	24°00'N	60°00'E
Omdurman, Sudan	90	15°38'N	32°27'E
Omsk, Russia	96	55°01'N	73°20'E
Onega, L., lake	85	62°00'N	36°00'E
Onitsha, Nigeria	90	6°08'N	6°47'E
Ontario, province, Can.	74	52°00'N	88°00'W
Ontario, L., lake	45	45°00'N	78°00'W
Oran, Algeria	90	35°42'N	0°39'W
Orange, river	91	28°00'S	20°00'E
Oregon, state, U.S.	50	44°00'N	121°00'W
Orenburg, Russia	84	51°50'N	55°03'E
Orinoco, river	79	8°00'N	65°00'W
Orizaba, Mexico	76	18°50'N	97°05'W
Orizaba, Pico de, peak	77	19°00'N	97°00'W
Orkney Is., islands	85	59°00'N	3°00'W
Orlando, FL	51	28°32'N	81°23'W
Oruro, Bolivia	78	17°57'S	67°06'W
Osaka, Japan	96	35°57'N	137°17'E
Oslo, Norway	84	59°55'N	10°47'E
Osterdal, river	85	62°00'N	14°00'E
Ostrava, Czech Rep.	84	49°50'N	18°17'E
Ottawa, Canada	74	45°24'N	75°41'W
Ottawa, river	75	46°00'N	78°00'W
Ouachita, river	55	34°00'N	92°00'W
Ouachita Mts., mountains	55	35°00'N	95°00'W
Ouagadougou, Burkina Faso	90	12°23'N	1°34'W
Oulu, Finland	84	65°02'N	25°26'E
Outer Hebrides Is., islands	85	58°00'N	7°00'W
Owen Sound, Canada	74	44°33'N	80°56'W
Owyhee, river	54	43°00'N	118°00'W
Oxnard, CA	50	34°12'N	119°11'W
Ozark Plat., plateau	55	36°00'N	93°00'W
Ozarks, L. of the, lake	55	38°00'N	93°00'W

P

Name	Page	Latitude	Longitude
Pachuca, Mexico	76	20°07'N	98°45'W
Pacific Ocean, ocean	14	30°00'N	140°00'W
Padang, Indonesia	96	0°55'S	100°21'E
Padre I., island	55	27°00'N	97°00'W
Pakistan, country	96	29°00'N	65°00'E
Palau, country	102	9°00'N	133°00'E
Palawan, island	97	9°30'N	118°30'E
Palembang, Indonesia	96	2°56'S	104°43'E
Palermo, Italy	84	38°08'N	13°21'E
Palikir, Fed. States of Micronesia	102	6°56'N	158°10'E
Palma de Mallorca, Spain	84	39°35'N	2°40'E
Palmyra Is., dependency, U.S.	102	6°00'N	162°00'W
Palmyra Is., islands	103	6°00'N	162°00'W
Pamirs, mountains	97	38°00'N	73°00'E
Pampas, plain	79	38°00'S	60°00'W
Panama, country	44	9°00'N	81°00'W
Panama Canal, canal	45	9°20'N	79°55'W
Panama City, Panama	44	9°00'N	79°32'W
Panama, G. of, gulf	79	8°00'N	79°00'W
Panama, Isth. of, isthmus	45	10°00'N	79°00'W
Pangnirtung, Canada	74	66°08'N	65°42'W
Pantelleria, island	85	37°00'N	12°00'E
Pánuco, river	77	22°00'N	98°00'W
Papua New Guinea, country	102	6°00'S	149°00'E
Paracas, peninsula	79	14°00'S	77°00'W
Paraguay, country	78	24°00'S	59°00'W
Paraguay, river	79	20°00'S	58°00'W
Paramaribo, Suriname	78	5°50'N	55°11'W
Paraná, Argentina	78	31°44'S	60°31'W
Paraná, river	79	22°00'S	53°00'W
Parañas Pt., cape	79	7°00'S	81°00'W
Paris, France	84	48°53'N	2°21'E
Parnaíba, Brazil	78	2°55'S	41°46'W
Parnaíba, river	79	7°00'S	44°00'W
Parry Is., islands	75	77°00'N	105°00'W
Pasley, C., cape	103	34°00'S	124°00'E
Passo Fundo, Brazil	78	28°15'S	52°24'W
Pasto, Colombia	78	1°13'N	77°17'W
Patagonia, region	79	46°00'S	70°00'W
Patras, Greece	84	38°16'N	21°44'E
Pavlodar, Kazakhstan	96	52°20'N	76°55'E
Peace, river	75	58°00'N	115°00'W
Peace River, Canada	74	56°15'N	117°14'W
Pearl, river	55	32°00'N	90°00'W
Pechora, river	85	67°00'N	52°00'E
Pechora, Russia	84	65°10'N	57°18'E
Pecos, river	54	35°00'N	104°00'W
Pécs, Hungary	84	46°05'N	18°14'E
Pee Dee, river	55	35°00'N	80°00'W
Peipus, L., lake	85	58°00'N	27°00'E
Pelly, river	75	63°00'N	135°00'W
Peloponese Pen., peninsula	85	38°00'N	23°00'E
Pelotas, Brazil	78	31°45'S	52°18'W
Pemba I., island	91	5°00'S	40°00'E
Pembroke, Canada	74	45°49'N	77°08'W
Pennines, The, mountains	85	54°00'N	2°00'W
Pennsylvania, state, U.S.	51	42°00'N	77°00'W
Penobscot, river	55	47°00'N	69°00'W
Pensacola Mts., mountains	15	84°00'S	55°00'W
Penza, Russia	84	53°10'N	45°00'E
Peoria, IL	51	40°42'N	89°35'W
Pereira, Colombia	78	4°45'N	75°41'W
Perm', Russia	84	57°59'N	56°18'E
Persian G., gulf	97	27°00'N	51°00'E
Perth, Australia	102	31°53'S	115°52'E
Peru, country	78	8°00'S	78°00'W
Petacalco Bay, bay	77	18°00'N	102°00'W
Peterborough, Canada	74	44°18'N	78°19'W
Petrolina, Brazil	78	9°22'S	40°33'W
Petropavlovsk-Kamchatskiy, Russia	96	53°05'N	158°34'E
Petrozavodsk, Russia	84	61°47'N	34°17'E
Phane Is., islands	97	14°00'N	123°00'E
Philippines, country	96	11°00'N	124°00'E
Philippine Sea, sea	97	15°00'N	133°00'E
Phnom Penh, Cambodia	96	11°33'N	104°54'E
Phoenix, AZ	50	33°27'N	112°04'W
Phoenix Is., islands	103	5°00'S	171°00'W
Piedmont, highlands	55	36°00'N	80°00'W
Piedras Negras, Mexico	76	28°42'N	100°32'W
Pierre, SD	50	44°22'N	100°21'W
Pietermaritzburg, S. Africa	90	29°37'S	30°23'E
Pikes Peak, peak	54	38°00'N	105°00'W
Pilcomayo, river	79	23°00'S	61°00'W
Pitcairn I., island	15	25°04'S	130°05'W
Pitcairn Is., dependency	16	25°04'S	130°05'W
Pittsburgh, PA	51	40°26'N	80°00'W
Piura, Peru	78	5°11'S	80°38'W
Platte, river	55	41°00'N	98°00'W
Plenty, Bay of, bay	103	37°00'S	177°00'E
Ploiesti, Romania	84	44°57'N	26°02'E
Plovdiv, Bulgaria	84	42°09'N	24°45'E
Po, river	85	45°00'N	11°00'E
Pocatello, ID	50	42°52'N	112°27'W
Podgorica, Montenegro	84	42°26'N	19°16'E
Poinsett, C., cape	15	66°00'S	113°00'E
Pointe-Noire, Rep. of Congo	90	4°48'S	11°52'E
Poland, country	84	51°00'N	21°00'E
Polynesia, region	103	2°00'S	163°00'W
Pond Inlet, Canada	74	72°42'N	77°47'W
Pontchartrain, L., lake	55	30°00'N	90°00'W
Poopó, L., lake	79	19°00'S	67°00'W
Popocatépetl, peak	77	19°00'N	99°00'W
Portage la Prairie, Canada	74	49°58'N	98°18'W
Port-au-Prince, Haiti	44	18°32'N	72°21'W
Port-Cartier, Canada	74	50°02'N	66°51'W
Port Elizabeth, S. Africa	90	33°57'S	25°35'E
Port-Gentil, Gabon	90	0°40'S	8°44'E
Port Harcourt, Nigeria	90	4°47'N	7°00'E
Port Hardy, Canada	74	50°43'N	127°31'W
Port Hedland, Australia	102	20°22'S	118°37'E
Portland, ME	51	43°40'N	70°15'W
Portland, OR	50	45°31'N	122°40'W
Port Louis, Mauritius	90	20°06'S	57°31'E
Port Moresby, Papua New Guinea	102	9°27'S	147°11'E
Porto, Portugal	84	41°09'N	8°37'W
Porto Alegre, Brazil	78	30°00'S	51°12'W
Porto-Novo, Benin	90	6°29'N	2°41'E
Pôrto Velho, Brazil	78	8°46'S	63°54'W
Port Said, Egypt	90	31°15'N	32°17'E
Portsmouth, United Kingdom	84	50°48'N	1°06'W
Port Sudan, Sudan	90	19°37'N	37°13'E
Portugal, country	84	40°00'N	8°00'W
Port-Vila, Vanuatu	102	17°44'S	168°24'E
Potomac, river	55	40°00'N	78°00'W
Potosí, Bolivia	78	19°36'S	65°45'W
Po Val., valley	85	45°00'N	10°00'E
Powder, river	54	45°00'N	106°00'W
Powell, L., lake	54	37°00'N	111°00'W
Poza Rica, Mexico	76	20°33'N	97°27'W
Poznan, Poland	84	52°24'N	16°55'E
Prague, Czech Rep.	84	50°06'N	14°25'E
Praia, Cape Verde	90	15°01'N	23°38'W
Pretoria, S. Africa	90	25°45'S	28°11'E
Prince Albert, Canada	74	53°10'N	105°45'W
Prince Albert Mts., mountains	15	75°00'S	158°00'E
Prince Charles I., island	75	67°00'N	77°00'W
Prince Charles Mts., mountains	15	74°00'S	63°00'E
Prince Edward I., island	75	46°00'N	64°00'W
Prince Edward Island, province, Can.	74	48°00'N	63°00'W
Prince George, Canada	74	53°52'N	122°46'W
Prince of Wales I., island	75	73°00'N	100°00'W
Prince Patrick I., island	75	77°00'N	120°00'W
Prince Rupert, Canada	74	54°18'N	130°18'W
Príncipe, island	91	2°00'N	8°00'E
Pripet, river	85	52°00'N	28°00'E
Pristina, Kosovo	84	42°40'N	21°10'N
Providence, RI	51	41°49'N	71°25'W
Provo, UT	50	40°14'N	111°39'W
Prut, river	85	48°00'N	28°00'E
Prydz Bay, bay	15	68°00'S	75°00'E
Pucallpa, Peru	78	8°23'S	74°32'W
Puebla, Mexico	76	19°03'N	98°12'W
Puebla, state, Mex.	76	18°00'N	97°00'W
Pueblo, CO	50	38°15'N	104°37'W
Puerto Ayacucho, Venezuela	78	5°40'N	67°37'W
Puerto Escondido, Mexico	76	15°52'N	97°06'W
Puerto Maldonado, Peru	78	12°37'S	69°12'W
Puerto Montt, Chile	78	41°28'S	72°58'W
Puerto Peñasco, Mexico	76	31°19'N	113°32'W
Puerto Rico, dependency, U.S.	44	18°00'N	66°00'W
Puerto Rico, island	45	18°00'N	66°00'W
Puerto Vallarta, Mexico	76	20°35'N	105°15'W
Puget Sound, bay	54	48°00'N	123°00'W
Punta Arenas, Chile	78	53°08'S	70°55'W
Purus, river	79	8°00'S	66°00'W
Putumayo, river	79	3°00'S	74°00'W
Puvirnituq, Canada	74	60°02'N	77°29'W
Pyeongyang, N. Korea	96	39°01'N	125°44'E
Pyrenees, mountains	85	43°00'N	1°00'E

Q

Name	Page	Latitude	Longitude
Qaraghandy, Kazakhstan	96	49°52'N	73°08'E
Qatar, country	96	26°00'N	52°00'E
Qattara Depression, depression	91	29°00'N	29°00'E
Qingdao, China	96	36°06'N	120°22'E
Qu'Appelle, river	75	52°00'N	104°00'W
Québec, Canada	74	46°48'N	71°13'W
Québec, province, Can.	74	52°00'N	72°00'W
Queen Charlotte Sound, bay	75	52°00'N	130°00'W
Queen Elizabeth Is., islands	75	80°00'N	109°00'W
Queen Maud Land, region	15	75°00'S	30°00'E
Queen Maud Mts., mountains	15	84°00'S	175°00'E
Queensland, state, Austl.	102	23°00'S	148°00'E
Quelimane, Mozambique	90	17°52'S	36°54'E
Querétaro, Mexico	76	20°36'N	100°24'W
Querétaro, state, Mex.	76	21°00'N	99°00'W
Quezon City, Philippines	96	14°44'N	121°02'E
Quintana Roo, state, Mex.	76	19°00'N	88°00'W
Quito, Ecuador	78	0°12'S	78°29'W
Quoddy Head, cape	55	45°00'N	67°00'W

R

Name	Page	Latitude	Longitude
Rabat, Morocco	90	33°59'N	6°51'W
Rabaul, Papua New Guinea	102	4°13'S	152°08'E
Race, C., cape	75	47°00'N	53°00'W
Rainier, Mt., peak	54	47°00'N	122°00'W
Raleigh, NC	51	35°46'N	78°38'W
Rancagua, Chile	78	34°10'S	70°47'W
Rankin Inlet, Canada	74	62°49'N	92°04'W
Rapid City, SD	50	44°05'N	103°14'W
Rarotonga I., island	103	21°00'S	160°00'W
Ras Dashen, peak	91	14°00'N	38°00'E
Rawson, Argentina	78	43°17'S	65°06'W
Recife, Brazil	78	8°04'S	34°57'W
Reconquista, Argentina	78	29°10'S	59°36'W
Red, river	75	49°00'N	98°00'W
Red, river	55	34°00'N	94°00'W
Red Deer, Canada	74	52°13'N	113°50'W
Red River of the North, river	55	48°00'N	97°00'W
Red Sea, sea	91	21°00'N	39°00'E
Regina, Canada	74	50°28'N	104°36'W
Reindeer L., lake	75	57°00'N	103°00'W
Reinga, C., cape	103	34°00'S	173°00'E
Reno, NV	50	39°32'N	119°49'W
Republican, river	55	40°00'N	99°00'W
Rep. of the Congo, country	90	1°00'N	16°00'E
Repulse Bay, Canada	74	66°32'N	86°09'W
Resistencia, Argentina	78	27°27'S	59°00'W
Resolute, Canada	74	74°41'N	94°54'W
Reunion, dependency, Fr.	90	21°00'S	56°00'E
Reunion, island	91	21°00'S	56°00'E
Revelstoke, Canada	74	51°00'N	118°11'W
Revillagigedo Is., islands	77	19°00'N	112°00'W
Reykjavík, Iceland	84	64°08'N	21°55'W
Reynosa, Mexico	76	26°05'N	98°17'W
Rhine, river	85	51°00'N	7°00'E
Rhine Delta, delta	85	52°00'N	3°00'E
Rhode Island, state, U.S.	51	43°00'N	72°00'W
Rhodes, island	85	36°00'N	28°00'E
Rhône, river	85	45°00'N	4°00'E
Ribeirão Prêto, Brazil	78	21°10'S	47°47'W
Riberalta, Bolivia	78	11°01'S	66°05'W
Richmond, VA	51	37°33'N	77°28'W
Rift Val., valley	91	2°00'N	38°00'E
Riga, Latvia	84	56°57'N	24°08'E
Riga, G. of, gulf	85	58°00'N	24°00'E
Riiser-Larsen Ice Shelf, ice shelf	15	73°00'S	20°00'W
Rimouski, Canada	74	48°27'N	68°31'W
Rio Branco, Brazil	78	9°56'S	67°48'W
Río Bravo del Norte, river	77	29°00'N	101°00'W
Río Cuarto, Argentina	78	33°06'S	64°20'W
Rio de Janeiro, Brazil	78	22°53'S	43°15'W
Río de la Plata, gulf	79	35°00'S	56°00'W
Río Gallegos, Argentina	78	51°38'S	69°14'W
Rio Grande, river	54	35°00'N	106°00'W
Rio Grande de Santiago, river	77	21°00'N	104°00'W
Rio Negro, river	79	1°00'S	65°00'W
Rivera, Uruguay	78	30°56'S	55°33'W
Riverside, CA	50	33°57'N	117°24'W
Rivière-du-Loup, Canada	74	47°49'N	69°33'W
Riyadh, Saudi Arabia	96	24°40'N	46°42'E
Roanoke, river	55	38°00'N	80°00'W
Roanoke, VA	51	37°16'N	79°57'W
Robson, Mt., peak	75	54°00'N	119°00'W
Rochester, MN	51	44°01'N	92°28'W
Rochester, NY	51	43°09'N	77°37'W
Rock, river	55	42°00'N	90°00'W
Rockefeller Plat., plateau	15	80°00'S	140°00'W
Rockford, IL	51	42°16'N	89°06'W
Rockhampton, Australia	102	23°25'S	150°31'E
Rocky Mts., mountains	45	50°00'N	116°00'W
Rojo, C., cape	77	22°00'N	97°00'W
Romania, country	84	47°00'N	25°00'E
Rome, Italy	84	41°54'N	12°29'E
Ronne Ice Shelf, ice shelf	15	80°00'S	60°00'W
Roosevelt I., island	15	79°00'S	162°00'W
Rosario, Argentina	78	32°56'S	60°41'W
Ross Ice Shelf, ice shelf	15	82°00'S	170°00'W
Ross I., island	15	77°00'S	168°00'E
Ross Sea, sea	15	74°00'S	170°00'W
Rostov-na-Donu, Russia	84	47°16'N	39°44'E
Roswell, NM	50	33°24'N	104°31'W
Rotterdam, Netherlands	84	51°55'N	4°29'E
Rouen, France	84	49°27'N	1°06'E
Rouyn-Noranda, Canada	74	48°14'N	79°01'W
Ruapeho Peak, peak	103	39°00'S	175°00'E
Rub' Al-Khali, desert	97	20°00'N	50°00'E
Rumbek, South Sudan	90	6°48'N	29°41'E
Russia, country	96	60°00'N	80°00'E
Russia, country	84	59°00'N	45°00'E
Ruvuma, river	91	12°00'S	38°00'E
Ruwenzori Mts., mountains	91	1°00'S	29°00'E
Rwanda, country	90	2°00'S	30°00'E
Ryazan', Russia	84	54°37'N	39°47'E
Rybinsk Res., lake	85	58°00'N	38°00'E
Ryukyu Is., islands	97	27°00'N	127°00'E

S

Name	Page	Latitude	Longitude
Saaremaa I., island	85	58°00'N	22°00'E
Sabine, river	55	33°00'N	95°00'W
Sable, C., cape	75	44°00'N	66°00'W
Sable I., island	75	44°00'N	60°00'W
Sacramento, CA	50	38°35'N	121°30'W
Sacramento, river	54	40°00'N	122°00'W
Saguenay, river	75	49°00'N	73°00'W
Sahara, desert	91	21°00'N	10°00'E
Sahel, region	91	12°00'N	13°00'E
Saimaa, L., lake	85	61°00'N	28°00'E
St. Anthony, Canada	74	51°22'N	55°36'W
St. Catharines, Canada	74	43°10'N	79°14'W
St. Clair, L., lake	55	43°00'N	83°00'W
St. Croix, river	55	46°00'N	93°00'W
Ste. Marie, Cap, cape	91	25°00'S	45°00'E
St. George, UT	50	37°06'N	113°35'W
St-Georges, Canada	74	46°07'N	70°41'W
St. George's Channel, strait	85	52°00'N	7°00'W
St. Helena, island	91	16°00'S	6°00'W
St. Helens, Mt., peak	54	46°00'N	122°00'W
St-Jean, Lac, lake	75	48°00'N	75°00'W
Saint John, Canada	74	45°18'N	66°01'W
St. John, river	75	47°00'N	68°00'W
St. John's, Canada	74	47°34'N	52°43'W
St. Johns, river	55	30°00'N	82°00'W
St. Kitts and Nevis, country	44	18°00'N	63°00'W
St. Lawrence, river	45	47°00'N	72°00'W
St. Lawrence, G. of, gulf	75	48°00'N	63°00'W
St. Lawrence I., island	54	63°00'N	170°00'W
St. Louis, MO	51	38°38'N	90°12'W
St-Louis, Senegal	90	16°00'N	16°29'W
St. Lucia, country	44	14°00'N	61°00'W
St. Martin, dependency, Fr./Neth.	44	19°00'N	62°00'W
St. Paul, MN	51	44°57'N	93°06'W
St. Petersburg, FL	51	27°46'N	82°41'W
St. Petersburg, Russia	84	59°56'N	30°19'E
St-Pierre and Miquelon, dependency, Fr.	44	47°00'N	56°00'W
St-Pierre and Miquelon, islands	45	47°00'N	56°00'W
St. Vincent and the Grenadines, country	44	13°00'N	61°00'W
St. Vincent, C., cape	85	37°00'N	9°00'W
Sakakawea, L., lake	54	48°00'N	102°00'W
Sakami, Lac, lake	75	54°00'N	78°00'W
Sakhalin, island	97	51°00'N	143°00'E
Salado, river	79	28°00'S	63°00'W
Salem, OR	50	44°57'N	123°02'W
Salerno, Italy	84	40°41'N	14°45'E
Salina Cruz, Mexico	76	16°11'N	95°11'W
Salinas, CA	50	36°41'N	121°39'W
Salmon, river	54	46°00'N	116°00'W
Salt, river	54	34°00'N	111°00'W
Salta, Argentina	78	24°48'S	65°25'W
Saltillo, Mexico	76	25°25'N	101°00'W
Salt Lake City, UT	50	40°46'N	111°53'W
Salto, Uruguay	78	31°23'S	57°57'W
Salton Sea, lake	54	33°00'N	116°00'W
Salvador, Brazil	78	12°59'S	38°30'W
Salween, river	97	21°00'N	98°00'E
Samara, Russia	84	53°17'N	50°13'E
Samarqand, Uzbekistan	96	39°42'N	66°58'E
Samoa, country	102	13°00'S	174°00'W
Samoa Is., islands	103	13°00'S	172°00'W
Sanaa, Yemen	96	15°23'N	44°14'E
San Ambrosio I., island	79	26°00'S	80°00'W
San Antonio, TX	50	29°25'N	98°30'W
San Antonio Pt., cape	77	30°00'N	116°00'W
San Bernardino, CA	50	34°06'N	117°17'W
San Carlos de Bariloche, Argentina	78	41°09'S	71°17'W
San Cristóbal, Venezuela	78	7°46'N	72°14'W
San Cristóbal de las Casas, Mexico	76	16°45'N	92°38'W
Sand Hills, hills	54	42°00'N	101°00'W
San Diego, CA	50	32°43'N	117°09'W
San Felipe, Mexico	76	31°02'N	114°50'W
San Félix I., island	79	26°00'S	80°00'W
San Francisco, CA	50	37°46'N	122°25'W
San Francisco Bay, bay	54	38°00'N	123°00'W
Sangre de Cristo, mountains	54	38°00'N	105°00'W
San Joaquin, river	54	37°00'N	121°00'W
San Jorge, G. of, gulf	79	46°00'S	66°00'W
San Jose, CA	50	37°20'N	121°54'W
San José, Costa Rica	44	9°55'N	84°05'W
San Juan, Puerto Rico	44	18°28'N	66°05'W
San Juan, river	54	37°00'N	107°00'W
San Lázaro, C., cape	77	25°00'N	112°00'W
San Lucas, Mexico	76	22°33'N	104°26'W
San Lucas, C., cape	77	23°00'N	110°00'W
San Luis Potosí, Mexico	76	22°10'N	100°59'W
San Luis Potosí, state, Mex.	76	23°00'N	100°00'W
San Luis Río Colorado, Mexico	76	32°28'N	114°47'W
San Marino, country	84	43°00'N	12°00'E
San Matías, G. of, gulf	79	42°00'S	65°00'W
San Miguel de Tucumán, Argentina	78	26°53'S	65°13'W
San Pedro, river	77	23°00'N	105°00'W
San Pedro de las Colonias, Mexico	76	25°45'N	102°57'W
San Salvador, El Salvador	44	13°42'N	89°11'W
San Salvador de Jujuy, Argentina	78	24°12'S	65°18'W
Santa Barbara, CA	50	34°25'N	119°42'W
Santa Cruz, Bolivia	78	17°47'S	63°11'W
Santa Cruz, river	79	50°00'S	70°00'W
Santa Fe, Argentina	78	31°37'S	60°42'W
Santa Fe, NM	50	35°41'N	105°56'W
Santa Isabel I., island	103	8°00'S	159°00'E
Santa Maria, Brazil	78	29°39'S	53°49'W
Santarém, Brazil	78	2°27'S	54°44'W
Santa Rosa, Argentina	78	36°35'S	64°17'W
Santa Rosalía, Mexico	76	27°20'N	112°17'W
Santiago, Chile	78	33°28'S	70°39'W
Santiago de Cuba, Cuba	44	20°02'N	75°49'W
Santiago del Estero, Argentina	78	27°48'S	64°16'W
Santo Domingo, Dominican Rep.	44	18°29'N	69°54'W
Santos, Brazil	78	23°56'S	46°17'W
São Francisco, river	79	13°00'S	42°00'W
São José do Rio Prêto, Brazil	78	20°49'S	49°20'W
São Luís, Brazil	78	2°33'S	44°14'W
São Paulo, Brazil	78	23°33'S	46°37'W
São Roque, C., cape	79	5°00'S	35°00'W
São Tomé, island	91	1°00'N	7°00'E
São Tomé, São Tomé and Príncipe	90	0°18'N	6°44'E
São Tomé and Príncipe, country	90	1°00'N	7°00'E
Sapporo, Japan	96	43°02'N	141°21'E
Sarajevo, Bos. & Her.	84	43°52'N	18°26'E
Saratov, Russia	84	51°31'N	45°55'E
Sardinia, island	85	40°00'N	9°00'E
Sarh, Chad	90	9°09'N	18°23'E
Sarnia, Canada	74	42°58'N	82°24'W
Saskatchewan, province, Can.	74	56°00'N	97°00'W
Saskatchewan, river	75	54°00'N	103°00'W
Saskatoon, Canada	74	52°09'N	106°40'W
Saudi Arabia, country	96	27°00'N	41°00'E
Sault Ste. Marie, Canada	74	46°31'N	84°20'W
Sault Ste. Marie, MI	51	46°30'N	84°21'W
Sava, river	85	45°00'N	18°00'E
Savannah, GA	51	32°05'N	81°06'W
Savannah, river	55	34°00'N	83°00'W
Sayan Mts., mountains	97	53°00'N	96°00'E
Scandinavian Mts., mountains	85	65°00'N	15°00'E
Scioto, river	55	40°00'N	83°00'W
Scotland, division, U.K.	84	58°00'N	5°00'W
Scott I., island	15	67°00'S	179°00'E
Seattle, WA	50	47°36'N	122°20'W
Sebastián Vizcaíno Bay, bay	77	29°00'N	115°00'W
Ségou, Mali	90	13°26'N	6°16'W
Seine, river	85	49°00'N	1°00'E
Sejong City, S. Korea	96	36°29'N	127°17'E
Semey, Kazakhstan	96	50°23'N	80°19'E
Sendai, Japan	96	38°16'N	140°54'E
Senegal, country	90	15°00'N	16°00'W
Senegal, river	91	15°00'N	13°00'W
Seoul, S. Korea	96	37°34'N	127°01'E
Sept-Îles, Canada	74	50°12'N	66°22'W
Serbia, country	84	44°00'N	22°00'E
Serowe, Botswana	90	22°23'S	26°42'E
Serra do Mar, mountains	79	23°00'S	45°00'W
Sevan, L., lake	85	41°00'N	45°00'E
Sevastopol', Ukraine	84	44°34'N	33°28'E
Severn, river	75	56°00'N	90°00'W
Severnaya Zemlya, islands	97	79°00'N	98°00'E
Seville, Spain	84	37°23'N	5°59'W
Seward Pen., peninsula	54	65°00'N	165°00'W
Seychelles, country	90	9°00'S	52°00'E
Seychelles Is., islands	91	8°00'S	52°00'E
Sfax, Tunisia	90	34°47'N	10°46'E
Shackleton Ice Shelf, ice shelf	15	64°00'S	100°00'E
Shanghai, China	96	31°12'N	121°28'E
Shasta, Mt., peak	54	42°00'N	122°00'W
Shawinigan, Canada	74	46°33'N	72°45'W
Sheffield, United Kingdom	84	53°22'N	1°28'W
Shenyang, China	96	41°49'N	123°30'E
Sherbrooke, Canada	74	45°24'N	71°53'W
Shetland Is., islands	85	60°00'N	1°00'W
Shikoku, island	97	33°00'N	133°00'E

Abbreviations

Arch.	Archipelago	Den.	Denmark	Isth.	Isthmus	N. Korea	North Korea	Sp.	Spain
Austl.	Australia	Dominican Rep.	Dominican Republic	It.	Italy	N.Z.	New Zealand	St., St-	Saint
Bos. & Her.	Bosnia & Herzegovina	fed. dist.	Federal District	Kos.	Kosovo	Pen.	Peninsula	Ste., Ste-	Sainte
C.	Cape	Fed. States of Micronesia	Federated States of Micronesia	L.	Lake	Plat.	Plateau	Str.	Strait
Can.	Canada			Liecht.	Liechtenstein	Pt.	Point	Terr.	Territory
Cen.	Central	Fr.	France	Mac.	Macedonia	R.	River	U.K.	United Kingdom
Cen. African Rep.	Central African Republic	Ft.	Fort	Mex.	Mexico	Rep.	Republic	U.S.	United States
		G.	Gulf	Mont.	Montenegro	Rep. of the Congo	Republic of the Congo	Val.	Valley
Czech Rep.	Czech Republic	Gr.	Greece	Mor.	Morocco				
Dem. Rep. of Congo	Democratic Republic of the Congo	I.	Island	Mt.	Mount	Res.	Reservoir		
		Is.	Islands	Mtn.	Mountain	Russ.	Russia	For U.S. two-letter state abbreviations, see pages 52–53.	
				Mts.	Mountains	S. Africa	South Africa		
				Neth.	Netherlands	S. Korea	South Korea		

Afghanistan
Islamic republic, SW Asia

Area: 250,000 sq. mi. (647,500 sq. km.)
Population: 31,890,000
Language(s): Dari, Pashtu

Monetary unit: afghani
Economy (pre-1980): agriculture (fruits and nuts), carpets, mining, natural gas, opium

After the fall of the Taliban in 2001, the newly established Afghan Interim Authority restored, in a modified form, the national flag first introduced in 1928. Black represents the dark ages of the past; red, the blood shed in the struggle for independence; and green, hope and prosperity for the future.

Albania
Republic, S Europe

Area: 11,100 sq. mi. (28,748 sq. km.)
Population: 3,601,000
Language(s): Albanian, Greek

Monetary unit: lek
Economy: agriculture (sugar beets and grapes), mining, oil, asphalt, textiles

On Nov. 28, 1443, the flag was first raised by Skanderbeg, the national hero. After independence from Turkish rule was proclaimed on Nov. 28, 1912, the flag was flown by various regimes, each of which identified itself by adding a symbol above the double-headed eagle. The current flag, which features only the eagle, was adopted on May 22, 1993.

Algeria
Republic, N Africa

Area: 919,950 sq. mi. (2,381,740 sq. km.)
Population: 33,333,000
Language(s): Arabic, French

Monetary unit: Algerian dinar
Economy: oil, natural gas, grapes, olives, dates, livestock, mining

In the early 19th century, during the French conquest of North Africa, Algerian resistance fighters led by Emir Abdelkader supposedly raised the current flag. Its colors and symbols are associated with Islam and the Arab dynasties of the region. The flag was raised over an independent Algeria on July 2, 1962.

Andorra
Coprincipality, SW Europe

Area: 181 sq. mi. (468 sq. km.)
Population: 71,800
Language(s): Catalan, French

Monetary unit: euro
Economy: tourism, international banking, cattle, sheep

The flag may date to 1866, but the first legal authority for it is unknown. The design was standardized in July 1993. Possible sources for its colors are the flags of neighboring Spain (red-yellow-red) and France (blue-white-red). The coat of arms incorporates both French and Spanish elements dating to the 13th century or earlier.

Angola
Republic, SW Africa

Area: 481,351 sq. mi. (1,246,700 sq. km.)
Population: 12,264,000
Language(s): Portuguese

Monetary unit: kwanza
Economy: subsistence farming, iron ore, oil, diamonds

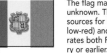

After Portugal withdrew from Angola on Nov. 11, 1975, the flag of the leading rebel group gained recognition. Inspired by designs of the Viet Cong and the former Soviet Union, it includes a star for internationalism and progress, a cogwheel for industrial workers, and a machete for agricultural workers. The black stripe is for the African people.

Antigua and Barbuda
Islands republic, Caribbean

Area: 171 sq. mi. (443 sq. km.)
Population: 69,500
Language(s): English

Monetary unit: East Caribbean dollar
Economy: tourism, light manufacturing, tropical fruits

When "associated statehood" was granted by Britain on Feb. 27, 1967, the flag was introduced, and it remained after independence (Nov. 1, 1981). Red is for the dynamism of the people, the V-shape is for victory, and the sun is for the climate. Black is for the majority population and the soil, blue is for the sea, and white is for the beaches.

Argentina
Republic, South America

Area: 1,068,296 sq. mi. (2,766,890 sq. km.)
Population: 40,302,000
Language(s): Spanish, English

Monetary unit: Argentine peso
Economy: agriculture, livestock, food processing, oil, natural gas, motor vehicles

The uniforms worn by Argentines when the British attacked Buenos Aires (1806) and the blue ribbons worn by patriots in 1810 may have been the origin of the celeste-white-celeste flag hoisted on Feb. 12, 1812. The flag's golden "sun of May" was added on Feb. 25, 1818, to commemorate the yielding of the Spanish viceroy in 1810.

Armenia
Republic, SW Asia

Area: 11,506 sq. mi. (29,800 sq. km.)
Population: 2,972,000
Language(s): Armenian

Monetary unit: dram
Economy: diamond-processing, machine tools, tires, mining, grapes

In 1885 an Armenian priest proposed adopting the "rainbow flag given to the Armenians when Noah's Ark came to rest on Mt. Ararat." On Aug. 1, 1918, a flag was sanctioned with stripes of red (possibly symbolizing blood), blue (for homeland), and orange (for courage and work). Replaced during Soviet rule, it was readopted on Aug. 24, 1990.

Australia
Continent republic, SE of Asia

Area: 2,967,893 sq. mi. (7,686,850 sq. km.)
Population: 20,434,000
Language(s): English

Monetary unit: Australian dollar
Economy: mining (gold, diamonds, uranium), gas, oil, food processing, wool, transport equipment

After Australian confederation was achieved on Jan. 1, 1901, the flag was chosen in a competition. Like the blue flags of British colonies, it displays the Union Jack in the canton. Also shown are the Southern Cross and a "Commonwealth Star." The design became official on May 22, 1909, and it was recognized as the national flag on Feb. 14, 1954.

Austria
Republic, cen. Europe

Area: 32,382 sq. mi. (83,870 sq. km.)
Population: 8,200,000
Language(s): German

Monetary unit: euro
Economy: machinery, ski equipment, motor vehicles, chemicals, mining (minerals, salt), iron, steel

The colors of the Austrian coat of arms date from the seal of Duke Frederick II in 1230. With the fall of the Austro-Hungarian Empire in 1918, the new Austrian republic adopted the red-white-red flag. The white is sometimes said to represent the Danube River. An imperial eagle, an Austrian symbol for centuries, is added to government flags.

Azerbaijan
Republic, SW Asia

Area: 33,436 sq. mi. (86,600 sq. km.)
Population: 8,120,000
Language(s): Azerbaijani

Monetary unit: Azerbaijani manat
Economy: oil, natural gas, oilfield equipment, steel, iron ore, agriculture (tea, fruit, tobacco)

In the early 20th century anti-Russian nationalists exhorted the Azerbaijanis to "Turkify, Islamicize, and Europeanize," and the 1917 flag was associated with Turkey and Islam. In 1918 the crescent and star (also symbols of Turkic peoples) were introduced. Suppressed under Soviet rule, the flag was readopted on Feb. 5, 1991.

Bahamas
Islands commonwealth, Caribbean

Area: 5,386 sq. mi. (13,950 sq. km.)
Population: 305,700
Language(s): English

Monetary unit: Bahamian dollar
Economy: tourism, banking, shellfish, pharmaceuticals, rum, fruit

The flag of The Bahamas was adopted on July 10, 1973, the date of independence from Britain. Several entries from a competition were combined to create the design. The two aquamarine stripes are for the surrounding waters, the gold stripe is for the sand and other rich land resources, and the black triangle is for the people and their strength.

Bahrain

Islamic kingdom, Persian Gulf

Area: 257 sq. mi. (665 sq. km.)
Population: 708,600
Language(s): Arabic

Monetary unit: Bahraini dinar
Economy: oil, petroleum refining, metal processing, banking, ship repairing

Red was the color of the Kharijite Muslims of Bahrain about 1820, and white was chosen to show amity with the British. The flag was recognized in 1933 but was used long before. The current flag law was adopted in 2002. The five white points represent the five pillars of Islam.

Bangladesh

Republic, S Asia

Area: 55,598 sq. mi. (144,000 sq. km.)
Population: 150,448,000
Language(s): Bengali, English

Monetary unit: taka
Economy: agriculture (rice, jute, tea), fertilizer, newsprint

The flag is dark green to symbolize Islam, plant life, and the hope placed in Bengali youth. Its original design included a red disk and a silhouette of the country. On Jan. 13, 1972, the silhouette was removed and the disk shifted off-center. The disk is the "rising sun of a new country" colored by the blood of those who fought for independence.

Barbados

Island republic, Caribbean

Area: 166 sq. mi. (431 sq. km.)
Population: 280,900
Language(s): English

Monetary unit: Barbadian dollar
Economy: tourism, sugar, molasses, rum, light manufacturing, electrical components

The flag was designed by Grantley Prescod, a Barbadian art teacher. Its stripes of blue-yellow-blue are for sea, sand, and sky. The black trident head was inspired by the colonial flag of Barbados, which featured a trident-wielding Poseidon, or Neptune, figure. The flag was first hoisted on Nov. 30, 1966, the date of independence from Britain.

Belarus

Republic, E cen. Europe

Area: 80,154 sq. mi. (207,600 sq. km.)
Population: 9,725,000
Language(s): Belarusian, Russian

Monetary unit: Belarusian ruble
Economy: machine tools, motor vehicles, mineral products, textiles, grains, flax, sugar beets

In 1951 the former Soviet republic created a striped flag in red (for communism) and green (for fields and forests), with the hammer, sickle, and star of communism. In 1991–95 an older design was used, but the Soviet-era flag was then altered and readopted without communist symbols. The vertical stripe is typical of embroidery on peasant clothing.

Belgium

Constitutional monarchy, NW Europe

Area: 11,787 sq. mi. (30,528 sq. km.)
Population: 10,309,800
Language(s): Dutch, French, German

Monetary unit: euro
Economy: engineering, scientific instruments, transportation equipment, textiles, processed food

A gold shield and a black lion appeared in the seal of Count Philip of Flanders as early as 1162, and in 1787 cockades of black-yellow-red were used in a Brussels revolt against Austria. After a war for independence, the flag was recognized on Jan. 23, 1831. By 1838 the design, which was influenced by the French tricolor, became standard.

Belize

Republic, Central America

Area: 8,867 sq. mi. (22,966 sq. km.)
Population: 294,400
Language(s): Spanish, Creole, English

Monetary unit: Belizean dollar
Economy: tourism, textiles, fish, sugar, bananas, citrus fruits, timber

The flag of Belize (former British Honduras) was based on the flag of the nationalist People's United Party. Its coat of arms shows a mahogany tree, a shield, and a Creole and a Mestizo. The red stripes, symbolic of the United Democratic Party, were added on independence day (Sept. 21, 1981), when the flag was first officially hoisted.

Benin

Republic, W Africa

Area: 43,483 sq. mi. (112,620 sq. km.)
Population: 8,078,000
Language(s): French

Monetary unit: West African States franc
Economy: subsistence agriculture, textiles, food processing (palm products, cotton, cocoa)

Adopted on Nov. 16, 1959, the flag of the former French colony used the Pan-African colors. Yellow was for the savannas in the north and green was for the palm groves in the south. Red stood for the blood of patriots. In 1975 a Marxist-oriented government replaced the flag, but after the demise of communism it was restored on Aug. 1, 1990.

Bhutan

Transitional state, S Asia

Area: 18,147 sq. mi. (47,000 sq. km.)
Population: 2,328,000
Language(s): Dzongkha (Tibetan)

Monetary unit: ngultrum
Economy: subsistence farming, animal husbandry, cement, wood products, fruits

The flag of Bhutan ("Land of the Dragon") features a dragon grasping jewels; this represents natural wealth and perfection. The white color is for purity and loyalty, the gold is for regal power, and the orange-red is for Buddhist sects and religious commitment. The flag may have been introduced as recently as 1971.

Bolivia

Republic, South America

Area: 424,162 sq. mi. (1,098,580 sq. km.)
Population: 9,119,000
Language(s): Spanish, Aymara, Quechua

Monetary unit: boliviano
Economy: mining, smelting, food, beverages (soybeans, coffee), natural gas

A version of the flag was first adopted on July 25, 1826, but on Nov. 5, 1851, the order of the stripes was changed to red-yellow-green. The colors were often used by the Aymara and Quechua peoples; in addition, red is for the valor of the army, yellow for mineral resources, and green for the land. The current flag law dates from July 14, 1888.

Bosnia and Herzegovina

Republic, SE Europe

Area: 19,741 sq. mi. (51,129 sq. km.)
Population: 4,552,000
Language(s): Bosnian, Croatian, Serbian

Monetary unit: marka
Economy: mining (iron ore, lead, zinc), vehicle assembly, textiles, wood products

The medium blue field is bisected by a yellow triangle (representing equality between the three peoples of the nation) with seven full and two half stars in white along the hypotenuse, intended to represent Europe. The half stars are intended to suggest the infinity of the star pattern.

Botswana

Republic, S Africa

Area: 231,803 sq. mi. (600,370 sq. km.)
Population: 1,816,000
Language(s): English, Setswana

Monetary unit: pula
Economy: mining (diamonds, copper), tourism, food processing, financial services

Adopted in 1966, the flag was designed to contrast symbolically with that of neighboring South Africa, where apartheid was then in effect. The black and white stripes in Botswana's flag are for racial cooperation and equality. The background symbolizes water, a scarce resource in the expansive Kalahari Desert.

Brazil

Republic, South America

Area: 3,284,426 sq. mi. (8,506,663 sq. km.)
Population: 190,011,000
Language(s): Portuguese

Monetary unit: real
Economy: agriculture (coffee, soybeans), livestock, mining, aircraft, motor vehicles, machinery

The original flag was introduced on Sept. 7, 1822, when Dom Pedro declared independence from Portugal. In 1889 the blue disk and the motto Ordem e Progresso ("Order and Progress") were added. The Brazilian states and territories are symbolized by the constellations of stars. Green is for the land, while yellow is for gold and other mineral wealth.

Brunei

Constitutional sultanate, SE Asia

Area: 2,228 sq. mi. (5,770 sq. km.)
Population: 374,600
Language(s): Malay, English

Monetary unit: Bruneian dollar
Economy: oil, natural gas production and refining, agriculture, forestry, fishing

When Brunei became a British protectorate in 1906, diagonal stripes were added to its yellow flag. The yellow stood for the sultan, while white and black were for his two chief ministers. Introduced in September 1959, the coat of arms has a parasol as a symbol of royalty and a crescent and inscription for the state religion, Islam.

Bulgaria

Republic, SE Europe

Area: 42,822 sq. mi. (110,910 sq. km.)
Population: 7,323,000
Language(s): Bulgarian

Monetary unit: lev
Economy: mining (coal, copper, zinc), chemicals, machinery, textiles

The flag was based on the Russian flag of 1699, but with green substituted for blue. Under communist rule, a red star and other symbols were added, but the old tricolor was reestablished on Nov. 27, 1990. The white is for peace, love, and freedom; green is for agriculture; and red is for the independence struggle and military courage.

Burkina Faso

Republic, W Africa

Area: 105,869 sq. mi. (274,200 sq. km.)
Population: 14,326,000
Language(s): French

Monetary unit: West African States franc
Economy: subsistence agriculture, cotton, livestock, gold

On Aug. 4, 1984, Upper Volta was renamed Burkina Faso by the revolutionary government of Thomas Sankara, and the current flag was adopted with Pan-African colors. The yellow star symbolizes leadership and revolutionary principles. The red stripe is said to stand for the revolutionary struggle, while the green stripe represents hope and abundance.

Burundi

Republic, E cen. Africa

Area: 10,745 sq. mi. (27,830 sq. km.)
Population: 8,391,000
Language(s): Kirundi, French

Monetary unit: Burundi franc
Economy: subsistence agriculture, coffee, tea, hides, assembly of imported components

The flag became official on June 28, 1967. Its white saltire (diagonal cross) and central disk symbolize peace. The red color is for the independence struggle, and green is for hope. The stars correspond to the national motto, "Unity, Work, Progress." They also recall the Tutsi, Hutu, and Twa peoples and the pledge to God, king, and country.

Cambodia

Constitutional monarchy, SE Asia

Area: 69,900 sq. mi. (181,040 sq. km.)
Population: 13,996,000
Language(s): Khmer

Monetary unit: riel
Economy: subsistence farming, tourism, textiles, rice milling, wood products

Artistic representations of the central ruined temple of Angkor Wat, a 12th-century temple complex, have appeared on Khmer flags since the 19th century. The current flag design dates to 1948. It was replaced in 1970 under the Khmer Republic and in 1976 under communist leadership, but it was again hoisted on June 29, 1993.

Cameroon

Republic, W cen. Africa

Area: 183,567 sq. mi. (475,440 sq. km.)
Population: 18,060,000
Language(s): French, English

Monetary unit: Central African States franc
Economy: petroleum products, aluminum, cocoa, coffee, textiles, timber, rubber

The flag was officially hoisted on Oct. 29, 1957, prior to independence (Jan. 1, 1960). Green is for the vegetation of the south, yellow for the savannas of the north, and red for union and sovereignty. Two yellow stars were added (for the British Cameroons) in 1961, but these were replaced in 1975 by a single star symbolizing national unity.

Canada

Republic, North America

Area: 3,851,809 sq. mi. (9,976,185 sq. km.)
Population: 33,390,000
Language(s): English, French

Monetary unit: Canadian dollar
Economy: motor vehicles, aircraft, industrial machinery, high-tech equipment, paper, pulp, food products

During Canada's first century of independence the Union Jack was still flown but with a Canadian coat of arms. The maple leaf design, with the national colors, became official on Feb. 15, 1965. Since 1868 the maple leaf has been a national symbol, and in 1921 a red leaf in the coat of arms stood for Canadian sacrifice during World War I.

Cape Verde

Islands republic, off W Africa

Area: 1,557 sq. mi. (4,033 sq. km.)
Population: 423,600
Language(s): Portuguese

Monetary unit: escudo
Economy: fish processing, textiles, salt mining, ship repair, sugar, fruits, coffee

After the elections of 1991, the flag was established with a blue field bearing a ring of 10 yellow stars to symbolize the 10 main islands of Cape Verde. The stripes of white-red-white suggest peace and national resolve. Red, white, and blue also are a symbolic link to Portugal and the United States. The new flag became official on Sept. 25, 1992.

Central African Republic

Republic, cen. Africa

Area: 240,534 sq. mi. (622,984 sq. km.)
Population: 4,369,000
Language(s): French, Sangho

Monetary unit: Central African States franc
Economy: subsistence farming, mining (diamonds, gold), timber, vehicle assembly

Barthélemy Boganda designed the flag in 1958. It combines French and Pan-African colors. The star is a guide for progress and an emblem of unity. The blue stripe is for liberty, grandeur, and the sky; the white is for purity, equality, and candor; the green and yellow are for forests and savannas; and the red is for the blood of humankind.

Chad

Republic, N cen. Africa

Area: 495,752 sq. mi. (1,284,000 sq. km.)
Population: 9,886,000
Language(s): Arabic, French

Monetary unit: Central African States franc
Economy: subsistence farming, livestock raising, oil, textiles, meatpacking

In 1958 a tricolor of green-yellow-red (the Pan-African colors) was proposed, but that design was already used by the Mali-Senegal federation, another former French colony. Approved on Nov. 6, 1959, the current flag substitutes blue for the original green stripe. Blue is for hope and sky, yellow for the sun, and red for the unity of the nation.

Chile

Republic, South America

Area: 292,258 sq. mi. (756,946 sq. km.)
Population: 16,285,000
Language(s): Spanish

Monetary unit: Chilean peso
Economy: mining (copper), timber, pulp, paper, chemicals, wine, fish processing

On Oct. 18, 1817, the flag was established for the new republic. The blue is for the sky, and the star is "a guide on the path of progress and honor." The white is for the snow of the Andes Mountains while the red recalls the blood of patriots. In the 15th century the Araucanian Indians gave red-white-blue sashes to their warriors.

China

Communist state, Asia

Area: 3,705,386 sq. mi. (9,596,960 sq. km.)
Population: 1,321,852,000
Language(s): Mandarin Chinese

Monetary unit: yuan
Economy: mining, steel, medical, high-tech equipment, textiles, consumer products

The flag was hoisted on Oct. 1, 1949. The red is for communism and the Han Chinese. The large star was originally for the Communist Party, and the smaller stars were for the proletariat, the peasants, the petty bourgeoisie, and the "patriotic capitalists." The large star was later said to stand for China, the smaller stars for minorities.

Colombia
Republic, South America

Area: 439,736 sq. mi. (1,138,910 sq. km.)
Population: 44,380,000
Language(s): Spanish
Monetary unit: Colombian peso
Economy: oil, mining (platinum, emeralds), textiles, chemicals, coffee, bananas, cocaine

In the early 19th century "the Liberator" Simon Bolivar created a yellow-blue-red flag for New Granada (which included Colombia, Venezuela, Panama, and Ecuador). The flag symbolized the yellow gold of the New World separated by the blue ocean from the red of "bloody Spain." The present Colombian flag was established on Nov. 26, 1861.

Comoros
Islands republic, off SE Africa

Area: 838 sq. mi. (2,170 sq. km.)
Population: 711,400
Language(s): Arabic, French
Monetary unit: Comoran franc
Economy: agriculture (vanilla, cloves, essential oils, copra), tourism, perfume distillation

The Comoros flag, adopted in the 1990s, contains the green triangle and crescent that are traditional symbols of Islam. The four stars and four horizontal stripes represent the country's main islands of Mwali, Njazidja, Nzwani and Mayotte, this last, a dependency of France, also claimed by Comoros.

Congo (Democratic Rep.)
Republic, Equatorial Africa

Area: 905,568 sq. mi. (2,345,410 sq. km.)
Population: 65,752,000
Language(s): French, Lingala
Monetary unit: Congolese franc
Economy: mining and processing (diamonds, copper, zinc), tobacco, palm oil, bananas, rubber

A new flag for the Democratic Republic of the Congo was unveiled on February 18, 2006, upon the adoption of a new constitution. This flag is similar in style to the one flown between 1963-1971, with a lighter blue color now used. The blue in the flag symbolizes peace; red the blood of the country's martyrs; yellow the country's wealth; and the star for the country's radiant future.

Congo (Republic)
Republic, Equatorial Africa

Area: 132,047 sq. mi. (342,000 sq. km.)
Population: 3,801,000
Language(s): French, local languages
Monetary unit: Central African States franc
Economy: petroleum, diamonds, plywood, peanuts, bananas, sugarcane, coffee

First adopted on Sept. 15, 1959, the flag uses the Pan-African colors. Green was originally said to stand for Congo's agriculture and forests, and yellow for friendship and the nobility of the people, but the red was unexplained. Altered in 1969 by a Marxist government, the flag was restored to its initial form on June 10, 1991.

Costa Rica
Republic, Central America

Area: 19,730 sq. mi. (51,100 sq. km.)
Population: 4,134,000
Language(s): Spanish
Monetary unit: Costa Rican colón
Economy: tourism, textiles, plastics, electronic, medical equipment, coffee, bananas, sugar

The blue and white stripes originated in the flag colors of the United Provinces of Central America (1823–40). On Sept. 29, 1848, the red stripe was added to symbolize sunlight, civilization, and "true independence." The current design of the coat of arms, which is included on government flags, was established in 1964.

Croatia
Republic, SE Europe

Area: 21,831 sq. mi. (56,542 sq. km.)
Population: 4,493,000
Language(s): Croatian
Monetary unit: kuna
Economy: chemicals, plastics, machine tools, electronics, petroleum refining, tourism

During the European uprisings of 1848, Croatians designed a flag based on that of Russia. In April 1941 the fascistic Ustasa used this flag, adding the checkered shield of Croatia. A communist star soon replaced the shield, but the current flag was adopted on Dec. 22, 1990. Atop the shield is a "crown" inlaid with historic coats of arms.

Cuba
Island communist state, Caribbean

Area: 42,803 sq. mi. (110,860 sq. km)
Population: 11,394,000
Language(s): Spanish
Monetary unit: Cuban peso
Economy: tourism, sugar, coffee, rice, cigars, textiles, cement

In the mid-19th century Cuban exiles designed the flag, which was later carried into battle against Spanish forces. It was adopted on May 20, 1902. The stripes were for the three military districts of Cuba and the purity of the patriotic cause. The red triangle was for strength, constancy, and equality, and the white star symbolized independence.

Cyprus
Island republic, E Mediterranean

The island of Cyprus is de facto divided between predominately Greek Republic of Cyprus (internationally recognized) and the predominantly Turkish northern third of the island (Turkish republic), recognized solely by Turkey and with the economy basically dependent on Turkey.

Area: (island) 3,571 sq. mi. (9,250 sq. km.)
Population: 788,500
Language(s): Greek, Turkish
Monetary unit: euro
Economy: tourism, food, beverage processing, cement, gypsum, ship repair, textiles, clay products

On Aug. 7, 1960, the Republic of Cyprus was proclaimed with a national flag of a neutral design. It bears the island in silhouette and a green olive wreath, for peace. In 1974 there was a Turkish invasion of the island. A puppet government, which adopted a flag based on the Turkish model, was set up on the northern third of Cyprus.

Czech Republic
Republic, cen. Europe

Area: 30,450 sq. mi. (78,866 sq. km.)
Population: 10,229,000
Language(s): Czech
Monetary unit: Czech koruna
Economy: machinery, transport equipment, chemicals, coal, steel, wheat, sugar beets, fruit

When Czechs, Slovaks, and Ruthenians united to form Czechoslovakia in 1918, a simple white-red bicolor flag was chosen; in 1920 it incorporated a blue triangle at the hoist. Czechoslovakia divided into Slovakia and the Czech Republic in 1993, but the latter country readopted the Czechoslovak flag as its own.

Denmark
Constitutional monarchy, N Europe

Area: 16,639 sq. mi. (43,094 sq. km.)
Population: 5,468,000
Language(s): Danish
Monetary unit: Danish krone
Economy: metal processing, chemicals, machinery, electronics, furniture, dairy products, oil, gas

A traditional story claims that the Danish flag fell from heaven on June 15, 1219, but the previously existing war flag of the Holy Roman Empire was of a similar design, with its red field symbolizing battle and its white cross suggesting divine favor. In 1849 the state and military flag was altered and adopted as a symbol of the Danish people.

Djibouti
Republic, E Africa

Area: 8,880 sq. mi. (23,000 sq. km.)
Population: 496,400
Language(s): Arabic, French
Monetary unit: Djiboutian franc
Economy: livestock herding, hides, salt, agricultural processing, fishing

First raised by anti-French separatists, the flag was officially hoisted on June 27, 1977. The color of the Afar people, green, stands for prosperity. The color of the Issa people, light blue, symbolizes sea and sky, and recalls the flag of Somalia. The white triangle is for equality and peace; the red star is for unity and independence.

Dominica
Island republic, Caribbean

Area: 291 sq. mi. (754 sq. km.)
Population: 72,400
Language(s): English
Monetary unit: East Caribbean dollar
Economy: bananas, cocoa, coconuts, coconut oil, copra, limes; soap

The flag was hoisted on Nov. 3, 1978, at independence from Britain. Its background symbolizes forests; its central disk is red for socialism and bears a sisserou (a rare local bird). The stars are for the parishes of the island. The cross of yellow, white, and black is for the Carib, Caucasian, and African peoples and for fruit, water, and soil.

Dominican Republic
Republic, Hispaniola, Caribbean

Area: 18,815 sq. mi. (48,730 sq. km.)
Population: 9,366,000
Language(s): Spanish

Monetary unit: Dominican peso
Economy: tourism, sugar processing, mining, textiles, cigars, consumer goods, coffee

On Feb. 28, 1844, Spanish-speaking Dominican revolutionaries added a white cross to the simple blue-red flag of eastern Hispaniola in order to emphasize their Christian heritage. On November 6 of that same year the new constitution established the flag but with the colors at the fly end reversed so that the blue and red would alternate.

Ecuador
Republic, South America

Area: 109,483 sq. mi. (283,560 sq. km.)
Population: 13,756,000
Language(s): Spanish, Quechua

Monetary unit: U.S. dollar
Economy: petroleum, textiles, wood products, chemicals, coffee, bananas, shrimp, cut flowers

Victorious against the Spanish on May 24, 1822, Antonio José de Sucre hoisted a yellow-blue-red flag. Other flags were later used, but on Sept. 26, 1860, the current flag design was adopted. The coat of arms is displayed on the flag when it is used abroad or for official purposes, to distinguish it from the flag of Colombia.

Egypt
Republic, NE Africa and Sinai Peninsula

Area: 386,662 sq. mi. (1,001,450 sq. km.)
Population: 80,335,000
Language(s): Arabic, English, French

Monetary unit: Egyptian pound
Economy: tourism, oil, mining, chemicals, salt, textiles, cotton, wheat, sugarcane

The 1952 revolt against British rule established the red-white-black flag with a central gold eagle. Two stars replaced the eagle in 1958, and in 1972 a federation with Syria and Libya was formed, adding instead the hawk of Quraysh (the tribe of Muhammad). On Oct. 9, 1984, the eagle of Saladin (a major 12th-century ruler) was substituted.

El Salvador
Republic, Central America

Area: 8,124 sq. mi. (21,040 sq. km.)
Population: 6,948,000
Language(s): Spanish

Monetary unit: U.S. dollar
Economy: petroleum, chemicals, fertilizer, textiles, light assembly, coffee, sugar, shrimp

In the early 19th century, a blue-white-blue flag was designed for the short-lived United Provinces of Central America, in which El Salvador was a member. On Sept. 15, 1912, the flag was reintroduced in El Salvador. The coat of arms in the center resembles that used by the former federation and includes the national motto, "God, Union, Liberty."

Equatorial Guinea
Republic, W cen. Africa

Area: 10,831 sq. mi. (28,051 sq. km.)
Population: 551,200
Language(s): Spanish, French

Monetary unit: Central African States franc
Economy: oil, gas, timber, subsistence farming, cocoa, coffee, palm oil, fishing

The flag was first hoisted at independence (Oct. 12, 1968). Its coat of arms shows the silk-cotton tree, or god tree, which recalls early Spanish influence in the area. The sea, which links parts of the country, is reflected in the blue triangle. The green is for vegetation, white is for peace, and red is for the blood of martyrs in the liberation struggle.

Eritrea
Transitional state, E Africa

Area: 46,842 sq. mi. (121,320 sq. km.)
Population: 4,907,000
Language(s): Arabic, local languages

Monetary unit: nakfa
Economy: subsistence farming, herding, food processing, textiles, small manufacturing, salt

Officially hoisted at the proclamation of independence on May 24, 1993, the national flag was based on that of the Eritrean People's Liberation Front. The red triangle is for the blood of patriots, the green is for agriculture, and the blue is for maritime resources. Around a central branch is a circle of olive branches with 30 leaves.

Estonia
Republic, N Europe

Area: 17,462 sq. mi. (45,226 sq. km.)
Population: 1,316,000
Language(s): Estonian, Russian

Monetary unit: euro
Economy: machinery, electronics, telecommunications, wood, paper, furniture, textiles

In the late 19th century an Estonian students' association adopted the blue-black-white flag. Blue was said to stand for the sky, black for the soil, and white for aspirations to freedom and homeland. The flag was officially recognized on July 4, 1920. It was replaced under Soviet rule, and readopted on Oct. 20, 1988.

Ethiopia
Republic, E Africa

Area: 435,186 sq. mi. (1,127,127 sq. km.)
Population: 76,512,000
Language(s): Amarigna, local languages

Monetary unit: birr
Economy: agriculture, food processing, hides, skins, gold, textiles, chemicals

The flag is red (for sacrifice), green (for labor, development, and fertility), and yellow (for hope, justice, and equality). Tricolor pennants were used prior to the official flag of Oct. 6, 1897, and a tricolor was flown by anti-government forces in 1991. On Feb. 6, 1996, the disk (for peace) and star (for unity and the future) were added.

Fiji
Islands republic, S Pacific

Area: 7,054 sq. mi. (18,270 sq. km.)
Population: 918,700
Language(s): English, Fijian, Hindustani

Monetary unit: Fijian dollar
Economy: subsistence farming, fishing, sugar, copra, fruit, gold, tourism

The national flag, introduced on Oct. 10, 1970, is a modified version of Fiji's colonial flag. It includes the Union Jack on a light blue field. The shield has the red cross of St. George on a white background, below a yellow lion, which holds a cocoa pod. Local symbols (sugar cane, coconuts, bananas, and the Fiji dove) are also shown.

Finland
Republic, N Europe

Area: 130,559 sq. mi. (338,145 sq. km.)
Population: 5,238,000
Language(s): Finnish, Swedish

Monetary unit: euro
Economy: timber, pulp, mining, electronics, scientific instruments, shipbuilding

In 1862, while Finland was under Russian control, a flag was proposed that would have a white background for the snows of Finland and blue for its lakes. The blue was in the form of a "Nordic cross" similar to those used by other Scandinavian countries. The flag was officially adopted by the newly independent country on May 29, 1918.

France
Republic, W Europe

Area: 210,025 sq. mi. (543,965 sq. km.)
Population: 60,876,000
Language(s): French

Monetary unit: euro
Economy: machinery, automobiles, aircraft, chemicals, engineering, food processing, wine, tourism

From 1789 blue and red, the traditional colors of Paris, were included in flags with Bourbon royal white. In 1794 the tricolor was made official. It embodied liberty, equality, fraternity, democracy, secularism, and modernization, but there is no symbolism attached to the individual colors. It has been the sole national flag since March 5, 1848.

Gabon
Republic, W cen. Africa

Area: 103,347 sq. mi. (267,667 sq. km.)
Population: 1,455,000
Language(s): French

Monetary unit: Central African States franc
Economy: oil, timber, mining (manganese, gold, uranium), cocoa, coffee, palm oil, ship repair

After proclaiming independence from France, Gabon adopted its national flag on Aug. 9, 1960. The central yellow stripe is for the Equator, which runs through the country. Green stands for the tropical forests that are one of Gabon's most important resources. Blue represents its extensive coast along the South Atlantic Ocean.

Gambia

Republic, W Africa

Area: 4,363 sq. mi. (11,300 sq. km.)
Population: 1,688,000
Language(s): English

Monetary unit: dalasi
Economy: agriculture (peanuts, palm kernels), hides, machine assembly, metalworking

The Gambia achieved independence from Britain on Feb. 18, 1965, under the current flag. The center stripe is blue to symbolize the Gambia River. The red stripe is for the sun and the equator. The green stripe is for agricultural produce, while the white stripes are said to stand for peace and unity.

Georgia

Republic, SW Asia

Area: 26,911 sq. mi. (69,700 sq. km.)
Population: 4,646,000
Language(s): Georgian, Russian

Monetary unit: lari
Economy: agriculture (citrus fruits, tea, hazelnuts, wine grapes), mining, chemicals, steel products

The five-cross design of the Georgian flag is believed to have been used in the Middle Ages. The central cross is the cross of St. George, the patron saint of Georgia. The red and white color is traditional, used in the flags of the independent kingdoms that eventually united to form Georgia. The current flag was adopted in 2004.

Germany

Republic, cen. Europe

Area: 137,847 sq. mi. (357,021 sq. km.)
Population: 82,401,000
Language(s): German

Monetary unit: euro
Economy: iron, steel, machine tools, electronics, wine and beer, chemicals, motor vehicles

In the early 19th century, German nationalists displayed black, gold, and red on their uniforms and tricolor flags. The current flag was used officially from 1848 to 1852 and readopted by West Germany on May 9, 1949. East Germany flew a similar flag but only the flag of West Germany was maintained upon reunification in 1990.

Ghana

Republic, W Africa

Area: 92,456 sq. mi. (239,460 sq. km.)
Population: 22,931,000
Language(s): English, local languages

Monetary unit: cedi
Economy: subsistence farming, mining (diamonds, gold), light manufacturing, cocoa, palm oil

On March 6, 1957, independence from Britain was granted and a flag, based on the red-white-green tricolor of a nationalist organization, was hoisted. A black "lodestar of African freedom" was added and the white stripe was changed to yellow, symbolizing wealth. Green is for forests and farms, red for the independence struggle.

Greece

Republic, S Europe

Area: 50,942 sq. mi. (131,940 sq. km.)
Population: 10,706,000
Language(s): Greek

Monetary unit: euro
Economy: tourism, food processing, mining, metal products, petroleum, textiles

In March 1822, during the revolt against Ottoman rule, the first Greek national flags were adopted; the most recent revision to the flag was made on Dec. 22, 1978. The colors symbolize Greek Orthodoxy while the cross stands for "the wisdom of God, freedom and country." The stripes are for the battle cry for independence: "Freedom or Death."

Grenada

Island republic, Caribbean

Area: 133 sq. mi. (344 sq. km.)
Population: 90,000
Language(s): English

Monetary unit: East Caribbean dollar
Economy: tourism, light assembly, banking, textiles, nutmeg, mace, bananas

Grenada's flag was officially hoisted on Feb. 3, 1974. Its background is green for vegetation and yellow for the sun, and its red border is symbolic of harmony and unity. The seven stars are for the original administrative subdivisions of Grenada. Nutmeg, a crop for which the "Isle of Spice" is internationally known, is represented as well.

Guatemala

Republic, Central America

Area: 42,043 sq. mi. (108,890 sq. km.)
Population: 12,728,000
Language(s): Spanish

Monetary unit: quetzal
Economy: coffee, bananas, sugar, timber, petroleum, chemicals, metals, rubber, textiles

The flag was introduced in 1871. It has blue and white stripes (colors of the former United Provinces of Central America) and a coat of arms with the quetzal (the national bird), a scroll, a wreath, and crossed rifles and sabres. Different artistic variations have been used but on Sept. 12, 1968, the present pattern was established.

Guinea

Republic, W Africa

Area: 94,926 sq. mi. (245,857 sq. km.)
Population: 9,948,000
Language(s): French

Monetary unit: Guinean franc
Economy: mining (bauxite, gold, diamonds), light manufacturing, bananas, coffee, pineapples

The flag was adopted on Nov. 12, 1958, one month after independence from France. Its simple design was influenced by the French tricolor. The red is said to be a symbol of sacrifice and labor, while the yellow is for mineral wealth, the tropical sun, and justice. Green symbolizes agricultural wealth and the solidarity of the people.

Guinea-Bissau

Republic, W Africa

Area: 13,946 sq. mi. (36,120 sq. km.)
Population: 1,473,000
Language(s): Portuguese

Monetary unit: West African States franc
Economy: cashews, peanuts, fish, seafood processing, timber, potential oil exports

The flag has been used since the declaration of independence from Portugal on Sept. 24, 1973. The black star on the red stripe was for African Party leadership, the people, and their will to live in dignity, freedom, and peace. Yellow was for the harvest and other rewards of work, and green was for the nation's vast jungles and agricultural lands.

Guyana

Republic, South America

Area: 83,000 sq. mi. (214,970 sq. km.)
Population: 769,000
Language(s): English

Monetary unit: Guyanese dollar
Economy: mining (bauxite, diamonds, gold), sugar, rum, shrimp, timber

Upon independence from Britain on May 26, 1966, the flag was first hoisted. The green stands for jungles and fields, white suggests the rivers which are the basis for the Indian word *guiana* ("land of waters"), red is for zeal and sacrifice in nation-building, and black is for perseverance. The flag is nicknamed "The Golden Arrowhead."

Haiti

Republic, Hispaniola, Caribbean

Area: 10,714 sq. mi. (27,750 sq. km.)
Population: 8,706,000
Language(s): Creole, French

Monetary unit: gourde
Economy: subsistence farming, sugar refining, flour milling, fruits, textiles, cement

After the French Revolution of 1789, Haiti underwent a slave revolt, but the French tricolor continued in use until 1803. The new blue-red flag represented the black and mulatto populations only. A black-red flag was used by various dictators, including François "Papa Doc" Duvalier and his son, but on Feb. 25, 1986, the old flag was reestablished.

Honduras

Republic, Central America

Area: 43,278 sq. mi. (112,090 sq. km.)
Population: 7,484,000
Language(s): Spanish

Monetary unit: lempira
Economy: coffee, bananas, sugar, tobacco, fishing, textiles, mining (zinc, silver)

Since Feb. 16, 1866, the Honduran flag has retained the blue-white-blue design of the flag of the former United Provinces of Central America, but with five central stars symbolizing the states of Honduras, El Salvador, Nicaragua, Costa Rica, and Guatemala. The flag design has often been associated with Central American reunification attempts.

Hungary

Republic, cen. Europe

Area: 35,919 sq. mi. (93,030 sq. km.)
Population: 9,956,000
Language(s): Hungarian

Monetary unit: forint
Economy: machinery, motor vehicles, pharmaceuticals, sugar beets, mining, textiles

The colors of the Hungarian flag were mentioned in a 1608 coronation ceremony, but they may have been used since the 13th century. The tricolor was adopted on Oct. 12, 1957, after the abortive revolution of 1956. The white is said to symbolize Hungary's rivers, the green its mountains, and the red the blood shed in its many battles.

Iceland

Island republic, off NW Europe

Area: 39,769 sq. mi. (103,000 sq. km.)
Population: 301,900
Language(s): Icelandic

Monetary unit: Icelandic krona
Economy: fishing and fish processing, aluminum, animal products, tourism, cement

Approval for an Icelandic flag was given by the king of Denmark on June 19, 1915; it became a national flag on Dec. 1, 1918, when the separate kingdom of Iceland was proclaimed. The flag was retained upon the creation of a republic on June 17, 1944. The design has a typical "Scandinavian cross".

India

Republic, S Asia

Area: 1,269,346 sq. mi. (3,287,590 sq. km.)
Population: 1,129,866,000
Language(s): Hindi, English

Monetary unit: Indian rupee
Economy: agriculture, mining, cut diamonds, crude oil, software services, textiles, machinery

Earlier versions of the flag were used from the 1920s, but the current flag was hoisted officially on July 22, 1947. The orange was said to stand for courage and sacrifice, white for peace and truth, and green for faith and chivalry. The blue wheel is a chakra, associated with Emperor Asoka's attempts to unite India in the 3rd century BC.

Indonesia

Republic, SE Asia

Area: 741,000 sq. mi. (1,919,440 sq. km.)
Population: 234,694,000
Language(s): Indonesian

Monetary unit: Indonesian rupiah
Economy: oil, natural gas, timber, plywood, rubber; tourism, cacao, nutmeg, palm oil, tea

Indonesia's red and white flag was associated with the Majapahit empire which existed from the 13th to the 16th century. It was adopted on Aug. 17, 1945, and it remained after Indonesia won its independence from The Netherlands in 1949. Red is for courage and white for honesty. The flag is identical, except in dimensions, to the flag of Monaco.

Iran

Islamic republic, SW Asia

Area: 636,296 sq. mi. (1,648,000 sq. km.)
Population: 65,398,000
Language(s): Farsi (Persian)

Monetary unit: Iranian rial
Economy: oil, natural gas, mining, metals, vegetables oils, caviar, textiles, carpets

The tricolor flag was recognized in 1906 but altered after the revolution of 1979. Along the central stripe are the Arabic words Allahu akbar ("God is great"), repeated 22 times. The coat of arms can be read as a rendition of the word Allah, as a globe, or as two crescents. The green is for Islam, white is for peace, and red is for valor.

Iraq

Republic, SW Asia

Area: 168,754 sq. mi. (437,072 sq. km.)
Population: 27,500,000
Language(s): Arabic, Kurdish

Monetary unit: Iraqi dinar
Economy: oil, natural gas, agriculture, livestock, textiles

Adopted on July 30, 1963, the Iraqi flag is based on the liberation flag first flown in Egypt in 1952. Red is for the willingness to shed blood, green is for Arab lands, black is for past suffering, and white is for purity. On Jan. 14, 1991, the Arabic inscription "God is Great" was added, and in 2008 the script was restyled.

Ireland

Republic, off NW Europe

Area: 27,135 sq. mi. (70,280 sq. km.)
Population: 4,109,000
Language(s): English, Irish Gaelic

Monetary unit: euro
Economy: engineering, machinery, tourism, brewing, distilling, mining, food products, textiles

In the 19th century various tricolor flags and ribbons became symbolic of Irish opposition to British rule. Many of them included the colors green (for the Catholics), orange (for the Protestants), and white (for the peace between the two groups). The tricolor in its modern form was recognized by the constitution on Dec. 29, 1937.

Israel

Republic, SW Asia

Area: 8,019 sq. mi. (20,770 sq. km.)
Population: 6,427,000
Language(s): Hebrew, Arabic

Monetary unit: Israeli shekel
Economy: high-technology, mining, textiles, chemicals, food processing, diamond cutting

Symbolic of the traditional tallit, or Jewish prayer shawl, and including the Star of David, the flag was used from the late 19th century. It was raised when Israel proclaimed independence on May 14, 1948, and the banner was legally recognized on Nov. 12, 1948. A dark blue was also substituted for the traditional lighter shade of blue.

Italy

Republic, S Europe

Area: 116,306 sq. mi. (301,230 sq. km.)
Population: 58,148,000
Language(s): Italian

Monetary unit: euro
Economy: iron, steel, ceramics, chemicals, fishing, textiles, automobiles, tourism, food processing

The first Italian national flag was adopted on Feb. 25, 1797, by the Cispadane Republic. Its stripes were vertically positioned on May 11, 1798, and thereafter it was honored by all Italian nationalists. The design was guaranteed by a decree (March 23, 1848) of King Charles Albert of Sardinia, ordering troops to carry the flag into battle.

Ivory Coast

Republic, W Africa

Area: 124,503 sq. mi. (322,460 sq. km.)
Population: 18,013,000
Language(s): French

Monetary unit: West African States franc
Economy: coffee, cocoa, palm oil, rubber, wood products, oil refining, diamonds, fishing

Adopted on Aug. 7, 1959, the flag of the former French colony has three stripes corresponding to the national motto (Unity, Discipline, Labor). The orange is for growth, the white is for peace emerging from purity and unity, and the green is for hope and the future. Unofficially the green is for forests and the orange is for savannas.

Jamaica

Island republic, Caribbean

Area: 4,244 sq. mi. (10,991 sq. km.)
Population: 2,780,000
Language(s): English

Monetary unit: Jamaican dollar
Economy: bauxite, alumina, tourism, tropical fruits, rum, cement, gypsum, telecommunications

The flag was designed prior to independence from Britain (Aug. 6, 1962). The black color stood for hardships faced by the nation, green for agriculture and hope, and yellow for the natural wealth of Jamaica. This was summed up in the phrase, "Hardships there are, but the land is green and the sun shineth."

Japan

Islands constit. monarchy, W Pacific

Area: 145,883 sq. mi. (377,835 sq. km.)
Population: 127,433,000
Language(s): Japanese

Monetary unit: yen
Economy: motor vehicles, electronics, optical equipment, chemicals, fishing, mining, textiles

The flag features a red sun on a cool white background. Traditionally, the sun goddess founded Japan in the 7th century BC and gave birth to its first emperor, Jimmu. Even today the emperor is known as the "Son of the Sun" and the popular name for the country is "Land of the Rising Sun." The current flag design was adopted on Aug. 5, 1854.

Jordan

Constitutional monarchy, SW Asia

Area: 35,637 sq. mi. (92,300 sq. km.)
Population: 6,053,000
Language(s): Arabic, English

Monetary unit: Jordanian dinar
Economy: phosphate mining, cement, chemicals, pharmaceuticals, wheat, fruits, olives, tourism

In 1917 Husayn ibn Ali raised the Arab Revolt flag. With the addition of a white seven-pointed star, this flag was adopted by Transjordan on April 16, 1928, and retained upon the independence of Jordan on March 22, 1946. White is for purity, black for struggle and suffering, red for bloodshed, and green for Arab lands.

Kazakhstan

Republic, W cen. Asia

Area: 1,049,155 sq. mi. (2,717,300 sq. km.)
Population: 15,285,000
Language(s): Kazakh, Russian

Monetary unit: tenge
Economy: oil, mining (manganese, titanium, gold), chemicals, agriculture, livestock, textiles

The flag was adopted in June 1992. Light blue is a traditional color of the nomads of Central Asia; it symbolizes peace and well-being. The golden sun and eagle represent freedom and the high ideals of the Kazakhs. Along the edge is a band of traditional Kazakh ornamentation; the band was originally in red but is now in golden yellow.

Kenya

Republic, E cen. Africa

Area: 224,962 sq. mi. (582,650 sq. km.)
Population: 36,914,000
Language(s): Kiswahili, English

Monetary unit: Kenyan shilling
Economy: coffee, cotton, tea, rice, mining (gold, salt), consumer goods, oil refining, tourism

Upon independence from Britain (Dec. 12, 1963), the Kenyan flag became official. It was based on the flag of the Kenya African National Union. Black is for the people, red for humanity and the struggle for freedom, green for the fertile land, and white for unity and peace. The shield and spears are traditional weapons of the Masai people.

Kiribati

Islands republic, W Pacific

Area: 313 sq. mi. (811 sq. km.)
Population: 107,800
Language(s): English, Kiribati

Monetary unit: Australian dollar
Economy: fishing, agriculture (coconuts, copra, tropical fruits), handicrafts, tourism

Great Britain acquired the Gilbert and Ellice Islands in the 19th century. In 1975 the Gilbert Islands separated from the Ellice Islands to form Kiribati, and a new flag was adopted based on the coat of arms granted to the islands in 1937. It has waves of white and blue, for the Pacific Ocean, as well as a yellow sun and a local frigate bird.

Korea, North

Communist state, E Asia

Area: 46,541 sq. mi. (120,540 sq. km.)
Population: 23,302,000
Language(s): Korean

Monetary unit: North Korean won
Economy: military products, mining (magnesite, precious metals), machinery, textiles

The traditional Korean Taeguk flag (still used by South Korea) was official in North Korea until July 10, 1948, when the current flag was introduced. Its red stripe and star are for the country's commitment to communism, while blue is said to stand for a commitment to peace. The white stripes stand for purity, strength, and dignity.

Korea, South

Republic, E Asia

Area: 38,023 sq. mi. (98,480 sq. km.)
Population: 49,045,000
Language(s): Korean, English

Monetary unit: South Korean won
Economy: electronics, motor vehicles, shipbuilding, chemicals, agriculture, mining, fishing

The flag was adopted in August 1882. Its white background is for peace, while the central emblem represents yin-yang (Korean: *um-yang*), the duality of the universe. The black bars recall sun, moon, earth, heaven and other Confucian principles. Outlawed under Japanese rule, the flag was revived in 1945 and slightly modified in 1950 and 1984.

Kosovo

Republic, SE Europe

Area: 4,203 sq. mi. (10,887 sq. km.)
Population: 2,126,708
Language(s): Albanian, Serbian

Monetary unit: euro
Economy: mining (lignite, lead, zinc, nickel, chrome, aluminum, magnesium), building materials

The flag of Kosovo, adopted at independence in February 2008, shows the shape of Kosovo in yellow on a medium blue field. Six white stars representing the country's major ethnic groups form an arc above the Kosovo silhouette. This design was chosen after a competition having nearly 1000 entries.

Kuwait

Constitutional monarchy, W Asia

Area: 6,880 sq. mi. (17,820 sq. km.)
Population: 2,506,000
Language(s): Arabic

Monetary unit: Kuwaiti dinar
Economy: oil, fishing, construction materials, industrial chemicals

The red flag of Kuwait, in use since World War I, was replaced by the current flag on Oct. 24, 1961, shortly after independence from Britain. The symbolism is from a poem written over six centuries ago. The green stands for Arab lands, black is for battles, white is for the purity of the fighters, and red is for the blood on their swords.

Kyrgyzstan

Republic, W cen. Asia

Area: 76,641 sq. mi. (198,500 sq. km.)
Population: 5,284,000
Language(s): Kyrgyz, Russian, Uzbek

Monetary unit: som
Economy: cotton, wheat, tobacco, wool, mining (gold, mercury, uranium, coal), machinery

The Kyrgyz flag replaced a Soviet-era design on March 3, 1992. The red recalls the flag of the national hero Mansas the Noble. The central yellow sun has 40 rays, corresponding to the followers of Mansas and the tribes he united. On the sun is the stylized view of the roof of a yurt, a traditional nomadic home that is now seldom used.

Laos

Communist state, SE Asia

Area: 91,429 sq. mi. (236,800 sq. km.)
Population: 6,522,000
Language(s): Lao, French, English

Monetary unit: kip
Economy: rice, corn, tobacco, fishing, timber, mining (tin, gypsum), opium

The Lao flag was first used by anti-colonialist forces from the mid-20th century. The white disk honored the Japanese who had supported the Lao independence movement, but it also symbolized a bright future. Red was said to stand for the blood of patriots, and blue was for the promise of future prosperity. The flag was adopted on Dec. 2, 1975.

Latvia

Republic, N Europe

Area: 24,938 sq. mi. (64,589 sq. km.)
Population: 2,260,000
Language(s): Latvian, Russian

Monetary unit: euro
Economy: wood, wood products, synthetic fibers, chemicals, machinery, electronics, processed foods

The basic flag design was used by a militia unit in 1279, according to a 14th century source. Popularized in the 19th century among anti-Russian nationalists, the flag flew in 1918 and was legally adopted on Jan. 20, 1923. Under Soviet control the flag was suppressed, but it was again legalized in 1988 and flown officially from Feb. 27, 1990.

Lebanon

Republic, SW Asia

Area: 4,015 sq. mi. (10,400 sq. km.)
Population: 3,926,000
Language(s): Arabic, French, English

Monetary unit: Lebanese pound
Economy: banking, agriculture (olives, tobacco), jewelry, cement, oil refining, metal fabricating

On Sept. 1, 1920, French-administered Lebanon adopted a flag based on the French tricolor. The current red-white flag was established by the constitution of 1943, which divided power among the Muslim and Christian sects. On the central stripe is a cedar tree, which is a biblical symbol for holiness, peace, and eternity.

Lesotho
Constitutional monarchy, S Africa

Area: 11,720 sq. mi. (30,355 sq. km.);
Population: 2,125,000
Language(s): Sesotho, English, Zulu

Monetary unit: loti
Economy: wool, mohair, diamonds, agriculture (corn, wheat, beans, sorghum), textiles

This flag was unfurled for the first time on October 4, 2006, to mark the occasion of Lesotho's 40th anniversary of independence from Britain. Lesotho states that the new flag shows it "at peace with itself and its neighbors". Blue signifies rain, white stands for peace, and green indicates prosperity. The black Basotho hat represents the country's indigenous people.

Liberia
Republic, W Africa

Area: ab. 43,000 sq. mi. (111,370 sq. km.)
Population: 3,196,000
Language(s): English, local languages

Monetary unit: Liberian dollar
Economy: rubber processing, rice, palm oil, coffee, cocoa, timber, iron ore, diamonds

In the 19th century land was purchased on the African coast by the American Colonization Society in order to return freed slaves to Africa. On April 9, 1827, a flag based on that of the United States was adopted, featuring a white cross. On Aug. 24, 1847, after independence, the cross was replaced by a star and the number of stripes was reduced.

Libya
Authoritarian state, N Africa

Area: 679,362 sq. mi. (1,759,540 sq. km.)
Population: 6,037,000
Language(s): Arabic, Italian, English

Monetary unit: Libyan dinar
Economy: oil, natural gas, iron, steel, textiles, barley, wheat, dates, olives, fruits

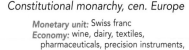

In 1947 three regions united to become the United Kingdom of Libya. A flag consisting of red, black, and green stripes with a centered white crescent and star became official in 1949. In 1969 the monarchy was overthrown by Muammar al-Qaddafi, who changed the flag to solid green. Following the overthrow of Qaddafi in 2011, the 1949 flag was reinstated.

Liechtenstein
Constitutional monarchy, cen. Europe

Area: 62 sq. mi. (160 sq. km.)
Population: 34,200
Language(s): German

Monetary unit: Swiss franc
Economy: wine, dairy, textiles, pharmaceuticals, precision instruments, tourism

The blue-red flag was given official status in October 1921. At the 1936 Olympics it was learned that this same flag was used by Haiti; thus, in 1937 a yellow crown was added, which symbolizes the unity of the people and their prince. Blue stands for the sky, red for the evening fires in homes. The flag was last modified on Sept. 18, 1982.

Lithuania
Republic, N Europe

Area: 25,174 sq. mi. (65,200 sq. km.)
Population: 3,575,000
Language(s): Lithuanian, Russian, Polish

Monetary unit: euro
Economy: dairy, livestock, food products, textiles, paper, machinery

The tricolor flag of Lithuania was adopted on Aug. 1, 1922. It was long suppressed under Soviet rule until its reestablishment on March 20, 1989. The yellow color suggests ripening wheat and freedom from want. Green is for hope and the forests of the nation, while red stands for love of country, sovereignty, and valor in defense of liberty.

Luxembourg
Constitutional monarchy, W Europe

Area: 998 sq. mi. (2,586 sq. km.)
Population: 480,200
Language(s): German, French

Monetary unit: euro
Economy: wine, livestock, iron and steel, chemicals

In the 19th century the national colors, from the coat of arms of the dukes of Luxembourg, came to be used in a tricolor of red-white-blue, coincidentally the same as the flag of The Netherlands. To distinguish it from the Dutch flag, the proportions were altered and the shade of blue was made lighter. It was recognized by law on Aug. 16, 1972.

Macedonia
Republic, SE Europe

Area: 9,781 sq. mi. (25,333 sq. km.)
Population: 2,056,000
Language(s): Macedonian, Albanian

Monetary unit: Macedonian denar
Economy: wheat, corn, tobacco, iron, steel, chromium, lead, zinc

A "starburst" flag replaced the communist banner on Aug. 11, 1992. The starburst was a symbol of Alexander the Great and his father, Philip of Macedon, but its use by Macedonia was opposed by Greece. Thus on Oct. 6, 1995, the similar "golden sun" flag was chosen instead. The gold and red colors originated in an early Macedonian coat of arms.

Madagascar
Island republic, off SE Africa

Area: 226,657 sq. mi. (587,040 sq. km.)
Population: 19,449,000
Language(s): Malagasy, French

Monetary unit: Madagascar ariary
Economy: tobacco, coffee, sugar, cloves, vanilla, sisal, livestock, graphite, soap

The Madagascar flag was adopted on Oct. 16, 1958, by the newly proclaimed Malagasy Republic, formerly a French colony. The flag combines the traditional Malagasy colors of white and red with a stripe of green. The white and red are said to stand for purity and sovereignty, while the green represents the coastal regions and symbolizes hope.

Malawi
Republic, SE Africa

Area: 45,745 sq. mi. (118,480 sq. km.)
Population: 13,603,000
Language(s): Chichewa, Chinyanja

Monetary unit: Malawian kwacha
Economy: tea, tobacco, peanuts, sorghum, sugar, fishing, textiles, cement

In 1964, independent Malawi adopted a flag that was striped black for the African people, red for the blood of the martyrs, and green for the vegetation and climate. A red setting sun was on the black stripe. A new flag in 2010, reordered the stripes to red-black-green and replaced the half sun with a full sun. The old flag was restored in 2012.

Malaysia
Constitutional monarchy, SE Asia

Area: 127,317 sq. mi. (329,750 sq. km.)
Population: 24,821,000
Language(s): Malay, English, Chinese

Monetary unit: ringgit
Economy: rubber, palm oil, cocoa, pineapples, natural gas, tin, electronics

The flag hoisted on May 26, 1950, had 11 stripes, a crescent, and an 11-pointed star. The number of stripes and star points was increased to 14 on Sept. 16, 1963. Yellow is a royal color in Malaysia while red, white, and blue indicate connections with the Commonwealth. The crescent is a reminder that the population is mainly Muslim.

Maldives
Islands republic, Indian Ocean

Area: 116 sq. mi. (300 sq. km.)
Population: 369,000
Language(s): Dhivehi, English

Monetary unit: rufiyaa
Economy: coconuts, millet, fishing, tourism

Maldivian ships long used a plain red ensign like those flown by Arabian and African nations. While a British protectorate in the early 20th century, the Maldives adopted a flag which was only slightly altered upon independence (July 26, 1965). The green panel and white crescent are symbolic of Islam, progress, prosperity, and peace.

Mali
Republic, W cen. Africa

Area: 478,767 sq. mi. (1,240,000 sq. km.)
Population: 11,995,000
Language(s): French; local languages

Monetary unit: West African States franc
Economy: food processing (sorghum, rice, millet), mining (phosphate, gold), livestock, leather goods

Designed for the Mali-Senegal union of 1959, the flag originally included a human figure, the Kanaga, in its center. In 1960 Senegal and Mali divided. Muslims in Mali objected to the Kanaga, and on March 1, 1961, the figure was dropped. Green, yellow, and red are the Pan-African colors and are used by many former French territories.

Malta
Island republic, Mediterranean

Area: 122 sq. mi. (316 sq. km.)
Population: 401,900
Language(s): Maltese, English

Monetary unit: euro
Economy: tourism, electronics, ship building and repair, potatoes, tomatoes, citrus fruit

The Maltese flag was supposedly based on an 11th-century coat of arms, and a red flag with a white cross was used by the Knights of Malta from the Middle Ages. The current flag dates from independence within the Commonwealth (Sept. 21, 1964). The George Cross was granted by the British for the heroic defense of the island in World War II.

Marshall Islands
Islands republic, W Pacific

Area: 70 sq. mi. (181 sq. km.)
Population: 61,800
Language(s): Marshallese, English

Monetary unit: U.S. dollar
Economy: subsistence agriculture, fishing, handicrafts, coconut products, breadfruit

The island nation hoisted its flag on May 1, 1979. The blue stands for the ocean. The white is for brightness while the orange is for bravery and wealth. The two stripes joined symbolize the Equator, and they increase in width to show growth and vitality. The rays of the star are for the municipalities; its four long rays recall a Christian cross.

Mauritania
Republic, W Africa

Area: 397,956 sq. mi. (1,030,700 sq. km.)
Population: 3,270,000
Language(s): Arabic, local languages

Monetary unit: ouguiya
Economy: mining (iron ore, copper), millet, rice, dates, livestock, fish processing

In 1958 Mauritania was granted autonomous status within the French Community. The current flag replaced the French tricolor on April 1, 1959, and no changes were made to the design at independence (Nov. 28, 1960). The green background of the flag and its star and crescent are traditional Muslim symbols that have been in use for centuries.

Mauritius
Island republic, Indian Ocean

Area: 788 sq. mi. (2,040 sq. km.)
Population: 1,251,000
Language(s): Creole, French, English

Monetary unit: Mauritian rupee
Economy: sugarcane, molasses, tea, tobacco, textiles, tourism

The Mauritius flag was officially adopted when the island gained independence from the United Kingdom in 1968. Designed by the College of Arms in Britain, red is symbolic of the country's struggle for independence; yellow, the bright future; green, the fertile land of the island, and blue, the Indian Ocean.

Mexico
Republic, North America

Area: 759,530 sq. mi. (1,967,183 sq. km.)
Population: 108,701,000
Language(s): Spanish

Monetary unit: Mexican peso
Economy: mining (silver, gold), oil, chemicals, motor vehicles, consumer goods, tourism

The green-white-red tricolor was officially established in 1821. Green is for independence, white for Roman Catholicism, and red for union. The emblem depicts the scene supposedly witnessed by the Aztecs in 1325: an eagle with a snake in its beak standing upon a cactus growing out of rocks in the water. The flag was modified on Sept. 17, 1968.

Micronesia
Islands federation, W Pacific

Area: 271 sq. mi. (702 sq km)
Population: 107,900
Language(s): English, local languages

Monetary unit: U.S. dollar
Economy: tourism, construction, fish processing, handicrafts (wood, pearls), bananas, black pepper

On Nov. 30, 1978, the flag of the former United States trust territory was approved by an interim congress. Based on the symbolism of the territory, the flag has stars for the four states of Micronesia. After sovereignty was granted in 1986, a dark blue background (for the Pacific Ocean) was substituted for the original "United Nations blue."

Moldova
Republic, E Europe

Area: 13,067 sq. mi. (33,843 sq. km.)
Population: 4,320,000
Language(s): Romanian, Russian

Monetary unit: Moldovan leu
Economy: food processing, cereals, fruits and vegetables, wine, sugar, machinery

By 1989, Moldovans protested against communist rule, and the traditional tricolor of blue-yellow-red, which had flown briefly in 1917–18, became a popular symbol. It replaced the communist flag in May 1990 and remained after independence in 1991. The shield has an eagle on whose breast are the head of a wild ox, a crescent, a star, and a flower.

Monaco
Constitutional principality, S Europe

Area: 0.75 sq. mi. (1.95 sq. km.)
Population: 32,700
Language(s): French, English, Italian

Monetary unit: euro
Economy: tourism

The flag of the Principality of Monaco, officially adopted in 1881, contains the heraldic colors of the ruling Grimaldi family. Those colors date to the 14th century and appear on the Grimaldi coat of arms as a series of red lozenges on a white background.

Mongolia
Republic, cen. Asia

Area: 603,909 sq. mi. (1,564,116 sq. km.)
Population: 2,952,000
Language(s): Khalkha Mongol

Monetary unit: togrog/tugrik
Economy: livestock, agriculture, animal products, cashmere, mining (coal, oil, copper, gold)

In 1945, the flag symbolizing communism (red) and Mongol nationalism (blue) was established. Near the hoist is a soyonba, a grouping of philosophical symbols (flame, sun, moon, yin-yang, triangles, and bars). Yellow traditionally stood for Lamaist Buddhism. On Jan. 12, 1992, a five-pointed star (for communism) was removed from the flag.

Montenegro
Republic, SE Europe

Area: 5,419 sq. mi. (14,026 sq. km.)
Population: 684,700
Language(s): Serbian, Bosnian, Albanian

Monetary unit: euro
Economy: steelmaking, aluminum, agricultural processing, tourism

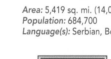

The flag of Montenegro was adopted on July 12, 2004. The flag is red with a gold coat of arms in the center. The coat of arms, based on that of the Petrovic dynasty, consists of a double-headed golden eagle with a crown above its head, holding a scepter in one claw and the orb in the other, with a breast shield containing a golden lion passant over green grass with blue sky above.

Morocco
Constitutional monarchy, NW Africa

Area: 172,414 sq. mi. (446,550 sq. km.)
Population: 33,757,000
Language(s): Arabic, French

Monetary unit: Moroccan dirham
Economy: food processing, wine, leather goods, fishing, mining (phosphates, copper, silver), tourism

After Morocco was subjected to the rule of France and Spain in the 20th century, the plain red flag, which had been displayed on its ships, was modified on Nov. 17, 1915. To its center was added the ancient pentagram known as the "Seal of Solomon." The flag continued in use even after the French granted independence in 1956.

Mozambique
Republic, SE Africa

Area: 309,496 sq. mi. (801,590 sq. km.)
Population: 20,906,000
Language(s): Portuguese, local languages

Monetary unit: metical
Economy: subsistence agriculture, cashew nuts, sugar, tea, coal, bauxite, aluminum, shrimp

In the early 1960s, anti-Portuguese groups adopted flags of green (for forests), black (for the majority population), white (for rivers and the ocean), gold (for peace and mineral wealth), and red (for the blood of liberation). The current flag was readopted in 1983; on its star are a book, a hoe, and an assault rifle.

Myanmar

Military state, SE Asia

Area: 261,970 sq. mi. (678,500 sq. km.)
Population: 47,374,000
Language(s): Burmese

Monetary unit: kyat
Economy: agricultural products (rice, peanuts, sugarcane), oil, mining (silver, lead, zinc), textiles

The design of the flag of Myanmar consists of three equal horizontal stripes of yellow (top), green, and red; centered on the green band is a large white five-pointed star that partially overlaps onto the adjacent colored stripes; the design revives the triband colors used by Burma from 1943-45, during the Japanese occupation.

Namibia

Republic, SW Africa

Area: 318,696 sq. mi. (825,418 sq. km.)
Population: 2,055,000
Language(s): English, Afrikaans

Monetary unit: Namibian dollar
Economy: diamonds, copper, zinc, lead, salt, sheep, fishing, food processing

The flag was adopted on Feb. 2, 1990, and hoisted on independence from South Africa, March 21, 1990. Its colors are those of the South West Africa People's Organization: blue (for sky and ocean), red (for heroism and determination), and green (for agriculture). The gold sun represents life and energy while the white stripes are for water resources.

Nepal

Constitutional monarchy, S Asia

Area: 54,363 sq. mi. (147,181 sq. km.)
Population: 28,902,000
Language(s): Nepali, local languages

Monetary unit: Nepalese rupee
Economy: agriculture (rice, wheat, jute, oilseed), livestock, carpets, tourism

Established on Dec. 16, 1962, Nepal's flag consists of two united pennant shapes; it is the only non-rectangular national flag in the world. In the upper segment is a moon with a crescent attached below; in the bottom segment appears a stylized sun. The symbols are for different dynasties and express a hope for the immortality of the nation. The crimson and blue colors are common in Nepali art.

Netherlands

Constitutional monarchy, NW Europe

Area: 16,033 sq. mi. (41,526 sq. km.)
Population: 16,571,000
Language(s): Dutch, Frisian

Monetary unit: euro
Economy: farming, food processing, horticulture, natural gas, chemicals, microelectronics

The history of the Dutch flag dates to the use of orange, white, and blue as the livery colors of William, Prince of Orange, and the use of the tricolor at sea in 1577. By 1660 the color red was substituted for orange. The flag was legalized by pro-French "patriots" on Feb. 14, 1796, and reaffirmed by royal decree on Feb. 19, 1937.

New Zealand

Islands republic, SW Pacific

Area: 103,738 sq. mi. (268,680 sq. km.)
Population: 4,116,000
Language(s): English, Maori

Monetary unit: New Zealand dollar
Economy: food processing, mining (coal, gold), natural gas, manufacturing, banking, insurance, tourism

The Maori of New Zealand accepted British control in 1840, and a colonial flag was adopted on Jan. 15, 1867. It included the Union Jack in the canton and the letters "NZ" at the fly end. Later versions used the Southern Cross. Dominion status was granted on Sept. 26, 1907, and independence on Nov. 25, 1947, but the flag was unchanged.

Nicaragua

Republic, Central America

Area: 49,998 sq. mi. (129,494 sq. km.)
Population: 5,675,000
Language(s): Spanish

Monetary unit: gold córdoba
Economy: coffee, sugar, shrimp, lobster, gold, machinery, chemicals, textiles

On Aug. 21, 1823, a blue-white-blue flag was adopted by the five member states of the United Provinces of Central America, which included Nicaragua. From the mid-19th century various flag designs were used in Nicaragua, but the old flag was readopted in 1908, with a modified coat of arms, and reaffirmed by law on Aug. 27, 1971.

Niger

Republic, W cen. Africa

Area: 489,192 sq. mi. (1,267,000 sq. km.)
Population: 12,895,000
Language(s): French, Hausa

Monetary unit: West African States franc
Economy: subsistence farming, uranium mining, cement, bricks, peanuts, cotton, rice

The flag of Niger was chosen on Nov. 23, 1959. The white color is for purity, innocence, and civic spirit. The orange is for the Sahara Desert and the heroic efforts of citizens to live within it, while the orange central disk represents the sun. The green color stands for agriculture and hope; it is suggestive of the Niger River valley.

Nigeria

Republic, W cen. Africa

Area: 356,669 sq. mi. (923,768 sq. km.)
Population: 135,031,000
Language(s): English, Hausa

Monetary unit: naira
Economy: subsistence farming, oil, rubber, hides, skins, mining (tin), automobile assembly

The Nigerian flag became official upon independence from Britain on Oct. 1, 1960. The flag design is purposefully simple in order not to favor the symbolism of any particular ethnic or religious group. Agriculture is represented by the green stripes while unity and peace are symbolized by the white stripe.

Norway

Constitutional monarchy, N Europe

Area: 125,182 sq. mi. (323,802 sq. km.)
Population: 4,628,000
Language(s): Norwegian

Monetary unit: Norwegian krone
Economy: gas, oil, food processing, fishing, timber, mining, chemicals, high-tech products, tourism

The first distinctive Norwegian flag was created in 1814 while the country was under Swedish rule. It was based on the red Danish flag with its white cross. In 1821 the Norwegian parliament developed the current flag design. From 1844 to 1899, six years before independence, the official flag included a symbol of Swedish-Norwegian union.

Oman

Sultanate, SE Arabian Peninsula

Area: 82,031 sq. mi. (212,460 sq. km.)
Population: 3,205,000
Language(s): Arabic, English, Urdu

Monetary unit: Omani rial
Economy: oil, natural gas, dates, cereals, limes, fishing

The flag dates to Dec. 17, 1970, and it was altered on Nov. 18, 1995. The white is for peace and prosperity, red is for battles, and green is for the fertility of the land. Unofficially, white recalls the imamate, red the sultanate, and green Al-Jabal Al-Akhdar ("The Green Mountain"). The coat of arms has two swords, a dagger, and a belt.

Pakistan

Republic, S Asia

Area: 310,403 sq. mi. (803,940 sq. km.)
Population: 164,742,000
Language(s): Urdu, Punjabi, English

Monetary unit: Pakistani rupee
Economy: textiles, food processing, pharmaceuticals, coal, gypsum, natural gas, fertilizer, chemicals

On Dec. 30, 1906, the All India Muslim League approved this typically Muslim flag, with its star and crescent. At independence (Aug. 14, 1947) a white stripe was added for minority religious groups. Also symbolized are prosperity and peace by the green and white colors, progress by the crescent, and knowledge and light by the star.

Palau

Islands republic, W Pacific

Area: 177 sq. mi. (458 sq. km.)
Population: 20,800
Language(s): Palauan, English, Filipino

Monetary unit: U.S. dollar
Economy: tourism, subsistence farming, fishing, textiles, handicrafts

Approved on Oct. 22, 1980, and hoisted on Jan. 1, 1981, the Palauan flag was left unaltered at independence in 1994. The golden disk represents the full moon, which is said on Palau to be propitious for fishing, planting, and other activities and gives the people "a feeling of warmth, tranquillity, peace, love, and domestic unity."

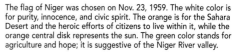

Panama
Republic, Central America

Area: 30,193 sq. mi. (78,200 sq. km.)
Population: 3,242,000
Language(s): Spanish, English

Monetary unit: balboa, U.S. dollar
Economy: Panama Canal, banking, flagship registry, tourism, food processing, textiles, cement

The Panamanian flag became official on July 4, 1904, after independence from Colombia was won through the intervention of the United States, which was determined to construct the Panama Canal. The flag was influenced by the United States, and its quartered design was said to symbolize the power sharing of Panama's two main political parties.

Papua New Guinea
Islands commonwealth, W Pacific

Area: 178,704 sq. mi. (462,840 sq. km.)
Population: 5,796,000
Language(s): Melanesian pidgin

Monetary unit: kina
Economy: subsistence farming, palm oil, plywood, copper, oil, silver, coffee, tea

The formerly German-, British-, and Australian-controlled territory officially recognized its flag on March 11, 1971, and flag usage was extended to ships at independence (Sept. 16, 1975). The colors red and black are shown extensively in local art and clothing. Featured emblems are a bird of paradise and the Southern Cross constellation.

Paraguay
Republic, South America

Area: 157,047 sq. mi. (406,750 sq. km.)
Population: 6,669,000
Language(s): Spanish, Guarani

Monetary unit: guarani
Economy: food processing (meat, sugar, vegetable oils), wood products, tobacco, cotton, cement, textiles

Under the dictator José Gaspar Rodríguez de Francia (1814–40) the French colors were adopted for the flag. The coat of arms (a golden star surrounded by a wreath) is on the obverse side, but the seal of the treasury (a lion, staff, and liberty cap, with the motto "Peace and Justice") is on the reverse; the flag is unique in this respect.

Peru
Republic, South America

Area: 496,226 sq. mi. (1,285,220 sq. km.)
Population: 28,675,000
Language(s): Spanish, Quechua, Aymara

Monetary unit: nuevo sol
Economy: mining (copper, zinc, silver), oil, petroleum products, fishing, cotton, sugar, coffee, coca

Partisans in the early 19th century adopted a red-white-red flag resembling that of Spain, but they soon made its stripes vertical. In 1825, the current design was established. The shield includes figures symbolic of national wealth—the vicuna (a relative of the alpaca), a cinchona tree, and a cornucopia with gold and silver coins.

Philippines
Archipelago republic, W Pacific

Area: 115,831 sq. mi. (300,000 sq. km.)
Population: 76,498,735
Language(s): Filipino, English

Monetary unit: Philippine peso
Economy: copra, fruit, sugar, timber, iron ore, gold, nickel, textiles, electronics assembly

In 1898, during the Spanish-American War, Filipinos established the basic flag in use today; it was officially adopted in 1936. The white triangle is for liberty. The golden sun and stars are for the three main areas of the Philippines: Luzon, the Visayan Islands, and Mindanao. The red color is for courage and the blue color is for sacrifice.

Poland
Republic, cen. Europe

Area: 120,728 sq. mi. (312,685 sq. km.)
Population: 38,518,000
Language(s): Polish

Monetary unit: zloty
Economy: machine building, iron and steel, coal mining, chemicals, shipbuilding, food processing

The colors of the Polish flag originated in its coat of arms, a white eagle on a red shield, dating from 1295. The precise symbolism of the colors is not known, however. Poland's simple flag of white-red horizontal stripes was adopted on Aug. 1, 1919. The flag was left unaltered under the Soviet-allied communist regime (1944 to 1990).

Portugal
Republic, W Europe

Area: 35,672 sq. mi. (92,391 sq. km.)
Population: 10,643,000
Language(s): Portuguese; Mirandese

Monetary unit: euro
Economy: fishing, cork, oil refining, chemicals, communications equipment, shipbuilding, wine, tourism

The central shield includes five smaller shields, for a victory over the Moors in 1139, and a red border with gold castles. Behind the shield is an armillary sphere (an astronomical device) recalling world explorations and the kingdom of Brazil. Red and green were used in many early Portuguese flags. The current flag dates to June 30, 1911.

Qatar
Emirate, E Arabian Peninsula

Area: 4,416 sq. mi. (11,437 sq. km.)
Population: 907,200
Language(s): Arabic, English

Monetary unit: Qatari rial
Economy: oil, natural gas, fishing, ammonia, fertilizers, cement, commercial ship repair

The 1868 treaty between Great Britain and Qatar may have inspired the creation of the flag. Qataris chose mauve or maroon instead of red (a more typical color among Arab countries) perhaps to distinguish it from the flag used in Bahrain. Passages from the Quran, in Arabic script, have sometimes been added to the flag.

Romania
Republic, E Europe

Area: 91,699 sq. mi. (237,500 sq. km.)
Population: 22,276,000
Language(s): Romanian, Hungarian

Monetary unit: Romanian leu
Economy: oil, natural gas, light machinery, motor vehicles, mining, timber, metallurgy, chemicals

In 1834, Walachia, an ancient region of Romania, chose a naval ensign with stripes of red, blue, and yellow. The modern Romanian tricolor was created in 1848 and flown for a brief time. In 1867, Romania reestablished the vertical tricolor, and with the fall of the 20th-century communist regime, it was defined on Dec. 27, 1989.

Russia
Republic, E Europe and N Asia

Area: 6,592,769 sq. mi. (17,075,272 sq. km.)
Population: 141,378,000
Language(s): Russian

Monetary unit: Russian ruble
Economy: oil, natural gas, transportation, medical, electronic equipment, chemicals, agriculture

Tsar Peter the Great visited the Netherlands in order to modernize the Russian navy, and in 1699, he chose a Dutch-influenced flag for Russian ships. The flag soon became popular on land as well. After the Russian Revolution, it was replaced by the communist red banner, but the tricolor again became official on Aug. 21, 1991.

Rwanda
Republic, E cen. Africa

Area: 10,169 sq. mi. (26,338 sq. km.)
Population: 9,908,000
Language(s): Kinyarwanda, French, English, Swahili

Monetary unit: Rwandan franc
Economy: cement, agricultural products, plastic goods, cigarettes, agriculture, minerals

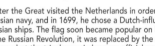

In 2001, Rwanda adopted a new flag, to promote national unity after the genocide of the early 1990s. The large blue stripe represents happiness and peace, and the smaller yellow and green stripes are for economic development and for prosperity. The sun with its 24 rays stands for unity, transparency, and enlightenment.

Saint Kitts and Nevis
Islands republic, Caribbean

Area: 101 sq. mi. (261 sq. km.)
Population: 39,300
Language(s): English

Monetary unit: East Caribbean dollar
Economy: tourism, sugar processing, electronic components, banking, beverages

On Sept. 18, 1983, at the time of its independence from Britain, St. Kitts and Nevis hoisted the current flag. It has green (for fertility), red (for the struggle against slavery and colonialism), and black (for African heritage). The yellow flanking stripes are for sunshine, and the two stars, one for each island, are for hope and liberty.

Saint Lucia

Island republic, Caribbean

Area: 238 sq. mi. (616 sq. km.)
Population: 170,600
Language(s): English, French dialect

Monetary unit: East Caribbean dollar
Economy: tourism, cocoa, spices, coconuts, bananas, beverages, electronic components

The flag was hoisted on March 1, 1967, when the former colony assumed a status of association with the United Kingdom; it was slightly altered in 1979. The blue represents Atlantic and Caribbean waters. The white and black colors are for racial harmony, while the black triangle also represents volcanoes. The yellow triangle is for sunshine.

Saint Vincent and the Grenadines

Archipelago republic, Caribbean

Area: 150 sq. mi. (389 sq. km.)
Population: 118,100
Language(s): English, French

Monetary unit: East Caribbean dollar
Economy: tourism, bananas, coconuts, spices, cement, fishing

At independence from Britain in 1979, a national flag was designed, but it was replaced by the current flag on Oct. 22, 1985. The three green diamonds are arranged in the form of a V. Green is for the rich vegetation and the vitality of the people, yellow is for sand and personal warmth, and blue is for sea and sky.

Samoa

Islands monarchy, SW Pacific

Area: 1,137 sq. mi. (2,944 sq. km.)
Population: 214,300
Language(s): Samoan, English

Monetary unit: tala
Economy: fishing, coconut oil and cream, copra, pineapples, automotive parts, textiles, beer

The first national flag of Samoa may date to 1873. Under British administration, a version of the current flag was introduced on May 26, 1948. On Feb. 2, 1949, a fifth star, as can be seen in the sky, was added to the Southern Cross. White in the flag is said to stand for purity, blue for freedom, and red for courage. The flag was left unaltered upon independence in 1962.

San Marino

Republic, enclave in Italy

Area: 24 sq. mi. (61 sq. km.)
Population: 29,600
Language(s): Italian

Monetary unit: euro
Economy: tourism, banking, textiles, electronics, ceramics, wine and cheeses

The colors of the flag, blue and white, were first used in the national cockade in 1797. The coat of arms in its present form was adopted on April 6, 1862, when the crown was added as a symbol of national sovereignty. Also in the coat of arms are three towers (Guaita, Cesta, and Montale) from the fortifications on Mount Titano.

São Tomé and Príncipe

Islands republic, off W Africa

Area: 386 sq. mi. (1,001 sq. km.)
Population: 199,600
Language(s): Portuguese

Monetary unit: dobra
Economy: cocoa and tropical fruits, some light construction, textiles, soap

The national flag was adopted upon independence from Portugal on July 12, 1975. Its colors are associated with Pan-African independence. The red triangle stands for equality and the nationalist movement. The stars are for the African population living on the nation's two main islands. Green is for vegetation and yellow is for the tropical sun.

Saudi Arabia

Islamic kingdom, Arabian Peninsula

Area: ab. 756,985 sq. mi. (2,149,690 sq. km.)
Population: 27,601,000
Language(s): Arabic

Monetary unit: Saudi riyal
Economy: oil and natural gas, gypsum, dates, wheat, commercial ship and aircraft repair

The Saudi flag, made official in 1932, but altered in 1968, originated in the military campaigns of Muhammad. The color green is associated with Fatima, the Prophet's daughter, and the Arabic inscription is translated as "There is no God but Allah and Muhammad is the Prophet of Allah." The saber symbolizes the militancy of the faith.

Senegal

Republic, W Africa

Area: 75,749 sq. mi. (196,190 sq. km.)
Population: 12,522,000
Language(s): French, local languages

Monetary unit: West African States franc
Economy: agricultural (peanuts) and fish processing, mining, petroleum refining

In a federation with French Sudan (now Mali) on April 4, 1959, Senegal used a flag with a human figure in the center. After the federation broke up in August 1960, Senegal substituted a green star for the central figure. Green is for hope and religion, yellow is for natural riches and labor, and red is for independence, life, and socialism.

Serbia

Republic, SE Europe

Area: 34,139 sq. mi. (88,361 sq. km.)
Population: 10,150,000
Language(s): Serbian

Monetary unit: Serbian dinar
Economy: machinery, electronics, chemicals, pharmaceuticals, electrical equipment, mining, agriculture

The Pan-Slavic colors (blue, white, and red) have been in the flag from Oct. 31, 1918. The coat of arms, centered vertically and shifted left of center, was added following the independence of Montenegro from the state union in 2004. On June 8, 2006, the new flag was hoisted in front of the United Nations building in New York City for the first time.

Seychelles

Islands republic, Indian Ocean

Area: 176 sq. mi. (455 sq. km.)
Population: 81,900
Language(s): Creole, English

Monetary unit: Seychelles rupee
Economy: fishing, tourism, food processing (coconuts, vanilla, cinnamon), boat building, printing

The former British colony underwent a revolution in 1977. The government was democratized in 1993, and on Jan. 8, 1996, a new flag was designed. The blue color is for sky and sea, yellow is for the sun, red is for the people and their work for unity and love, white is for social justice and harmony, and green is for the land and natural environment.

Sierra Leone

Republic, W Africa

Area: 27,699 sq. mi. (71,740 sq. km.)
Population: 6,145,000
Language(s): English, Creole

Monetary unit: leone
Economy: diamonds, small-scale manufacturing, petroleum refining, coffee, cocoa, ginger

Under British colonial control, Sierra Leone was founded as a home for freed slaves. With independence on April 27, 1961, the flag was hoisted. Its stripes stand for agriculture and the mountains (green); unity and justice (white); and the aspiration to contribute to world peace, especially through the use of the natural harbor at Freetown (blue).

Singapore

Island republic, SE Asia

Area: 267 sq. mi. (693 sq. km.)
Population: 4,553,000
Language(s): Mandarin Chinese, Malay, English

Monetary unit: Singapore dollar
Economy: banking, electronics, chemicals, oil drilling equipment, petroleum and rubber processing, shipbuilding

On Dec. 3, 1959, the flag was acquired, and it was retained after separation from Malaysia on Aug. 9, 1965. The red and white stripes stand for universal brotherhood, equality, purity, and virtue. The crescent symbolizes the growth of a young country, while the five stars are for democracy, peace, progress, justice, and equality.

Slovakia

Republic, cen. Europe

Area: 18,859 sq. mi. (48,845 sq. km.)
Population: 5,448,000
Language(s): Slovak, Hungarian

Monetary unit: euro
Economy: metal products, nuclear fuel, chemicals, electrical and optical apparatus, rubber products

In 1189, the kingdom of Hungary (including Slovakia) introduced a double-barred cross in its coat of arms; this symbol was altered in 1848–49 by Slovak nationalists. After a period of communist rule, the tricolor was made official in 1989. On Sept. 3, 1992, the shield was added to the white-blue-red flag to differentiate it from the flag of Russia.

Slovenia
Republic, S cen. Europe

Area: 7,827 sq. mi. (20,273 sq. km.)
Population: 2,009,000
Language(s): Slovenian, Serbo-Croatian

Monetary unit: euro
Economy: metal products, lead and zinc smelting, electronics, wood products, textiles, chemicals

Under the current flag, Slovenia proclaimed independence on June 25, 1991, but it was opposed for a time by the Yugoslav army. The flag is the same as that of Russia and Slovakia except for the coat of arms. It depicts the peaks of Triglav (the nation's highest mountain), the waves of the Adriatic coast, and three stars on a blue background.

Solomon Islands
Archipelago republic, SW Pacific

Area: 10,985 sq. mi. (28,450 sq. km.);
Population: 566,800
Language(s): Melanesian dialect, English

Monetary unit: Solomon Islands dollar
Economy: fishing, timber, copra, rice, palm oil, cocoa

The flag was introduced on Nov. 18, 1977, eight months before independence from Britain. The yellow stripe stands for the sun. The green triangle is for the trees and crops of the fertile land, while the blue triangle symbolizes rivers, rain, and the ocean. The five stars represented the original five districts of the island.

Somalia
Transitional state, E Africa

Area: 246,201 sq. mi. (637,657 sq. km.)
Population: 9,119,000
Language(s): Somali, Arabic

Monetary unit: Somali shilling
Economy: sugar refining, textiles, wireless communication, livestock, bananas, hides, fish

From the mid-19th century, areas in the Horn of Africa with Somali populations were divided between Ethiopia, France, Britain, and Italy. On Oct. 12, 1954, with the partial unification of these areas, the flag was adopted with a white star, each point referring to a Somali homeland. The colors were influenced by the colors of the United Nations.

South Africa
Republic, S Africa

Area: 471,011 sq. mi. (1,219,912 sq. km.)
Population: 44,000,000
Language(s): Afrikaans, English, local languages

Monetary unit: rand
Economy: mining (platinum, gold, chromium, diamonds), machinery, textiles, chemicals, automobiles, livestock

With the decline of apartheid, the flag was hoisted on April 27, 1994, and confirmed in 1996. Its six colors collectively represent Zulus, English or Afrikaners, Muslims, supporters of the African National Congress, and other groups. The Y-symbol stands for "merging history and present political realities" into a united and prosperous future.

South Sudan
Republic, E cen. Africa

Area: 239,284 sq. mi. (619,746 sq. km.)
Population: 8,260,500
Language(s): Arabic, English

Monetary unit: South Sudan pound
Economy: oil, teak, gold

The flag of the Sudan People's Liberation Movement was adopted following the 2005 end of the second civil war. The colors of the horizontal bars resemble those of the Kenya flag. Black represents the people, red is for blood shed to achieve liberation, green represents agriculture, and white is in hope of peace. The blue of the triangle represents the Nile and the star represents unity in South Sudan.

Spain
Constitutional monarchy, SW Europe

Area: 194,897 sq. mi. (504,782 sq. km.)
Population: 40,448,000
Language(s): Castilian Spanish, Catalan

Monetary unit: euro
Economy: textiles, metal products, chemicals, shipbuilding, automobiles, tourism, pharmaceuticals, medical equipment

The colors of the flag have no official symbolic meaning. Introduced in 1785, by King Charles III, the flag was changed only under the Spanish Republic (1931–39). Under different regimes, however, the coat of arms has been altered. The current design dates from Dec. 18, 1981, with the death of Francisco Franco and the resurgence of democracy.

Sri Lanka
Island republic, off SE India

Area: 25,332 sq. mi. (65,610 sq. km.)
Population: 20,926,000
Language(s): Sinhala, Tamil, English

Monetary unit: Sri Lankan rupee
Economy: rubber processing, tea, telecommunications, insurance, banking, gemstones, textiles, tourism

From the 5th century BC, the Lion flag was a symbol of the Sinhalese people. The flag was replaced by the Union Jack in 1815, but readopted upon independence in 1948. The stripes of green (for Muslims) and orange (for Hindus) were added in 1951. In 1972, four leaves of the Bo tree were added as a symbol of Buddhism; the leaves were altered in 1978.

Sudan
Military state, E cen. Africa

Area: 728,216 sq. mi. (1,886,079 sq. km.)
Population: 31,118,500
Language(s): Arabic

Monetary unit: Sudanese pound
Economy: oil, cotton processing, textiles, petroleum refining, pharmaceuticals

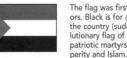

The flag was first hoisted on May 20, 1970. It uses Pan-Arab colors. Black is for al-Mahdi (a leader in the 1800s) and the name of the country (sudan in Arabic means black); white recalls the revolutionary flag of 1924 and suggests peace and optimism; red is for patriotic martyrs, socialism, and progress; and green is for prosperity and Islam.

Suriname
Republic, South America

Area: 63,039 sq. mi. (163,270 sq. km.)
Population: 470,800
Language(s): Dutch, English, Surinamese

Monetary unit: Suriname dollar
Economy: bauxite and gold mining, alumina production, oil, food processing (fish, shrimp)

Adopted on Nov. 21, 1975, four days before independence from the Dutch, the flag of Suriname features green stripes for jungles and agriculture, white for justice and freedom, and red for the progressive spirit of a young nation. The yellow star is symbolic of the unity of the country, its golden future, and the people's spirit of sacrifice.

Swaziland
Kingdom, SE Africa

Area: 6,704 sq. mi. (17,363 sq. km.)
Population: 1,133,000
Language(s): Swati, English

Monetary unit: lilangeni
Economy: mining (coal, asbestos), wood pulp, sugar, soft drink concentrates, textiles

The flag dates to the creation of a military banner in 1941, when Swazi troops were preparing for the Allied invasion of Italy. On April 25, 1967, it was hoisted as the national flag. The crimson stripe stands for past battles, yellow for mineral wealth, and blue for peace. Featured are a Swazi war shield, two spears, and a "fighting stick."

Sweden
Constitutional monarchy, N Europe

Area: 173,732 sq. mi. (449,964 sq. km.)
Population: 9,031,000
Language(s): Swedish

Monetary unit: Swedish krona
Economy: steel, chemicals, paper, tourism, precision equipments, processed foods, motor vehicles

From the 14th century, the coat of arms of Sweden had a blue field with three golden crowns, and the earlier Folkung dynasty used a shield of blue and white wavy stripes with a gold lion. The off-center "Scandinavian cross" was influenced by the flag of the rival kingdom of Denmark. The current flag law was adopted on July 1, 1906.

Switzerland
Republic, cen. Europe

Area: 15,942 sq. mi. (41,290 sq. km.)
Population: 7,555,000
Language(s): French, German, Italian, Romansh

Monetary unit: Swiss franc
Economy: machinery, watches, precision instruments, chemicals, textiles, food products, dairy, wines

The Swiss flag is ultimately based on the war flag of the Holy Roman Empire. Schwyz, one of the original three cantons of the Swiss Confederation, placed a narrow white cross in the corner of its flag in 1240. This was also used in 1339 at the Battle of Laupen. Following the 1848 constitution, the flag was recognized by the army, and it was established as the national flag on land on Dec. 12, 1889.

Syria

Authoritarian state, SW Asia

Area: 71,498 sq. mi. (185,180 sq. km.)
Population: 19,315,000
Language(s): Arabic, Kurdish, Armenian

Monetary unit: Syrian pound
Economy: petroleum, textiles, food processing, phosphate mining, cement

In 1918 the Arab Revolt flag flew over Syria, which joined Egypt in the United Arab Republic in 1958, and based its new flag on that of the Egyptian revolution of 1952; its stripes were red-white-black, with two green stars for the constituent states. In 1961 Syria broke from the union, but it readopted the flag on March 29, 1980.

Tajikistan

Republic, W cen. Asia

Area: 55,251 sq. mi. (143,100 sq. km.)
Population: 7,077,000
Language(s): Tajik, Russian

Monetary unit: somoni
Economy: mining (aluminum, zinc), chemicals, cement, cotton, fruits, vegetable oil, textiles

Following independence from the Soviet Union in 1991, Tajikistan developed a new flag on Nov. 24, 1992. The green stripe is for agriculture, while red is for sovereignty. White is for the main crop—cotton. The central crown contains seven stars representing unity among workers, peasants, intellectuals, and other social classes.

Tanzania

Republic, E Africa

Area: 364,900 sq. mi. (945,087 sq. km.)
Population: 39,384,000
Language(s): Swahili, English, Arabic

Monetary unit: shilingi
Economy: agriculture (coffee, sugar, cashews, cloves), food processing, mining (diamonds, coal, salt)

In April 1964 Tanganyika and Zanzibar united, and in July their flag traditions melded to create the current design. The black stripe is for the majority population, while green is for the rich agricultural resources of the land. Mineral wealth is reflected in the yellow narrow borders, while the Indian Ocean is symbolized by blue.

Thailand

Constitutional monarchy, SE Asia

Area: 198,457 sq. mi. (514,000 sq. km.)
Population: 65,068,000
Language(s): Thai, English

Monetary unit: baht
Economy: tourism, textiles, jewelry, electronic components, food processing, mining (tungsten, tin)

In the 17th century, the flag of Thailand was plain red, and Thai ships in 1855 displayed a flag with a central white elephant as a symbol of good fortune. The Thai king replaced the elephant with two white stripes in 1916 and added the blue stripe on Sept. 28, 1917. Red symbolizes the blood of patriots, white is for Buddhism, and blue is for royal guidance.

Timor-Leste

Republic, Timor Island, W Pacific

Area: 5,794 sq. mi. (15,007 sq. km.)
Population: 1,085,000
Language(s): Tetum, Portuguese, Indonesian

Monetary unit: U.S. dollar
Economy: printing, soap, handicrafts, coffee, sandalwood, potential oil exports

Timor-Leste's flag consists of two isosceles triangles, one black and one yellow, overlapping on a red background. The black stands for obscurantism that needs to be overcome; the yellow for the trace of colonialism. The red background is for the struggle for liberation. The white star is the symbol of peace.

Togo

Republic, W Africa

Area: 21,925 sq. mi. (56,785 sq. km.)
Population: 5,702,000
Language(s): French, local languages

Monetary unit: West African States franc
Economy: cocoa, coffee, cotton, phosphate mining, cement, handicrafts, textiles

On April 27, 1960, Togo became independent from France under the current flag. Its stripes correspond to the administrative regions and symbolize that the population depends on the land for its sustenance (green) and its own labor for development (yellow). The red is for love, fidelity, and charity, while the white star is for purity and unity.

Tonga

Archipelago constit. mon., SW Pacific

Area: 289 sq. mi. (748 sq. km.)
Population: 117,000
Language(s): Tongan, English

Monetary unit: pa'anga
Economy: agriculture (tropical fruits, vanilla beans, coffee, ginger, black pepper), tourism, fishing

The colors red and white were popular in the Pacific long before the arrival of Europeans. The Tonga constitution (Nov. 4, 1875) established the flag, which was created by King George Tupou I with the advice of a missionary. The cross was chosen as a symbol of the widespread Christian religion, and the color red was related to the blood of Jesus.

Trinidad and Tobago

Islands republic, Caribbean

Area: 1,980 sq. mi. (5,128 sq. km.)
Population: 1,057,000
Language(s): English, French, Spanish

Monetary unit: Trinidad & Tobago dollar
Economy: oil, natural gas, asphalt, chemicals, tourism, fishing, citrus fruits, bananas, coffee, sugar

Hoisted on independence day, Aug. 31, 1962, the flag symbolizes earth, water, and fire as well as past, present, and future. Black also is a symbol of unity, strength, and purpose. White recalls the equality and purity of the people and the sea that unites them. Red is for the sun, the vitality of the people and nation, friendliness, and courage.

Tunisia

Republic, N Africa

Area: 63,170 sq. mi. (163,610 sq. km.)
Population: 10,276,000
Language(s): Arabic, French

Monetary unit: Tunisian dinar
Economy: petroleum, mining (phosphate, iron ore), tourism, textiles, citrus fruit, dates, almonds, olives

The Tunisian flag, established in 1835, contains the crescent and moon, a symbol used by the Ottoman Empire but dating from the ancient Egyptians and Phoenicians. More as a cultural than a religious symbol, the crescent and star came to be associated with Islam because of its widespread adoption in Muslim nations.

Turkey

Republic, SE Europe and SW Asia

Area: 301,384 sq. mi. (780,580 sq. km.)
Population: 71,159,000
Language(s): Turkish, Kurdish

Monetary unit: Turkish lira
Economy: textiles, food processing (fruit, nuts), tobacco, cotton, iron and steel, cement, chemicals

In June 1793 the flag was established for the navy, although its star had eight points instead of the current five (since about 1844). This design was reconfirmed in 1936 following the revolution led by Ataturk. Various myths are associated with the symbolism of the red color and the star and crescent, but none really explains their origins.

Turkmenistan

Authoritarian state, W cen. Asia

Area: 188,457 sq. mi. (488,100 sq. km.)
Population: 5,097,000
Language(s): Turkmen, Russian, Uzbek

Monetary unit: Turkmen manat
Economy: oil, natural gas, cotton, fruit, sheep, silk, textiles

The flag was introduced on Feb. 19, 1992. Its stripe contains intricate designs for five Turkmen tribes. Its green background is for Islam, and its crescent symbolizes faith in a bright future. The stars are for the human senses and the states of matter (liquid, solid, gas, crystal, and plasma). On Feb. 19, 1997, an olive wreath was added to the stripe.

Tuvalu

Archipelago monarchy, SW Pacific

Area: 10 sq. mi. (26 sq. km.)
Population: 12,000
Language(s): Tuvaluan, English, Samoan

Monetary unit: Tuvaluan dollar
Economy: subsistence farming (tropical fruits) and fishing, handicrafts

On Oct. 1, 1978, three years after separating from the Gilbert Islands, Tuvalu became independent under the current flag. The stars represent the atolls and islands of the country. The Union Jack recalls links with Britain and the Commonwealth. Replaced by supporters of republicanism on Oct. 1, 1995, the flag was reinstated on April 11, 1997.

Uganda

Republic, E cen. Africa

Area: 91,136 sq. mi. (236,040 sq. km.)
Population: 30,263,000
Language(s): English, local languages

Monetary unit: Ugandan shilling
Economy: coffee, tea, sugar, fish and fish products, gold, copper, cotton, flowers, cement, steel

The crested crane symbol was selected by the British for Uganda. The flag, established for independence on Oct. 9, 1962, was based on the flag of the ruling Uganda People's Congress (which has three black-yellow-red stripes), with the addition of the crane in the center. Black stands for the people, yellow for sunshine, and red for brotherhood.

Ukraine

Republic, E Europe

Area: 233,090 sq. mi. (603,700 sq. km.)
Population: 46,300,000
Language(s): Ukrainian, Russian

Monetary unit: hryvnia
Economy: coal, metals, machinery and transport equipment, chemicals, sugar, sunflowers, livestock

The first national flag of Ukraine, adopted in 1848, had equal stripes of yellow over blue and was based on the coat of arms of the city of Lviv. In 1918 the stripes were reversed to reflect the symbolism of blue skies over golden wheat fields. A red Soviet banner flew from 1949, but it was replaced by the blue-yellow bicolor on Jan. 28, 1992.

United Arab Emirates

Emirate federation, SE Arabian Peninsula

Area: about 32,000 sq. mi. (83,600 sq km.)
Population: 4,444,000
Language(s): Arabic, Persian, English

Monetary unit: Emirati dirham
Economy: oil, fishing, aluminum, commercial ship repair, dates, vegetables, limes, textiles

On Dec. 2, 1971, six small Arab states formed the United Arab Emirates, and a seventh state joined on Feb. 11, 1972. The flag took its colors from the Arab Revolt flag of 1917. The colors are included in a 13th-century poem which speaks of green Arab lands defended in black battles by blood-red swords of Arabs whose deeds are pure white.

United Kingdom

Constit. monarchy, off NW Europe

Area: 94,526 sq. mi. (244,820 sq. km.)
Population: 60,776,000
Language(s): English, Welsh, Scottish Gaelic
Monetary unit: British pound

Economy: transportation, communications equipment, petroleum, publishing, consumer goods, food production

Within the Union Jack are combined the crosses of St. George (a symbol of England), St. Andrew (Scotland), and St. Patrick (Ireland). Its earliest form, called the "Union Flag," or "Great Union," was designed in 1606. The current flag design has been in use since Jan. 1, 1801, when Great Britain and Ireland were joined.

United States

Republic, North America

Area: 3,620,067 sq. mi. (9,375,974 sq. km.)
Population: 301,140,000
Language(s): English, Spanish

Monetary unit: U.S. dollar
Economy: transportation, communications equipment, petroleum, publishing, consumer goods, food production

The Stars and Stripes has white stars corresponding to the states of the union (50 since July 4, 1960), as well as stripes for the 13 original states. The first unofficial national flag, hoisted on Jan. 1, 1776, had the British Union flag in the canton. The official flag dates to June 14, 1777; its design was standardized in 1912 and 1934.

Uruguay

Republic, South America

Area: 68,039 sq. mi. (176,220 sq. km.)
Population: 3,461,000
Language(s): Spanish

Monetary unit: Uruguayan peso
Economy: food processing, meatpacking, electrical, transportation equipment, petroleum, textiles, chemicals

The flag adopted on Dec. 16, 1828, combined symbols of Argentina with the flag pattern of the United States. It was last altered on July 11, 1830. On the canton is the golden "Sun of May," which was seen on May 25, 1810, as a favorable omen for anti-Spanish forces in Buenos Aires, Argentina. The stripes are for the original Uruguayan departments.

Uzbekistan

Authoritarian state, W cen. Asia

Area: 172,742 sq. mi. (447,400 sq. km.)
Population: 27,780,000
Language(s): Uzbek, Russian, Tajik

Monetary unit: Uzbekistani som
Economy: cotton, oil, natural gas, gold, copper, chemicals, machinery

The flag of the former Soviet republic was legalized on Nov. 18, 1991. The blue is for water but also recalls the 14th-century ruler Timur. The green is for nature, fertility, and new life. The white is for peace and purity; red is for human life force. The stars are for the months and the Zodiac, while the moon is for the new republic and Islam.

Vanuatu

Archipelago republic, SW Pacific

Area: 4,710 sq. mi. (12,200 sq. km.)
Population: 212,000
Language(s): Bislama, local languages

Monetary unit: vatu
Economy: fishing, financial services, tourism, copra, cocoa, coffee

The flag was hoisted upon independence from France and Britain, on July 30, 1980. Black is for the soil and the people, green for vegetation, and red for local religious traditions such as the sacrifice of pigs. On the triangle are two crossed branches and a full-round pig's tusk, a holy symbol. The horizontal "Y" is for peace and Christianity.

Venezuela

Republic, South America

Area: 352,145 sq. mi. (912,050 sq. km.)
Population: 26,024,000
Language(s): Spanish

Monetary unit: bolivar
Economy: oil, natural gas, iron ore, gold, chemicals, motor vehicles, food processing, textiles

The Venezuelan flag was adopted on March 18, 1864. Yellow was originally said to stand for the gold of the New World, separated by the blue of the Atlantic Ocean from "bloody Spain," symbolized by red. The stars are for the original seven provinces. In the upper hoist corner, the national arms are added to flags which serve the government.

Vietnam

Communist state, SE Asia

Area: 127,244 sq. mi. (329,560 sq.km.)
Population: 85,262,000
Language(s): Vietnamese, English

Monetary unit: dong
Economy: rice, corn, coffee, sugarcane, fishing, textiles, rubber, coal, steel, fertilizer, cement

On Sept. 29, 1945, Vietnamese communists adopted the red flag in use today. On July 4, 1976, following the defeat of the American-sponsored government in the south, the flag became official throughout the nation. The five points of the star are said to stand for the proletariat, peasantry, military, intellectuals, and petty bourgeoisie.

Yemen

Republic, S Arabian Peninsula

Area: 203,850 sq. mi. (527,970 sq. km.)
Population: 22,231,000
Language(s): Arabic

Monetary unit: Yemeni rial
Economy: agriculture, petroleum refining, textiles, leather goods, food processing, handicrafts

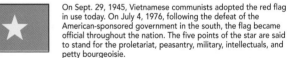

Revolutions broke out in North Yemen in 1962 and in South Yemen in 1967. In 1990 the two states unified, and that May 23 the tricolor was adopted, its design influenced by the former United Arab Republic. The black is for the dark days of the past, white for the bright future, and red for the blood shed for independence and unity.

Zambia

Republic, S cen. Africa

Area: 290,586 sq. mi. (752,614 sq. km.)
Population: 11,477,000
Language(s): English, local languages

Monetary unit: Zambian kwacha
Economy: mining (copper, gold, cobalt), corn, tobacco, peanuts, cotton, livestock, textiles

Zambia separated from British rule on Oct. 24, 1964. Its flag, based on the flag of the United National Independence Party, has a green background for agriculture, red for the freedom struggle, black for the African people, and orange for copper. The orange eagle appeared in the colonial coat of arms of 1939. It symbolizes freedom and success.

Zimbabwe

Republic, S cen. Africa

Area: 150,804 sq. mi. (390,580 sq. km.)
Population: 12,311,000
Language(s): English, local languages

Monetary unit: multiple currencies (including U.S. dollar and South African rand)
Economy: mining (coal, gold, platinum), wood products, cement, chemicals, fertilizer, textiles

On April 18, 1980, elections brought the black majority to power under the current flag. The black color is for the ethnic majority, while red is for blood, green for agriculture, yellow for mineral wealth, and white for peace and progress. At the hoist is a red star (for socialism) and the ancient "Zimbabwe Bird" from the Great Zimbabwe ruins.

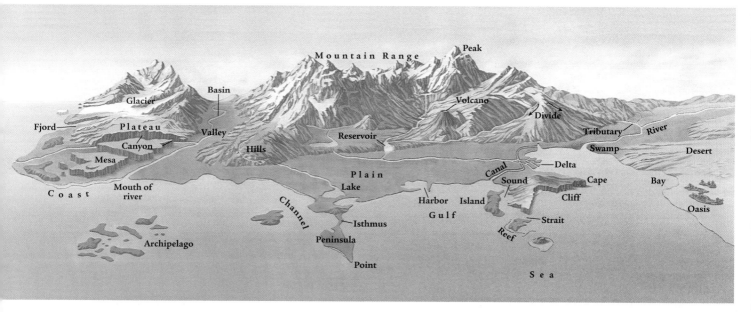

Glossary

This glossary provides brief definitions of some of the geographical terms and foreign terms used in this atlas. It does not include names of peoples, languages, religions, and geologic eras. For definitions of those terms, please refer to a standard dictionary such as *Merriam-Webster's Intermediate Dictionary* or *Merriam-Webster's Collegiate® Dictionary.*

In addition, this glossary includes information about a small set of place-names that are used in the atlas but whose meaning may not be immediately self-explanatory from the maps, graphs, or text in which they appear. More detailed information on place-names can be found in *Merriam-Webster's Geographical Dictionary.*

acid rain : rain having increased acidity caused by atmospheric pollutants

agglomeration : a cluster containing a large city and the populated areas surrounding it

alpine : of or relating to mountains

Altiplano : the region comprising a series of high plains in western Bolivia and extending into southeastern Peru

amphitheater : a flat or gently sloping area surrounded by abrupt slopes

Anatolia : the part of Turkey comprising the peninsula forming the western extremity of Asia

An Nafud : a desert in northern Saudi Arabia

aqueduct
1 : a conduit for carrying a large quantity of flowing water
2 : a structure for conveying a canal over a river or hollow

archipelago : a group of islands

arid : having insufficient rainfall to support agriculture

Arnhem Land : a coastal region of northern Australia containing a large aboriginal reservation

atoll : a coral island consisting of a reef surrounding a lagoon

bab — an Arabic word meaning "strait"

bank
1 : an undersea elevation rising especially from the continental shelf
2 : the rising ground bordering a lake, river, or sea
3 — see SANDBANK

basin
1 a : a large or small depression in the surface of the land or in the ocean floor
b : the entire tract of country drained by a river and its tributaries
c : a great depression in the surface of Earth occupied by an ocean
2 : a broad area of Earth beneath which the strata dip usually from the sides toward the center

bay — see INLET

bight : a bay formed by a bend in a coast

biodiversity : biological diversity in an environment as indicated by numbers of different species of plants and animals

Bosporus : the strait connecting the Sea of Marmara with the Black Sea

Brittany : an historical region in northwestern France

broadleaf : composed of plants having leaves that are not needles

canal : an artificial waterway for navigation or for draining or irrigating land

canyon : a deep narrow valley with steep sides and often with a stream flowing through it

cap — a French word meaning "cape"

cape : a point or extension of land jutting out into water as a peninsula or as a projecting point

cascade : one of a series of steep usually small falls of water

cataract : steep rapids in a river

causeway : a raised way across wet ground or water

cay : a low island or reef of sand or coral

Central America : the narrow southern portion of North America comprised of Guatemala, El Salvador, Honduras, Nicaragua, Costa Rica, Panama, and Belize

channel : a strait or narrow sea between two close land areas

city : an inhabited place usually of greater size or importance than a town

cliff : a very steep, vertical, or overhanging face of rock, earth, or ice

coast : the land near a shore

collectivity — see TERRITORIAL COLLECTIVITY

colony : a distant territory belonging to or under the control of a nation

coniferous : composed of plants having needle-shaped leaves

continent : one of the six or seven great divisions of land on Earth

continental shelf : a shallow submarine plain of varying width forming a border to a continent and typically ending in a comparatively steep slope to the deep ocean floor

country
1 : an indefinite usually extended expanse of land
2 : a state or nation or its territory

crown land : land belonging to a monarchy and yielding revenues that the reigning sovereign is entitled to

crust : the outer part of Earth composed essentially of crystalline rocks

current : a part of the ocean moving continuously in a certain direction

Cyrenaica : the easternmost part of Libya settled by ancient Greeks

Dalmatia : a region on the Adriatic coast

Damaraland : the plateau region of central Namibia

Dardanelles : the strait connecting the Sea of Marmara with the Aegean Sea

dasht — a Persian word meaning "desert"

deciduous : composed of plants having leaves that fall off seasonally or at a certain stage of development in the life cycle

defile : a narrow passage or gorge

deforestation : the action or process of clearing of forests

delta : the triangular or fan-shaped piece of land made by deposits of mud and sand at the mouth of a river

density : the average number of individuals per unit of space

dependency : a territorial unit under the jurisdiction of a nation but not formally annexed by it

depression : an area of land in which the central part lies lower than the margin

desert : arid land with usually little vegetation that is incapable of supporting a considerable population without an artificial water supply

diaspora : the movement, migration, or scattering of a people away from an established or ancestral homeland

division : a portion of a territorial unit marked off for a particular purpose (as administrative or judicial functions)

duchy : the territory of a duke or duchess

elevation
1 : the height above sea level
2 : a place that rises above its surroundings

eminence : a natural elevation

emirate : the state or jurisdiction of an emir (a ruler in an Islamic country)

enclave : a foreign territorial unit enclosed within a larger territory [The difference between an *enclave* and an *exclave* is one of perspective. An enclosed territorial unit is an enclave with respect to the territory that surrounds it, but it is an exclave of the country to which it belongs.]

endangered species : a species threatened with extinction

Equator : the great circle of Earth that is everywhere equally distant from the North Pole and the South Pole and divides the surface into Northern Hemisphere and Southern Hemisphere

erg : a desert region of shifting sand

escarpment : a long cliff or steep slope separating two comparatively level or more gently sloping surfaces and resulting from erosion or faulting

estuary : an arm of the sea at the lower end of a river

Eurasian : of Europe and Asia

European Union : an economic, scientific, and political organization consisting of Belgium, France, Italy, Luxembourg, Netherlands, Germany, Denmark, Greece, Ireland, United Kingdom, Spain, Portugal, Austria, Finland, Sweden, Cyprus, Czech Republic, Estonia, Hungary, Latvia, Lithuania, Malta, Poland, Slovakia, Slovenia, Bulgaria, and Romania.

evergreen : composed of plants having foliage that remains green and functional through more than one growing season

exclave : a portion of a country separated from the main part and surrounded by foreign territory — compare ENCLAVE

fjord : a narrow inlet of the sea between cliffs or steep slopes

free association : a relationship affording sovereignty with independent control of internal affairs and foreign policy except defense

geothermal : produced by the heat of the Earth's interior

geyser : a spring that throws forth intermittent jets of heated water and steam

glacier : a large body of ice moving slowly down a slope or valley or spreading outward on a land surface

Gobi : the desert in a plateau region in southern Mongolia and extending into China

Gondwana : the hypothetical land area believed to have once connected the Indian Subcontinent and the landmasses of the Southern Hemisphere

gorge : a narrow steep-walled canyon or part of a canyon

Gran Chaco : the thinly populated swampy region of South America divided between Argentina, Bolivia, and Paraguay

great circle : a circle on the surface of the Earth a portion of which is the shortest distance between any two points

grid : a network of uniformly spaced horizontal and perpendicular lines (as for locating points on a map)

gulf — see INLET

habitat : a place or environment where a plant or animal naturally or normally lives and grows

harbor : a protected part of a body of water that is deep enough to furnish anchorage; *esp* : one with port facilities

headland : a point of usually high land jutting out into a body of water

headstream : a stream that is the source of a river

hemisphere : the northern or southern half of the Earth as divided by the Equator or the eastern or western half as divided by a meridian

highland : elevated or mountainous land

hill — see MOUNTAIN

Horn of Africa : the easternmost projection of land in Africa

humid : characterized by perceptible moisture

hydroelectric : relating to electricity produced by waterpower

ice cap : an area having a cover of perennial ice and snow

ice field : a glacier flowing outward from the center of an extensive area of relatively level land

ice shelf : an extensive ice cap originating on land but continuing out to sea beyond the depths at which it rests on the sea bottom

indigenous : having originated in a particular region or environment

Indochina : the peninsula comprised of Myanmar, Thailand, Laos, Cambodia, Vietnam, and the western part of Malaysia

inlet
1 : a recess in the shore of a larger body of water [In this sense, *inlet* is a general term for *bay* or *gulf*. The chief difference between a bay and a gulf is one of size. A bay is usually smaller than a gulf.]
2 : a narrow water passage between peninsulas or through a barrier island leading to a bay or lagoon

intermittent lake : a lake that is sometimes dry

intermittent stream : a stream that is sometimes dry

intermontane : situated between mountains

International Date Line : the line coinciding approximately with the meridian 180 degrees from the Prime Meridian fixed by international agreement as the place where each calendar day first begins

island : an area of land surrounded by water and smaller than a continent

islet : a little island

isthmus : a narrow strip of land connecting two larger land areas

jebel — an Arabic word meaning "mountain"

key : any of the coral islets off the southern coast of Florida

kill : a channel — used chiefly in place-names in Delaware, Pennsylvania, and New York

kingdom : a major territorial unit headed by a king or queen

kum — a Turkic word meaning "desert"

Labrador : a peninsula divided between the Canadian provinces of Quebec and Newfoundland and Labrador

lac — a French word meaning "lake"

lagoon : a shallow sound, channel, or pond near or connected with a larger body of water

laguna — a Spanish word meaning "lagoon" or "lake"

lake : a considerable inland body of standing water

landform : a natural feature of a land surface

landmass : a large area of land

Lapland : the region north of the Arctic Circle divided between Norway, Sweden, Finland, and Russia

legend : an explanatory list of the symbols on a map or chart

Llano Estacado : the plateau region of eastern and southeastern New Mexico and western Texas

Llanos : the region of vast plains in northern South America that is drained by the Orinoco River and its tributaries

locality : a specific location

loch : a lake in Scotland

lough : a lake in Ireland

lowland : low or level country

magnetic pole : either of two small regions which are located respectively in the polar areas of the Northern Hemisphere and the Southern Hemisphere and toward which a compass needle points from any direction throughout adjacent regions

marine : influenced or determined by proximity to the sea

marsh : a tract of soft wet land

massif : a principal mountain mass

Melanesia : the islands in the southwestern Pacific northeast of Australia and south of the Equator

mesa : an isolated relatively flat-topped natural elevation usually less extensive than a plateau

Mesopotamia : the historical region between the Tigris and Euphrates rivers

metropolitan : constituting the chief or capital city and sometimes including its suburbs

Micronesia : the widely scattered islands of the western Pacific east of the Philippines

midlatitude : of the area approximately between 30 to 60 degrees north or south of the Equator

mineral : a naturally occurring crystalline element or compound that has a definite chemical composition and results from processes other than those of plants and animals

monarchy : a nation or state having a government headed by a hereditary chief of state with life tenure

mountain
1 : an elevated mass of land that projects above its surroundings [Among the many types of natural land elevations, a distinction needs to be made between *hill, mountain,* and *peak*. A hill is likely to be lower than a mountain or peak and typically has a rounded summit. A mountain is larger and projects more conspicuously than a hill, while a peak is usually a prominent type of mountain having a well-defined summit.]
2 : an elongated ridge

mouth : the place where a stream enters a larger body of water

municipality : a primarily urban political unit

narrows : a strait connecting two bodies of water

national park : an area of special scenic, historical, or scientific importance set aside and maintained by a national government

notch : a deep close pass

novaya — a Russian word meaning "new"

oasis : a fertile or green area in an arid region

occidental — a Spanish word meaning "western"

ocean : any of the large bodies of water into which the whole body of salt water that covers much of Earth is divided

Oceania : the lands of the central and southern Pacific

Okavango : a large marsh in northern Botswana

oriental — a Spanish word meaning "eastern"

Pampas : the extensive generally grass-covered plains region of South America lying east of the Andes Mountains

Pangaea : the hypothetical land area believed to have once connected the landmasses of the Southern Hemisphere with those of the Northern Hemisphere

pass : a low place in a mountain range

passage : a place through which it is possible to pass

Patagonia : a barren tableland mostly in Argentina

peak — see MOUNTAIN

peninsula : a portion of land nearly surrounded by water

per capita : per unit of population

pico — a Spanish word meaning "peak"

piedmont : the area lying or formed at the base of mountains

plain
1 : an extensive area of level or rolling treeless country
2 : a broad unbroken expanse

plate : any of the large movable segments into which Earth's crust is divided

plateau : a usually extensive land area having a relatively level surface raised sharply above adjacent land on at least one side
[Sometimes the word is used synonymously with *tableland.*]

point : a place having a precisely indicated position

polar : of or relating to the region around the North Pole or the South Pole

polder : a tract of lowland reclaimed from a body of water

pole : either extremity of Earth's axis

Polynesia : the islands of the central Pacific

pool
1 : a small and rather deep body of water
2 : a quiet place in a stream
3 : a body of water forming above a dam

Prime Meridian : the meridian of 0 degrees longitude which runs through the original site of the Royal Greenwich Observatory at Greenwich, England and from which other longitudes are reckoned

princely state : a state governed by a prince in pre-independent India

principality : the territory of a prince

profile : a drawing showing comparative elevations of land surface along a given strip

projection : an estimate of a future possibility based on current trends

promontory
1 : a high point of land or rock projecting into a body of water
2 : a prominent mass of land overlooking or projecting into a lowland

protectorate : a political unit dependent on the authority of another

punta — a Spanish word meaning "point"

race : a narrow channel through which a strong or rapid current of water flows

rain forest
1 : a tropical woodland with an annual rainfall of at least 100 inches (254 centimeters) and marked by lofty trees forming a continuous canopy
2 : woodland of a usually rather mild climatic area that receives heavy rainfall and that usually includes numerous kinds of trees with one or two types that dominate

range : a series of mountains

reef : a chain of rocks or coral or a ridge of sand at or near the surface of water

region
1 : a primary administrative subdivision of a country
2 : an indefinite area of Earth
3 : a broad geographical area distinguished by similar features

republic
1 : a political unit having a form of government headed by a chief of state who is not a monarch

2 : a political unit having a form of government in which supreme power resides in a body of citizens entitled to vote and is exercised by elected officers and representatives responsible to them and governing according to law
3 : a constituent political and territorial unit of a country

reservation : a tract of public land set aside for a special use

reservoir : an artificial lake where water is collected and kept in quantity for use

ridge
1 : a range of hills or mountains
2 : an elongate elevation on an ocean bottom

rift valley : an elongated valley formed by the depression of a block of the Earth's crust between two faults or groups of faults of approximately parallel orientation

rio — a Spanish word meaning "river"

river : a natural stream of water of usually considerable volume

roadstead : a place less enclosed than a harbor where ships may ride at anchor

Rub' al-Khali : the vast desert region of the southern Arabian Peninsula

rural : of or relating to the country

Sahel : the semidesert southern fringe of the Sahara that stretches from Mauritania to Chad

san — a Spanish word meaning "saint"

sandbank : a large deposit of sand forming a shoal

santa; santo — Spanish words meaning "saint"

são — a Portuguese word meaning "saint"

savanna : a tropical or subtropical grassland containing scattered trees

scale : an indication of the relationship between the distances on a map and the corresponding actual distances

Scandinavia
1 : the peninsula occupied by Norway and Sweden
2 : the region of northern Europe comprising Denmark, Norway, and Sweden and often including Finland and Iceland

scrubland : land covered with vegetation chiefly consisting of stunted trees or shrubs

sea
1 : a more or less landlocked body of salt water
2 : an ocean
3 : an inland body of water

semiarid : having from about 10 to 20 inches (25 to 51 centimeters) of annual precipitation

semidesert : an arid area that has some of the characteristics of a desert but has greater annual precipitation

serra — a Portuguese word meaning "mountain range"

shan — a Chinese word meaning "mountain range"

shield : the ancient mass of hard rock that forms the core of a continent

shoal : a ridge or large deposit of sand that makes the water shallow

shore : the land bordering a usually large body of water

Siberia : a vast region mostly in Russia extending from the Pacific Ocean to the Ural Mountains

sierra — a Spanish word meaning "mountain range"

site : the location of some particular thing

sound
1 : a long broad inlet of the ocean generally parallel to the coast
2 : a long passage of water connecting two larger bodies of water or separating a mainland and an island

source : the point of origin of a stream of water

spa : a town or resort with mineral springs

spring : a source of water issuing from the ground

state
1 : a sovereign politically organized body of people usually occupying a definite territory
2 : one of the constituent units of a nation having a federal government

steppe
1 : one of the vast usually level and treeless tracts in southeastern Europe or Asia
2 : arid land found usually in regions of extreme temperature range

strait : a comparatively narrow passageway connecting two large bodies of water

strata : layers having parallel layers of other kinds above or below or both above and below

subarctic : characteristic of regions bordering the Arctic Circle

subcontinent : a major subdivision of a continent

subduction zone : an area in which the edge of one of Earth's plates descends below the edge of another

subsistence agriculture : a system of farming that provides all or almost all the goods required by the farm family usually without any significant surplus for sale

subtropical : characteristic of regions bordering on the tropics

Sudd : the lowland swamp region of southern Sudan

sultanate : a state or nation governed by a sultan

supercontinent : a former large continent from which other continents are believed to have broken off and drifted away

swamp : a tract of wetland often partially or intermittently covered with water

tableland : a broad level elevated area [Sometimes the word is used synonymously with *plateau*.]

territorial collectivity : a French overseas territorial unit enjoying some degree of local authority and having a status lesser than an overseas department but greater than an overseas territory

territory
1 a : a geographical area belonging to or under the jurisdiction of a governmental authority
b : an administrative subdivision of a country
c : a part of the U.S. not included within any state but organized with a separate legislature
d : a geographical area dependent on an external government but having some degree of autonomy
2 : an indeterminate geographical area

tidewater : low-lying coastal land

Tierra del Fuego : an archipelago divided between Argentina and Chile

time zone : a geographic region within which the same standard time is used

tract : a stretch of land

Transcaucasia : the region in southeastern Europe south of the Caucasus Mountains and between the Black and Caspian seas

trench : a long, narrow, and usually steep-sided depression in the ocean floor

tributary : a stream feeding a larger stream or a lake

Tripolitania : an historical region of northern Africa originally a Phoenician colony

tropic : either of the regions lying between the two parallels of the Earth's latitude that are approximately 23 $\frac{1}{2}$ degrees north of the Equator (Tropic of Cancer) and approximately 23 $\frac{1}{2}$ degrees south of the Equator (Tropic of Capricorn)

tundra : a treeless plain having permanently frozen subsoil and vegetation consisting chiefly of mosses, lichens, herbs, and very small shrubs

union territory : a centrally administered subdivision of India consisting of an island group, the area surrounding a city, or an area containing a linguistic minority

unitary district : one of the administrative subdivisions of Scotland since 1996

upland : high land especially at some distance from the sea

urban : of or relating to the city

valley
1 : an elongated depression of Earth's surface usually between ranges of hills or mountains
2 : an area drained by a river and its tributaries

volcán — a Spanish word meaning "volcano"

volcano : a mountain composed wholly or in part of material ejected from a vent in the Earth's crust

Wallachia : an historical region in Romania

waterway : a navigable body or course of water

wilderness : a region uncultivated and uninhabited by human beings and more or less in its natural state

woodland : land covered with woody vegetation